Health, Behavior
and the Community
(PGPS-76)

Pergamon Titles of Related Interest

Goldstein, Sprafkin & Gershaw—*Skill Training for Community Living: Applying Structured Learning Therapy*

Krasner—*Environmental Design and Human Behavior: A Handbook of Theory and Application*

Meacher—*New Methods of Mental Health Care*

Mushkin & Dunlop—*Health: What Is It Worth? Measures of Health Benefits*

Nietzel—*Crime and Its Modification: A Social Learning Perspective*

Nietzel & Winett—*Behavioral Approaches to Community Psychology*

Rapoport—*Human Aspects of Urban Form: Towards a Man-Environment Approach to Urban Form and Design*

Health, Behavior and the Community

An Ecological Perspective

Ralph Catalano

Pergamon Press

NEW YORK • OXFORD • TORONTO • SYDNEY • FRANKFURT • PARIS

Pergamon Press Offices:

U.S.A.	Pergamon Press Inc., Maxwell House, Fairview Park, Elmsford, New York 10523, U.S.A.
U.K.	Pergamon Press Ltd., Headington Hill Hall, Oxford OX3 0BW, England
CANADA	Pergamon of Canada Ltd., 150 Consumers Road, Willowdale, Ontario M2J 1P9, Canada
AUSTRALIA	Pergamon Press (Aust) Pty. Ltd., P O Box 544, Potts Point, NSW 2011, Australia
FRANCE	Pergamon Press SARL, 24 rue des Ecoles, 75240 Paris, Cedex 05, France
FEDERAL REPUBLIC OF GERMANY	Pergamon Press GmbH, 6242 Kronberg/Taunus, Pferdstrasse 1, Federal Republic of Germany

Copyright © 1979 Pergamon Press Inc.

Library of Congress Cataloging in Publication Data

Catalano, Ralph, 1946-
    Health, behavior, and the community.

    (Pergamon general psychology series)
    Includes index.
    1. Social change. 2. Social problems. 3. Exter-
nalities (Economics) I. Title.
HM101.C37   1979   362'.042   78-23714
ISBN 0-08-022972-7
ISBN 0-08-022971-9 pbk.

Printed in the United States of America

To June, my parents, and Gunnar Myrdal

Contents

Introduction

This volume is intended to introduce students interested in public health, mental health, law, urban planning, public administration, or social work, to the complex interdependencies of the contemporary community. The hope is that this introduction will reduce the unexpected impacts of ill-informed remedies which may control one problem but which worsen or create others. The book's content and organization reflect two more specific goals. The less ambitious end is to present an historical overview of the explanations used to guide attempts to control illness, abnormal behavior, and crime. These overviews are found in Chapters 5, 6, and 7, which are written as semi-independent modules as well as part of the larger whole.

The more ambitious goal of the book is to demonstrate that while researchers and practitioners often deal with health and behavioral problems as discrete events, no problem arises, worsens, or disappears independently in the community. This goal is pursued by introducing the "ecological perspective" which is the basis for an emerging attempt to coordinate the efforts of the community service professions. The ecological perspective is traced from its best known antecedents to its recent influence on explanations of health and behavioral problems. The basic assumption of the ecological perspective, that the human community is a complex system of interdependencies analogous to natural eco-systems, is described and critiqued.

Bringing this material together in a reasonably brief and coherent way requires the introduction of a structuring device. Thomas Kuhn's construct of "disciplinary matrix" has been chosen to organize the historical overviews and demonstrate the influence of scientific theories on the community service professions. A disciplinary matrix summarizes the historical succession of dominant explanations and research techniques held by those studying and attempting to control a given problem. Chapter 1 is a description of the concept of disciplinary matrix and an explanation of how it will be used in the remainder of the book. The discussion of the matrix is necessarily abstract. Experience with over 2,000 students indicates, however, that the concepts are easily mastered to the level sufficient for understanding the remainder of the book. The less sophisticated student need only grasp the ordering function of the matrix, while the more advanced will doubtless benefit from the discussion of wider implications.

The essentials of the ecological perspective as applied to the human community are described in Chapters 2, 3, and 4. Chapter 2 is an introduction to the biological underpinnings of the perspective through basic descriptions of natural selection, ecosystems, and homeostasis.

The economic principles assumed in the application of the ecosystem model to human communities are explained in Chapter 3. The material does not assume prior familiarity with economics. The discussion elaborates on the concept of "social cost" or "externality," and demonstrates that the health and behavioral impacts of community change can be viewed as unaccounted costs. The emphasis is on the fact that the sum of many economically "rational" individual decisions is not necessarily a healthy, efficient community. The chapter ends with a discussion of the historical realization that the health and behavioral costs of community change must be accounted.

Sociology's early attempts to predict the health and behavioral outcomes of community change are described in Chapter 4. The discussion focuses on the "Chicago School's" seminal work in human ecology which provides the basis for the ecological perspective.

Chapters 5, 6, and 7 are historical overviews of the study of ill-health, abnormal behavior, and crime. While the chapters are intended to be as self-contained as possible, the disciplinary matrix concept and ecological perspective tie them closely to the introductory and closing chapters of the book.

Chapter 8 returns to the concept of social cost and discusses the use of ecological principles to identify the health and behavioral costs of community change. The historical evolution of American communities from urban centers to metropolitan regions is described to demonstrate the predicament created by making seemingly rational decisions without considering external costs. The dilemmas faced by American school systems are used as specific examples. The implications of socio-economic segregation and fiscal disparities are discussed from an ecological perspective. The chapter includes a discussion of remedial interventions at the community and regional levels. Students are warned of the possible unintended outcomes caused by pursuing intuitive remedies and by the unwillingness of individuals to bear the social costs of their indecisions.

Various levels of intervention in ecological processes are discussed in Chapter 9. The likelihood of successfully adding social cost accounting to decisions at the national and community levels is assessed, as is its use by community service professionals.

The reader should realize at the outset that the goals of the book required considerable information reduction. While every effort has been made to include the most seminal and representative concepts, the summary nature of the presentations will doubtless disappoint some advanced scholars in each of the fields covered. The author would remind them that the modern educational system rapidly conditions the serious student to be concerned with narrowly defined issues. This book was designed to take full advantage of the limited occasions in which the student is expected to reflect on the convergence, rather than divergence, of disciplines.

The following people are among the many who gave their time to make this volume possible. The author is indebted to Gunnar Myrdal, Gerald Karaska, John Monahan, Robert Meier, and Betty Olson for reviewing the chapters dealing with their respective disciplines. Editing volunteered by Rose Nappi, Wesley Marx and Michael Markowitz was extremely helpful. John Monahan's help in the search for a publisher led to Pergamon. Diane Langmack's patience and competence took the anxiety and confusion out of preparing the manuscript. Sylvia Halpern and Angela Clark of Pergamon Press made it possible for the manuscript to become a book.

The preparation of this book would no doubt have been abandoned on several occasions had it not been for the encouragement and suggestions of my wife. Her unselfish sacrifice of time during the preparation of this volume will always serve the author as a model of devotion.

Health, Behavior
and the Community
(PGPS-76)

1 Gestalt, Paradigm, and Disciplinary Matrix

Amos Hawley (1968, p. vii), a human ecologist, has written:

> Virtually every scholar is heir to an intellectual tradition having an ancient past and a future that reaches well beyond him. In that tradition are not only certain major themes but also numerous derivations and corollaries, some clear and recognizable, others lurking in an inchoate state. The scholar is guided by that lore to the posture he adopts, the problems he chooses for study, and the way in which he formulates them.

The influence of intellectual tradition upon the quality of ongoing research has long been a subject of some concern for the natural and social scientist. This concern has increased in recent years as the number of multidisciplinary academic programs grows, and the difficulties inherent in conducting interdisciplinary research become more apparent. This situation has led to a renewed interest in what is often labeled "Sociology of Knowledge," or "Intellectual History," or, more traditionally, "Philosophy of Science." This chapter describes one outgrowth of this interest and allied research—the concept of paradigm. Understanding paradigm is important, for the remainder of this book will use the concept to explain the ecology of crime, mental illness, and poor health. The

1

concept will also be used to demonstrate that the disciplines of community psychology, criminology, and public health are adopting, or can adopt, ecological analyses. "Paradigm" may seem abstract at first but will become familiar as it is encountered in examples and in Chapters 5, 6 and 7. The student should remember that a paradigm consists of an explanation and the tools used to test and teach it. These tools include "analogies," "conventions," and "exemplars," all of which are explained in Chapter 1.

Students often ask if paradigm is just another term for "theory". While a paradigm must begin with, and always be based on, theory, the concepts differ in two important ways. Theory usually refers to an explanation of a phenomenon, whether or not that explanation has been tested or widely accepted. For a theory to be raised to paradigm status several prerequisites must be met. One is that the theory's accuracy be tested through research procedures which can be replicated. A second is that this testing lead to the theory's becoming the most widely accepted explanation among the scientists interested in the phenomenon being studied. A paradigm, therefore, is more than just a theory. It is a theory which has become dominant in a discipline and, in the process, has spawned research conventions which are passed on to succeeding generations of students.

The second concept introduced in the chapter is "disciplinary matrix." As will be discovered in succeeding pages, this construct is basically a summary of the historical succession of paradigms used to study a particular phenomenon. Explanations of crime, for example, have changed over the centuries as have the tools criminologists use in their research and teaching. A disciplinary matrix of criminology compares the succession of paradigms so that important differences stand out.

Keep in mind that the concepts of paradigm and disciplinary matrix are not the primary subject of this book. One need not be a philosopher of science to benefit from the volume. On the other hand, understanding the organizing function of the paradigm and disciplinary matrix concepts will make the book much easier to master. The student who makes the effort to grasp the more subtle elements of the discussion will also realize that the concepts give meaning to a wider and more profound range of issues than those dealt with in the following eight chapters.

GESTALT

The best way to begin explaining paradigm is by considering three classic experiments in the psychology of perception. A subject is seated in a room opposite a machine apparently designed to move a small light bulb in a precisely measured fashion. The room is darkened and the observer asked to estimate how far the light moves in any direction. Although the light remains stationary, the subject soon reports that it is moving in one direction or another.

A simply printed letter C is flashed on a screen before an observer who has been asked to identify the figures shown to him. The subject reports seeing a circle until the length of the exposure is considerably increased.

A drawing in which more than one familiar scene can be discerned is shown to several subjects. Each reports seeing only one or the other until asked to look more closely or told that there are other easily discerned scenes in the drawing.

These seemingly simple tests cast light on a proposition of tremendous importance to understanding our cognitive functions: what we see is often determined by what we think we are seeing. In the first case, for example, the observer expected the light to move because before the room was darkened he saw an elaborate machine apparently designed to move the bulb. He had an "idea" of how the machine worked and the idea affected what he saw.

In the second case, the "idea" of a circle as one of the possible figures the observer could see actually led him to report seeing a whole circle when in fact it was the letter "C."

In the last case, the observer does not see more than one scene, because the idea that the drawing represents what he first recognized precludes his seeing other things.

Through experience with and learning about things, we develop abstract pictures of what they look like and what they do. We then use these abstract pictures to identify new things we experience. Once something new is identified as like something previously experienced, we assume it will do what the others like it do. Psychologists interested in this phenomenon call these abstract pictures "gestalts." Joseph Royce (1964, p. 92), has written:

> The essence of the answer to the question of how we perceive is that we perceive *gestalts*. That is, we do not perceive a thousand and one minutiae which are there, but rather we tend to see certain "wholes", certain total configurations, some of which we have perhaps named, such as tree, mountain, car and house . . .

As indicated by our examples, we can anticipate a gestalt identification using only a few of the characteristics peculiar to the type of previously experienced things. So the shape of a circle led our second observer to assume the letter C was a circle. Other cases of inaccurate identifications can be more serious. Upon returning from the popcorn counter at the theater, for example, you might put your arm around someone who, in the dark, appears very much like the man or woman with whom you came, but who is actually someone else. In either case your mistake can be an educational experience in that you have learned, for better or worse, that the gestalt you previously used to identify certain objects is not discriminating enough under some conditions.

The process by which gestalts evolve has been the subject of investigation by students of human maturation. Jean Piaget, who has spent a lifetime investigating the way in which infants and children organize reality, has theorized that the child goes through two phases of cognitive development. The first, or "assimilation," phase is dominated by a "grasping and sucking" pattern, which leads the infant to interpret all that he perceives as like a nursing bottle which should be grasped and brought to his mouth for sucking. The infant is attempting to impose his gestalt on what he perceives. This phase gives way to "accommodation" which is the realization that not everything perceived can be grasped and sucked. When the infant alters his gestalt to accommodate this realization the maturation process begins. Piaget claims that maturation, or the increasing realization that reality will not always lend itself to the gestalt one seeks to impose on it, is a process which continues throughout life.

The process of individual maturation, whereby one adjusts his gestalts to accommodate reality, is similar to the development of science. Man at first explains external phenomena, stars for example, in terms of his own experience. So a formation of stars becomes a warrior or a bull. Like the infant, as the astronomer's power of observation increases, he realizes his original gestalt identification was not accurate. Stars do not act as men do. Astronomy must "mature" through accommodation and develop new gestalts to organize its observation of the stars.

The Stages of Scientific Progress

Thomas Kuhn (1970), as a philosopher of science and an historian, was much interested in the contradiction between the gradual, step-by-step accumulation of knowledge usually attributed to the natural sciences, and the often-cited scientific "revolutions" such as Copernican astronomy or Einsteinian physics. In an effort to resolve this puzzle, Kuhn studied the historical development of the natural sciences. He found that the development of the natural sciences has not been a constant, or linear, progression, in which knowledge is slowly, steadily added to a sound base. Rather, progress has often been sudden, with changes that sweep away the very foundations of existing theory.

Kuhn argues that scientific progress goes through a four-stage cycle. The first, or "pre-normal," stage exists when individuals or small groups of researchers pursue knowledge of the same phenomena, but do not communicate among themselves. Each might use different terms and measures to describe the same subject. More importantly, each uses different theories to organize his investigation. The result is that little overall progress is made, because whatever these isolated researchers learn is not shared, or passed on to new researchers who must use considerable energy and resources rediscovering old knowledge.

Kuhn (1970, p. 208), using the study of light as an example, describes the preparadigmatic stage as follows:

> One group took light to be particles emanating from material bodies; for another it was a modification of the medium that intervened between the body and the eye; still another explained light in terms of an interaction of the medium with an emana-

tion from the eye; and there were combinations and modifications besides ... Anyone examining a survey of physical optics before Newton may well conclude that,
though the field's practitioners were scientists, the net result of their activity was less
than science. Being able to take no common body of belief for granted, each writer
on physical optics felt forced to build his field anew from its foundations.

The preparadigmatic stage gives way to more productive science when isolated
groups of researchers realize they have similar interests and that communication
and development of common language and techniques will facilitate progress.
This cooperation eventually leads to what Kuhn calls "normal science," or the
process of adding to a shared body of knowledge through theorizing and experi-
menting. What makes the normal stage different from the pre-normal is the
acceptance of common terminology, testing procedures, measurement
techniques, and, most importantly, basic assumptions about the nature of the
subject being studied. These basic assumptions, such as "The earth is the center
of the universe around which the sun moves," determine the meaning the ex-
perimenter assigns to his data. So an astronomer who believed the sun moved
about the earth understood a 24-hour day to be the period of the sun's orbit
around the earth. Astronomers, as a group, were interested in measuring the
sun's orbit and testing theories dealing with solar movement. Over time, astronomy generated a body of knowledge based on the earth-is-center assumption,
and this knowledge was passed along to each succeeding generation of
astronomers.

The normal stage gives way to the third or "crisis" stage when more sophisticated observational techniques generate new data which cannot be explained, or
ordered, by the old assumptions. For example, as new telescopes and measuring
devices led to observations which could not be explained by the earth-is-center
assumption astronomers began to question its accuracy. The result of this
questioning was Copernicus' theory that the sun was stationary and that the
earth and planets moved around it. Such a revolutionary assumption was not
immediately accepted by all Copernicus' colleagues. The fact that ancient beliefs
suddenly became obsolete made Copernicus few friends. In fact, the Pope was so
afraid the new assumption would throw man into confusion, he forced
Copernicus to disavow his theory. It was too late, however, for the theory was so
much better at explaining observations that acceptance was inevitable.

As in astronomy, the crisis stage ended with the adoption of new assumptions. Kuhn calls this re-organizing the "revolution" stage. This revolution leads
to a new stage of normal science, and the cycle begins again.

This description of Kuhn's findings introduces the concept which will be used
to organize the remaining chapters of this book.

THE CONCEPT OF PARADIGM

The key to Kuhn's explanation of scientific progress is the underlying assumption, such as "The earth is the center of the universe," which generates the common terminology and techniques. Kuhn calls this assumption, or set of assumptions, a "paradigm." Paradigm, or lack of it, defines Kuhn's stages. A paradigm is what unites the isolated researchers of a preparadigmatic period into the self-aware group that conducts normal science. In the normal stage, the paradigm provides a context, or *gestalt*, in which research is conducted and knowledge accumulated. When a group of investigators accepts a paradigm and proceeds into the stage of normal science, knowledge usually increases rapidly. A group with a paradigm and body of knowledge to augment and pass on to students becomes a "discipline." The investigations and research conducted by disciplines are highly organized. New students are introduced to the existing knowledge and latest research, with the expectations that some of them will solve the next logical problem growing from the last found solution. This situation is similar to puzzle-solving. The discipline points out puzzles or problems that are to be solved and proceeds to solve them using the insights gained from the paradigm. This process of selection and solution is guided by what the group sees as a "relevant problem." Here lies the connection between the gestalt theory described earlier and Kuhn's paradigms.

The group uses its paradigm very much as a gestalt. That is, the paradigm tends to determine which situations are seen as puzzles or problems deserving of the researcher's time. Kuhn (1970, p. 37) writes:

> ... One of the things a scientific community acquires with a paradigm is a criterion for choosing problems ... To a great extent these are the only problems that the community will admit as scientific or encourage its members to undertake ... One of the reasons why normal science seems to progress so rapidly is that its practitioners concentrate on problems that only their lack of ingenuity should keep them from solving.

The implications of paradigms acting as gestalts goes beyond the mere selection of problems to be solved. It is the gestalt function of the paradigm that leads to the crisis stage and the revolution. The crisis stage is brought on by the failure of an existing paradigm to explain anomalies. In the course of normal science, certain phenomena occur that are not expected. "Expected" is the key term, for a gestalt leads one to anticipate, or even impose order on, observations. (For example, the experiment in which a whole circle is seen even though the subject is shown the letter "C.")

As the paradigm leads to fuller knowledge, as the more obvious problems are solved, researchers begin to turn to more particular applications and look for more particular phenomena. This new research usually produces anomalies which are explained by adjusting the paradigm. After these adjustments, the research continues, and more anomalies are discovered. These, perhaps, are not so easily explained; the gestalt cannot be forced upon them.

At this point, investigators begin to question the validity of the new adjustment. The crisis is then precipitated and is not resolved until either the objections raised are satisfied by an acceptable adjustment to the old paradigm, or until a new paradigm is developed.

Kuhn goes to great length to explain the gestalt function of paradigm, including the discussion of a number of the gestalt theorists' experiments. He describes an experiment in which special playing cards are prepared so that there are anomalous cards, such as a black five of hearts or red five of spades. These cards, along with normal cards, are flashed before subjects who are asked to identify each. All subjects at first react by identifying the black five of hearts, for example, as either a five of hearts or a five of spades without commenting on the anomaly. As the exposure time is increased, some become hesitant to identify the card but eventually do, again incorrectly. When the time is greatly increased, some notice the anomaly; others continue to make the same mistakes, and others note that something is wrong but cannot identify the inconsistency.

Commenting on the experiment, Kuhn (1970, p. 112) writes:

> Either as a metaphor or because it reflects the nature of the mind, that psychological experiment provides a wonderfully simple and cogent schema for the process of scientific discovery. In science, as in the playing card experiment, novelty emerges only with difficulty, manifested by resistance, against a background provided by expectation. Initially, only the anticipated and usual are experienced even under circumstances where anomaly is later to be observed. Further acquaintance, however, does result in awareness of something wrong or does relate the effect to something that has gone wrong before. That awareness of anomaly opens a period in which conceptual categories are adjusted until the initially anomalous has become the anticipated. At this point the discovery has been completed. I have already urged that the process or one very much like it is involved in the emergence of all fundamental scientific novelties. Let me now point out that, recognizing the process, we can at last begin to see why normal science, as pursuit not directed to novelties and tending at first to suppress them, should nevertheless be so effective in causing them to arise.

Three primary assertions have been made in this chapter. The first is that when we observe the world either as ordinary men and women or as scientists, what we see is influenced by "gestalts" or ideas of what exists. These gestalts grow from previous experience with, and learned explanations of, reality. The second is that disciplines, or groups of researchers who share a body of knowledge, have paradigms which are necessary to the progress of normal science. A paradigm, however, can function as a gestalt and lead researchers to see things that are not there, or to ignore things that are. The third primary assertion is that disciplines, like people, go through a maturation process of rejecting paradigms no longer reasonable in the light of new experiences, and of accepting new, more accommodating gestalts. This maturation process of disciplines consists of a cycle of pre-normal to normal science. With these basic axioms as a foundation, we can move on to developing a means of applying the concept of paradigm to Public Health, Abnormal Psychology and Criminology.

THE DISCIPLINARY MATRIX

The primary criticism of Kuhn's work was that his description of paradigm was vague and needed more definition. Responding to the need for more clarity, Kuhn devised the "Disciplinary Matrix." Kuhn insisted that a paradigm could not be separated from the people who used it. So, while the concept had an abstract sense similar to the basic assumptions or gestalts noted earlier, it also had a sociological sense which reflected a discipline's need for communication, organization, and perpetuation through teaching students. To capture both the abstract and sociological senses, Kuhn suggested that paradigm be conceptualized as consisting of four elements. The first of these is the *basic assumptions* about the discipline's subject. These assumptions are usually stated in the form of general laws. The basic assumptions of pre-Copernican, or Ptolemeic, astronomy, for example, would be:
1. The earth is the center of the universe.
2. The sun moves around the earth.
3. The sun takes 24 hours to complete its orbit around the earth.

The second paradigm element is the *analogies* the discipline uses to clarify its basic assumptions. For example, you might begin to explain an automobile engine to someone by showing them a scale model which allows you to demonstrate how pistons move and what a crankshaft is. The model is essentially an analogy, in that you are saying it is "like" a real engine. An understanding of the model leads to an understanding of the engine. An analogy does not have to be an exact replica of the subject. Soccer, for example, could be explained to someone by saying it is like ice hockey played without ice or sticks.

The Ptolemeic paradigm of astronomy demonstrated its basic assumptions by using a globe representing the earth being circled by another globe representing the sun. By placing a candle in the sun's globe, day and night could be explained by moving the "sun" around the earth. By analogizing the universe to the model, the basic assumptions became clearer to the student.

The third element of a paradigm is the *conventions* its adherents adopt to facilitate experimentation and communication. These conventions include epistemology, descriptive mode, research setting, and unit of analysis.

"Epistemology" refers to the discipline's assumptions concerning the sources of knowledge. These assumptions vary along a continuum, one extreme of which is "empirical" epistemology. Empiricists contend that knowledge comes only from the identification, measurement, and classification of phenomena external to the scientist. In general, the empiricist believes that a subject cannot be studied if its identification and measurement cannot be replicated. At the other extreme of the epistemological continuum is the "intuitional" assumption. Intuitional epistemology contends that knowledge can be gained from insights not based on replicable investigative methods or explicit measurements. A good physician, for example, may be able to diagnose an illness from little measurable explicit data. The physician may not be able to explicitly describe the clue or the logic which led to the diagnosis, and, therefore, may not be able to teach others to replicate the procedure.

Communications among researchers can range from mathematical measurements and calculations to verbal descriptions. This convention, or "descriptive mode," will be divided into quantitative, which refers to mathematical measurement, and qualitative, which refers to verbal descriptions. It should be noted that the quantitative qualitative dichotomy is not the same as the empirical-intuitive differentiation. Empirical sciences may use qualitative descriptions, and intuited data can be described quantitatively.

A third convention, "research setting," deals with a discipline's experiments or theory-testing exercises. Some sciences deal with questions best answered in the laboratory where the environment can be carefully controlled. A chemist, for example, must have a laboratory to conduct his research. Other questions, such as those dealt with by geologists or archeologists, can only be answered by field observation. The paradigms we deal with in this book will be characterized as laboratory, if their research is done there, and as naturalistic, if done in the field.

The last convention arises from whether a discipline analyzes individual subjects, or the interrelationships among subjects, to answer the questions raised by its basic assumptions. Psychology, for example, has traditionally studied the individual to answer questions about human behavior. Sociology, because its questions relate to behavior as shaped by the interrelationships among individuals, must study groups. The convention describing this difference is referred to as the "level of analysis," and is usually either "individual" or "aggregate."

The last element of Kuhn's paradigm elements is *exemplars*. An exemplar is the presentation of a paradigm's assumptions, analogies, and conventions most often used to introduce students to a discipline. Exemplars are the classic works of a discipline, usually written by the field's most influential figures. In many cases, these works were those that lifted a field from pre-normal to normal science, or precipitated the revolution stage.

These exemplars play a very important role in the progress of science, for a paradigm's gestalt function is passed on to students through a discipline's exemplar. In other words, the exemplar teaches the student to see what his professors see when conducting research. Kuhn (1970, p. 144) writes:

> One of the fundamental techniques by which the members of a group, whether an entire culture or a specialists' sub-community within it, learn to see the same things

when confronted with the same stimuli is by being shown examples of situations that their predecessors in the group have already learned to see as like each other and as different from other sorts of situations.

The exemplar of Ptolemeic astronomy is Ptolemy's calendar, which was based on the earth-is-center assumption, and used by astronomers for centuries to predict celestial phenomena. The calendar and the assumptions underlying it were first described in Ptolemy's *Almagest*.

The four elements can be arrayed in matrix form to allow comparison of a discipline's succession of paradigms (Table 1-1).

Kuhn calls a table comparing the progression of a discipline's paradigms a Disciplinary Matrix. Disciplinary matrices for the paradigm progressions of Public Health, Abnormal Psychology, and Criminology will be constructed in subsequent chapters to demonstrate the historic and potential contributions of the ecological paradigm.

Paradigm and the Remaining Chapters

Kuhn's theory of paradigm progression and his disciplinary matrix have been introduced for several purposes. Among these purposes is to make obvious the need for more comprehensive paradigms by demonstrating the inadequacies of traditional approaches to training community service professionals. These approaches have attempted to either extend one discipline's paradigm beyond its primary subject to the community, or to assemble the community-oriented work of several disciplines into one curriculum.

An example of the unidisciplinary approach has been the training of community psychologists, which assumes the student should be primarily a psychologist with an interest in applied work. Students, therefore, are exposed to exemplars of psychology and learn to see the world as a psychologist would. The fault in this is that psychology's basic assumptions, analogies, conventions, and exemplars are concerned with measuring and explaining individual behavior as a function of internal, or very immediate, influences. This "person" oriented paradigm is of little help in measuring or explaining the economic and political forces which shape the larger environmental determinants of emotional stability.

The multidisciplinary approach typical of, for example, urban planning education, has not been any more successful. In this case, students are exposed to the paradigms of several disciplines in classes such as urban economics, urban sociology, and urban geography. This arrangement leads to the impossible demand that the student see different things when confronted with the same data. The result is that the student chooses one field in which to specialize, and becomes similar to the unidiscipline trained professional.

The result of uni- and multidisciplinary training has been the confusing and disconcerting situation in which several "experts" will attribute a problem to different causes and recommend conflicting, if not counteracting, remedies.

Table 1-1. Disciplinary Matrix of Astronomy

PARADIGM	BASIC ASSUMPTIONS	ANALOGIES	CONVENTIONS	EXEMPLARS
Ptolemeic ("Geocentric")	1. The earth is the center of the universe. 2. The Sun moves around the earth. 3. The Sun requires 24 hours to orbit the earth.	A model with earth at the center and the Sun in orbit	1. Empirical epistemology 2. Quantitative description 3. Naturalistic research 4. Aggregate level of analysis	*The Almagest* (Alexandria, c. 150 A.D.)
Copernican ("Heliocentric")	1. The Sun is the center of the universe. 2. The earth and the planets move around the Sun. 3. The earth requires 365¼ days to orbit the Sun.	A model with the Sun at the center and the earth in orbit	1. Empirical epistemology 2. Quantitative description 3. Naturalistic research 4. Aggregate level of analysis	*De Revolutionibus Orbium Coelestium* ("On the Revolutions of the Heavenly Spheres," Leipzig, 1543)

The process of paradigm progression will also be used to introduce the ecological paradigm, and describe its emergence from the work of biologists, economists and sociologists. A disciplinary matrix of the ecological paradigm will be constructed for comparison with other paradigms applied to community problems.

2 The Biological Basis of the Ecological Paradigm

One of the goals of this book is to suggest that many health and behavioral problems are precipitated by the process of adjusting to change in physical and social environments. Ecologists, or those who study adjustment, or adaptation, to environmental change, have developed a paradigm to further their work. This "ecological" paradigm was first used to analyze phenomena in the sub-human community, but eventually was borrowed by social scientists to help them understand human adaptation. The following three chapters describe several basic ecological principles and how these principles were first applied to human communities. This chapter introduces several concepts that were borrowed from biology in the 1920s to help establish a "human ecology" or the study of human adaptation to the environment. Chapter 3 describes the economic principles used by the first human ecologists to compare the sub-human community to the city. The explanations for illness and abnormal behavior suggested by the comparison are summarized in Chapter 4.

The ecosystem concept was developed to help ecologists explain changes in the size, mix, spatial distribution and behavior of sub-human populations in a given geographic area. The concept proved so useful in helping ecologists understand change in sub-human communities that sociologists inevitably borrowed it to determine if it could help explain change in human communities.

Several concepts dealing with the mechanics of change in an ecosystem will be described here. Key concepts dealing with change, and described in the following pages, are "perturbation," "homeostasis," and "equilibrium."

Students should also remember that the living components of the ecosystem have a *spatial* and a *trophic* order. Spatial order refers to where, in a map sense, different species are found in an ecosystem. Trophic order refers to the food chain or the complex set of interdependencies by which energy flows through the ecosystem. These two concepts are important for several reasons. The most important is that changes in either the spatial or trophic order require the organism in an ecosystem to adapt to new circumstances. The adaptation process, as will be suggested in subsequent chapters, can trigger health and behavioral problems.

DARWIN'S PERSPECTIVE ON LIFE

Just as Copernicus accomplished a scientific revolution in astronomy by radically altering the accepted model of the universe, Charles Darwin helped to bring about a fundamental revolution in biology by offering an entirely new perspective on the nature of life. This new perspective was described in *On the Origins of the Species* which was published in 1859. Three main components of the "Darwinian Revolution" are: the recognition of the "struggle for existence" in nature; the commitment to objective, "value-neutral" observation; and an understanding of the extremely long time periods required by evolutionary processes.

From reading Malthus' famous *Essay on the Principles of Population* (1798), Darwin acquired the idea that the number of individuals in any species inevitably tend to outrun the available food supply. In the resulting struggle for existence, extinction is always a real possibility for the species, as well as for the individual. Paraphrasing Darwin, present being is no assurance of future existence. To survive, an organism must avoid threats and take advantage of every opportunity. As a naturalist, Darwin was a keen observer of the sophisticated strategies for survival that were apparent in the behavior of living things. In the context of its environment, an organism's behavior tends to be "adaptive," that is, it "makes sense."

The second basic component of Darwin's perspective was its scientific detachment. Most of the "natural historians" who came before Darwin perceived the forms, interrelationships, and behavior of plants and animals in terms of human analogies, human motivations, and human belief systems. The "Social Darwinists," who wrote in the decades following the publication of *On the Origins of the Species*, also projected their values onto nature. Using ideas like the "survival of the fittest," they sought to justify the existing social and political order of the Victorian world by appealing to "scientific evidence." Darwin, however, did not collect his data to prove pre-conceived theory. The outlines of the theory emerged gradually over a period of many years as he amassed a vast body of field notes and observations. Whatever Darwin's beliefs were concerning the origin and purpose of life, they were carefully kept out of his published scientific writings. His successors and critics, who used On the Origins of the Species as an occasion for pro- and antireligious propaganda, were usually less objective.

Finally, Darwin recognized the importance of time. In the nineteenth century, geologists were only beginning to realize the antiquity of the earth by analyzing the successive layers of rock laid down over millions of years. But people are "tempo-centric," believing that only the events of the present time really matter as far as the future is concerned. A widely accepted estimate, in Darwin's time, placed the creation of the earth in 4004 B.C., based on computations from the generations listed in the Bible. Darwin saw nature as a process rather than a product, and emphasized that present biological facts could only be understood by considering the cumulative impact of small influences and minute variations operating over eons of time.

From this basic perspective, Darwin and his contemporaries Thomas Huxley (1825-1895) and Alfred Wallace (1823-1913), developed the concept of "evolution." "Stated simply, evolution means that the typical characteristics of a species will be determined over long periods of time, by the relative success of differing individuals in the struggle for existence. Darwin called the mechanism by which "favorable" variations tend to be preserved, and "unfavorable" ones destroyed, natural selection.

Natural Selection

To understand the revolutionary impact of the concept of natural selection, we need to examine the earlier concept of evolution which it replaced. This early, intuitive evolutionary theory was proposed in 1809 by the French naturalist Jean Lemarck. According to Lamarck, each organism in nature possesses an unconscious inner drive to achieve perfection. In striving to meet the demands of a changing environment, organisms gradually alter their behavior, and even their physical form. Giraffes stretch their necks to reach the topmost leaves on trees. Bats, by stretching the webbing between their fingers, gradually develop wings and master the art of flight. Rabbits, dependent on keen hearing for survival, develop larger and larger ears, and so forth. The key element in Lamarck's theory, however, is that these changes in each organism, or acquired traits, can be transmitted to future generations. Of course, our present understanding of genetics indicates that acquired traits cannot be inherited, and as laboratory biologists demonstrated this fact in countless experiments throughout the nineteenth century, the Lamarckian view of evolution lost credibility. But the puzzle remained: how to account for the variety and diversity of living species, and their precise adaptation to environmental factors without recourse to a divine master plan?

It remained for Darwin to solve the puzzle. From a study of the variations that naturally occur among domesticated species of animals and plants, he realized that no two organisms are ever *exactly* alike. By carefully selecting and crossing the most desirable traits in each generation, animal breeders had created new varieties: more productive crops, flowers with brighter colors, cattle that yielded more milk or beef, dog breeds adapted to specialized purposes. Taking the familiar fact of selective breeding as a model, or *analogy*, Darwin argued that nature also selects certain variations and discards others, not by conscious purpose, like the breeder, but "automatically" through the effects of environmental forces on the process of competition in the struggle for existence.

To make these ideas more concrete, imagine a herd of giraffes that is sufficiently mobile to avoid most of the threats to survival in its immediate environment, like predators, floods, or fires. Suppose, however, that a flood did not subside, that a geological change made their old grazing area a lake. Mobility may have allowed most of the herd to survive the immediate threat, but now the herd has to survive in a new environment. The vegetation might be different, requiring a change in feeding behavior. Assume that giraffes need fresh leaves to survive, and that the new area had taller trees than the old. The taller individuals would not have to adjust very much, but the shorter members of the herd would not find enough nutrition to survive.

As the shorter giraffes die out, the herd becomes smaller and the average height will be taller. The characteristics of the group have been altered, but no individual animal has stretched its neck.

The solid curve in Fig. 2-1 shows a distribution of heights in our herd. Statisticians call such a bell-shaped curve a "normal distribution," and it is very commonly found in measuring phenomena in the natural world. As shown, the *mean* (or average) height is 12 feet, while the range is from 8 to 16 feet. This distribution emerges over a long period of time, because any giraffes shorter than 8 feet, or taller than 16 feet, cannot compete for leaves as successfully as those between the extremes. Since height is genetically determined (taller parents will tend to have taller offspring), the distribution will remain relatively stable over time. The "average" giraffes will have more offspring than either extreme, simply because there are, by definition, more "average" giraffes.

The dashed curve in Fig. 2-1 shows the distribution of heights after the herd has moved to the area of taller trees. Most 8-foot animals have died, so few will be born in the subsequent generations. By the same process, more of the giraffes taller than 16 feet will survive, because there are now more leaves available to that group alone. As more of the taller giraffes survive to have offspring that will tend to resemble their parents, we see that the average height has become 13 feet, and the range is now from 9 to 17 feet.

The gradual process by which the average characteristics of a population change as individuals adjust, or fail to adjust, to their environment is called *natural selection*. Natural selection takes time to produce appreciable changes;

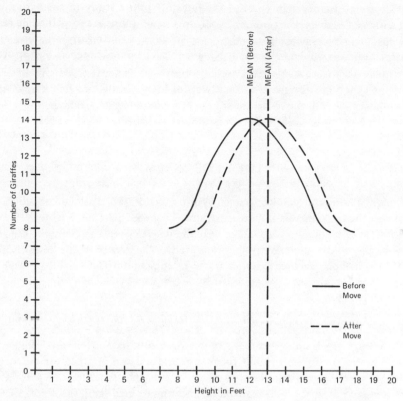

Fig. 2-1. Distribution of heights in a giraffe herd before and after migration to an environment of taller trees.

how much time, or how many generations of individuals, depends on the amount of change in the environment, and the natural variability of characteristics occurring in the group. Darwin never understood the reasons why variations occur spontaneously among the offspring of living things. The discovery of the laws of genetics, and the understanding of the mechanism of mutation were still unknown when Darwin wrote. It was sufficient for his theory that such processes *did* occur, and could be observed in nature.

It must be remembered that natural selection is *place-specific*. The process cannot be understood without investigating the changing environmental factors that affect the different groups of a species. In the Galapagos Islands, off the west coast of South America, Darwin noted that slight environmental differences between islands only a few miles apart had produced recognizably different varieties of turtles from the same ancestral species.

Of course, the environment always includes other organisms; some may be dangerous predators or parasites, some may coexist peaceably, and others may provide some positive benefit to the survival of another species (a relationship biologists call *symbiosis*). Imagine a group of lions that prey upon our giraffes. The change in the environment might not affect the lions directly, but once the giraffes have moved, the lions will have to follow, or else find new sources of nutrition. Darwin characterized these complex interrelationships among organisms and their environments as the "web of life." Changes in one part of this web impact on all the other members, reverberating throughout the entire structure. The "web of life" concept is the basis of all ecological studies.

THE ECOSYSTEM

Imagine a barren and desolate desert. Without water, there is no plant or animal life, even though minerals and nutrients may be present. At some remote time in the past, imagine that an earthquake near the desert causes the center of the area to sink, and uplifts the surrounding mountains. The center of the desert is now at the water table level and ground water reaches the surface, making it slightly moist. Soon we find cacti, or other hardy desert plants growing at the spot in the center (Fig. 2-2a).

Why? There are millions of spores and seeds of all kinds borne by the winds, or carried by migratory birds, over the desert. These seeds constantly fall on the sand, but never germinate because the environmental conditions are wrong: not enough water for most, too hot for many, and soil too infertile for nearly all. Cacti, however, need little moisture, lots of sun, and sandy soil to germinate, take root, and survive. In that central patch of moistened sand, the seeds of cacti will survive, even though similar seeds, and those of other species, had not succeeded there before.

Assume that some climatic shift increases the rainfall in the surrounding mountains, so that the water table rises, increasing the moisture available at the central spot. Soon we would find that the original stand of cacti disappeared, and there is now a circle of cacti growing a few yards around the original site (Fig. 2-2b). What has happened is that the sand in which the cacti had been growing became too wet for new cacti seeds to germinate; no new plants grew there, and the old ones eventually died, as their roots rotted in soil too wet for their survival.

The formerly dry sand a few yards around the old site, however, is permeated by increased moisture, becoming as damp as the old spot had been. In this circular band, seeds scattered from the old plants, or from some distant place by the wind, can now germinate and survive, thereby forming the circle of cacti we observe.

Something also happens in the wetter central area where the cacti used to thrive. There we find chapparal (a mixture of low, tough, hardy shrubs common in the natural vegetation of many areas of Southern California). The chapparal

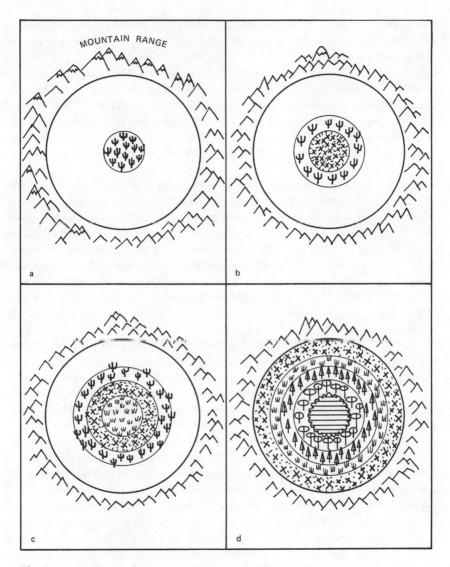

Fig. 2-2. a: Desert at time 1 (cactus). b: Time 2 (chapparal and cactus). c: Time 3 (grasses, chapparal and cactus). d: Time 4 (pond, hardwoods, softwoods, grasses and chapparal).

that previously could not survive because of lack of moisture can now thrive in the wetter central spot, which has also been enriched by the decomposed cacti that formerly thrived there.

If the desert remains static in terms of its water supply, sunlight, and soil fertility, the types and locations of plants found there may remain fairly constant. But nothing in nature is constant. The earth is always shifting; climates always changing—imperceptibly to the average observer, but changing none the less. As plants die and decompose, the soil becomes richer. Our desert's environment does not remain constant, and, of course, neither, therefore, can the organisms that live there.

Assume that the principal changes in the desert are increases in available water and in soil fertility. The central spot develops a small water hole as rainfall in the mountains increases, and the soil grows richer as chapparal and cacti die and decompose. As a result, the cacti will not survive in the old circular bands as the sand there becomes too wet. It will thrive, however, in a circle more distant from the water as that formerly dry area becomes damp with moisture now permeating further from the water hole. The chapparal that formerly grew on the central site will also die because its soil becomes too wet. It will, however, reappear in a circle formerly occupied by the cacti, for that area will be just right for the chapparal.

Between the chapparal and the water hole will appear a new plant type whose seeds could not previously survive there (Fig. 2-2c).

As the water hole becomes a pond, the process will continue, and new bands will occur in circles around the banks, and the cacti will constantly "move" further and further from the center, followed by the chapparal and plants which succeeded it.

It should be noted, no individual plant is actually "moving." Through natural selection, the type of organism best suited to a particular circular band becomes dominant there. Since no location remains the same, the pattern of most suitable plants shifts over time. The process reflects the fact that the organism best able to cope with the threats, and utilize the supports peculiar to a place, will eventually dominate there.

Eventually the cacti will reach the edges of the desert (Fig. 2-2d) and find no more dry areas. The cacti will, therefore, disappear. At this point, perhaps, the place could no longer be called a "desert" for it will be green and filled with plants that require water and fertile soil.

The increasing water supply probably meant that weather conditions had changed and that rain clouds appeared more often, meaning there were fewer days of bright sunlight. The chapparal would also disappear, but other plant species would have appeared. Trees, softwoods at first and eventually hardwoods, could appear making the former desert a forest.

There are a number of terms used by biologists to describe the process outlined in the example. The area and the things that live there are called an "ecosystem." It is a geographic area which supports a community of plants and animals. An ecosystem can be defined by physical boundaries, such as mountains, or by characteristics, such as altitude, soil types, or temperature. A particular combination or community of plants and animals will usually be characteristic of ecosystems having similar qualities.

The ingredients in an ecosystem which determine the types of plants that will thrive there are called the "abiotic" elements. Water, minerals, sunlight, and organic composition of the soil are among the abiotic elements.

The plant and animal life that exists in an ecosystem is called the "biotic" element. The ecosystem in our example would have been supporting animal life. And in the same way that the plant life changed as the abiotic elements shifted, the animal life also would have changed.

Animals, of course, have considerably more mobility than do plants, adding considerable complexity to the biotic changes. If, for example, a certain type of rodent thrived best in desert conditions and its environment began changing, it could move to an area where the conditions remained within the parameters of the rodent's ability to adjust. In the example, a rodent could scurry over the hills bounding our valley to the next ecosystem which may or may not be more desert-like.

Chances are that the forces that changed the rodent's old ecosystem are not local. The changes most likely occurred over an area larger than the animal's ability to migrate. In this case those members of the rodent population that have genetically controlled variations enabling them to withstand less desert-like conditions will survive while the rest disappear. The rodent population will become dominated by those that possess the genes that produce larger size. The result will be the "evolution" of the rodent from its former desert characteristics to the type of rodent found more commonly in forests.

Of course, it is possible that a species cannot move far enough, or have enough variation among its members, to allow survival in the face of environmental changes. It will then become extinct.

Trophic Organization

In any ecosystem, complex relationships develop not only between the biotic and abiotic elements but also among the biotic elements themselves. Plants are eaten by insects and by animals who also eat other animals. Larger animals eat insects and smaller animals. Animals and plants decompose and excrete and fertilize other plants. These nutritional relationships are called "food webs," or trophic organizations, and become quite complex. An example of a trophic organization is the interdependency that develops among the biotic elements of the chapparal ecosystem of Southern California and Baja, Mexico (Fig. 2-3).

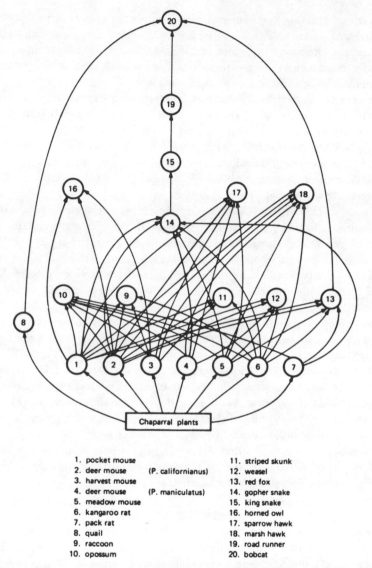

Fig. 2-3. The basic foodweb of the chaparral ecosystem. Deliberately omitted from this is a shrub-mule deer-cougar food chain, which is now sometimes absent because of human disturbance of this ecosystem resulting from the hunting of both animals. Earlier hunters from middle Pleistocene times are believed to have disrupted yet other food chains of this ecosystem by exterminating such animals as sloths, camels and horses and thus causing their predators such as "lion" and saber-toothed cat also to pass to extinction.

The chaparral ecosystem we have today, even in areas where we refer to it as "undisturbed," has been vastly and irreversibly changed by approximately 20,000 years of human occupation.

Omitted from this diagram entirely are insects. Every animal in this foodweb probably eats one or more insect species at some stage. (From Boughey, A. *Fundamental Ecology.* London: Intext, 1971. Reproduced by permission.)

Predicting the Pattern and Behavior of Biotic Elements

As described in our example, the biotic elements of an ecosystem assume a spatial arrangement determined by the abiotic elements and the dictates of the food web. Each member of the biotic community becomes dominant in an area best suited to it. A group's area is called its "niche." In our example, the niches, as viewed from above, form a circle which grows as water permeates further from the water hole. The process of expansion creates zones in transition, in which one group becomes dominant while another is dying out. How large the transitionary zones are depends, in theory at least, on how quickly the niches are changing, or how fast the amount of moisture in the soil increases.

Ecologists, or biologists specializing in the study of interrelationships among species, use a tool called a "gradient" which helps them describe the spatial arrangements in an ecosystem. Figure 2-4 is a simplified gradient. It shows a cross-cut, or earth-level side view, of one side of an African ecosystem. The river, at the left, supplies the moisture which permeates out through the soil, creating niches dominated by the plant groups and the animals best suited to the area.

This pattern can remain relatively stable over what we would consider a long period of time. This means the abiotic elements are changing very slowly, so the types of biotic elements present and their arrangement change slowly. Under such conditions, the food web becomes established and predator-prey, symbiotic, and parasitic relationships create a biotic population which remains roughly constant in its size and proportional makeup of species. This arrangement of biotic elements, or trophic organization, appears to be self-regulating. That is, the complex interdependencies preclude one species from completely depleting its prey, or from going without symbiotic or parasitic partners.

Under such conditions, the ecosystem can be studied to determine how much energy in the form of sunlight, how much nutrition from the soil, and how much water are needed to support the size and mix of the biotic elements. Such stable conditions also allow the study of biotic behavior, or what plants and animals do. On the simplest level, one can say that all biotic elements do is motivated by the drive to perpetuate the species. This involves behavior intended to maintain the current population, such as feeding and territorial defense, as well as mating behavior intended to bring forth a succeeding generation.

In a stable ecosystem, the feeding behavior of any group can be watched and eventually an understanding of the trophic organization developed. The role or function of each species in the generation and distribution of nutrition can be identified. Knowing this, we can predict who will prey on whom, where, and at what time.

A second aspect of behavior that can be studied in a stable ecosystem is individual and group behavior motivated by threats to territory. Each organism adjusts to a particular place in which it is most secure. Any threats to the stability or predictability of that place are resisted. Social rank is often measured by how large or how well protected an individual's territory is. Interaction

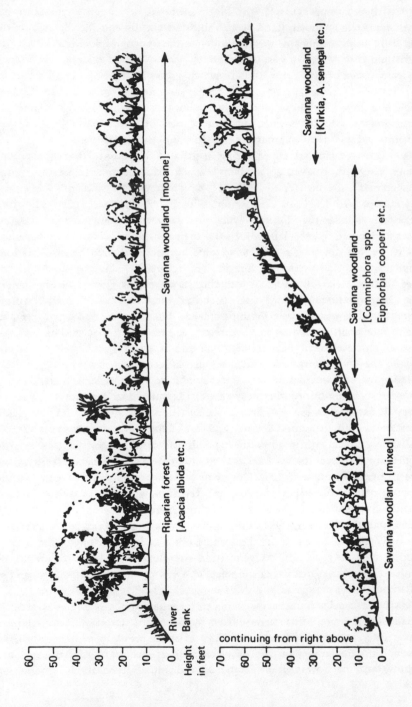

Fig. 2-4. A catena vegetation pattern illustrating variation in the plant communities of a savanna in South Central Africa. In this relatively undisturbed area plant community types conform to a topographical pattern related to the depth of soil and the availability of water there. The vegetation catena conforms closely to the soil catena pattern which determines it. (From Boughey, A., 1971. Reproduced by permission.)

among individuals motivated by territoriality leads to social patterns which apparently follow generalized laws.

Under stable conditions, mating behavior can also be studied and predicted. The drive to procreate is very strong and, when the mating season arrives, social and feeding behavior can be changed greatly. Understanding the mating behavior of the species, therefore, is essential to predicting behavior.

Perturbation

We have seen that the abiotic elements control the size, makeup, and spatial distribution of the biotic elements. In the preceding section, the patterns and behavior that we described were based on fairly constant, or slowly changing, abiotic elements, but we are most interested in the dynamics of change. That is: what happens to the trophic organization when the rate of abiotic change accelerates?

Biologists call agents which enter an ecosystem and alter its organization "perturbations." These can include, for example, the arrival of man or of new animal species escaping change in their old ecosystem, or changes in energy, moisture, or other abiotic elements.

Returning to our example of the desert ecosystem, the introduction of water was a perturbation which disrupted prior stability. Whatever balance had previously existed among insects and other organisms was disrupted. Cacti appeared and led to more perturbations in the form of decaying plants. If the amount of moisture had stabilized, balance would have been restored, creating a new spatial pattern and trophic organization. This organization would have new species such as the cacti, and would lack the old which did not have enough variation in its population to survive. New feeding, territorial, and mating behavior would result from the pattern changes and addition of new members.

Since abiotic elements are never constant, ecologists must become familiar with the effects of perturbations. Many techniques, including computer modeling, are used to describe ecosystems and predict what will happen to spatial arrangements and behavior when perturbations are introduced. Beyond its purely scientific value, the ability to predict such effects is important to decision makers who must weigh, for example, the economic benefits of building a dam against its impact on natural systems.

Invasion and Succession

In the desert ecosystem that we described, one could predict roughly what would happen as the perturbation of increased moisture was introduced. As the moisture permeates outward, each circle-like niche would shift outward by expanding its circumference. Individuals at the outer edge of each circle would invade into the area that was formerly best suited to another plant type. This would form a zone in transition where both the invader and invaded exist side by side until the former succeeds to dominance. This process of invasion and succession is often hastened by some characteristic of the invader plant which makes it even more difficult for the remaining members of the old species to survive. For example, the invading plant may be taller, blocking the sunlight of the old plants, or the invader may emit a vapor, which destroys the seeds of other plants more quickly than the change in soil moisture.

While the inner edge of a plant group is being invaded, its outer edge is invading the next group, creating another zone in transition. So each niche is invading outward while being invaded on its inner side. New species, moreover, are being introduced at the banks of the pond as more fertile niches form there. The result is a set of expanding circular niches which continue to expand as long as the perturbations of slowly increasing moisture and fertility are maintained.

Animals, insects, and their behavior are greatly affected by this perturbation. Their niches must also change, causing invasions and successions and constant adjustment in the trophic organization as new members enter and old die out.

Catastrophic or sudden changes in abiotic elements make the patterns and behavior of the biotic elements difficult to predict. The trophic organization is disrupted. Food webs break down. Former symbiotic partners might prey on each other. The disappearance of old prey leads predators to find new sources of nutrition. Niches and territory may become impossible to defend. Mating habits change. Under such conditions, biotic elements may be predictable only in the sense that they can be expected to do things not usually observed in a stable ecosystem.

SYSTEMS TERMINOLOGY

The concepts described in the present chapter have been given names that will be used in the following chapters and in many other works dealing with ecological principles. An ecosystem has "boundaries" within which elements interact with each other to reach balance. These boundaries are often geographically defined, and the interacting elements are the biotic members and abiotic conditions. The balance sought by the elements is called "equilibrium." In our example, when the abiotic elements were constant and the trophic organization stable, so that the behavior of the biotic elements was predictable, the ecosystem could be described as "in equilibrium."

When a perturbation was introduced, the situation was one of "disequilibrium." The process by which the biotic elements seek to return to equilibrium with each other and the abiotic elements is called "homeostasis."

Restated in systems terminology, the earlier assertions regarding perturbation and predictability yield the following principles. The biotic elements of an ecosystem seek equilibrium with the abiotic elements. Homeostatic processes, such as invasion and succession, create more or less predictable biotic patterns and behavior. The further an ecosystem is from equilibrium, the less predictable is behavior; the closer to equilibrium, the more predictable.

THE IMPORTANCE OF BIOLOGICAL CONCEPTS
TO THE ECOLOGICAL PARADIGM

The concepts that have been introduced in this chapter are important because they were used by the Chicago School to devise the ecological paradigm. When introduced to data describing the spatial arrangement and behavior of human communities, Park, McKenzie, and their colleagues recognized patterns similar to those of natural ecosystem. This similarity led to the analogy between human and plant communities which is the historic precursor to the ecological paradigm.

Biology, however, is only one of the disciplines which contribute to the ecological paradigm and, therefore, the Social Ecology. The other chief contributors that must be considered are economics and sociology.

3 The Economic Basis of the Ecological Paradigm

The ecosystem concept proved to be such a powerful predictor of change in sub-human communities that, by the 1920s, sociologists were applying it to the human community. The sociological use of the concept assumed that the human community had characteristics analogous to abiotic and biotic elements as well as to trophic and spatial organization. This assumption was based on economic theories dealing with the nature, location and growth of cities. This chapter describes these theories and how they demonstrate the need for understanding the health and behavioral costs of community change.

The student should pay special attention to several concepts. The first is "division of labor" or the complex set of economic interdependencies among producers, consumers, managers, laborers, etc. This set of interdependencies, upon which the community depends for its material means of support, was seen by sociologists as analogous to the biotic element or trophic organization of the ecosystem.

Another important concept is "economic base" which refers to the role a community plays in the regional or national system of collection, production, and distribution. The economic base of the community, for reasons discussed here, was viewed by the ecologists as similar to the abiotic elements of the ecosystem.

A third key concept is "geometry of industrial location" or the process by which the economic bases of communities are established and changed.

Perhaps the two most important topics in this chapter are "highest and best use" and "social cost." These concepts will give the student an insight into the market theory of economics which influences many decisions regarding community change in America. Once the market model and its flaws are understood, the need for an ecological approach to the study of illness and abnormal behavior will become clear.

While most people think of money when they hear "economics," the scope of the discipline is much broader. On the broadest level, economics can be described as the science concerned with man's allocation of any scarce good. Such goods include all the material things usually purchased with money, as well as less tangible goods, such as prestige, power, or security. Security, in fact, is what underlies much of what we ordinarily consider to be economically motivated behavior. The drive to insure that we will, in the near or distant future, be in a circumstance we find acceptable is a very powerful explainer of human behavior. It is the common denominator of human and sub-human species, for, as noted in Chapter 2, much of what animals or plants do can be understood as part of a strategy to insure their survival. In the same fashion that sub-human communities develop into trophic organizations, human communities are means for individuals and groups to increase their security. It is this similarity which led the early human ecologists to analogize the metropolis to the ecosystem.

PREINDUSTRIAL MARKET CENTERS

The Emergence of Preindustrial Market Centers

While there are probably as many reasons for the appearance of cities as there are cities, some theories based on observation, common sense, and logic have become widely accepted explanations of man's tendency to aggregate into communities. Consider the question "Why do people not exist as independent, isolated individuals?" The most obvious answer is that survival of the species requires physical proximity of its members. The procreative process would be impossible without social interaction. Beyond the interaction necessary to allow procreation, sustained proximity is a necessary characteristic of the human family which is the basic human trophic organization. The preindustrial family was an economic unit in which each member played a role crucial to the survival of the whole. In fact, children in the so-called "underdeveloped" areas are still seen as means to increase the survival chances of their parents (Hawley, 1973).

Given the family unit, and occasional extra-family contact to allow for mate selection, is there a need for greater density and interaction of population? Could not family farms spread miles apart, and mate selection be accomplished with minimal interaction?

For people to exist in dispersed family units without interaction, except for mating, the following conditions would have to prevail. First, each family would have to be physically strong enough, and each farm fertile enough, to produce all that is needed for survival. Second, no one could have social, political, or religious needs requiring interaction beyond the immediate family. These conditions obviously do not exist. Even if the political, religious, or social needs of man disappeared, it would be very difficult for any family to produce all it needs to maintain itself at a level of existence recognizable as human. Even if the family members were talented enough, it is not likely they could find a location with resources in a form easily enough worked to allow them to produce all they wanted, given limited time and physical energy.

Individual vulnerability and limited ability to work leads to the division of labor and the emergence of human communities. Faced with the reality that an individual family, no matter how talented, would find it difficult to produce all it needed to survive, man has become specialized. Specialization means that someone with the talent or inclination to farm, and with a farm suited to growing vegetables, becomes a vegetable farmer. Another with the land and aptitude for dairy farming becomes a dairyman. Others concentrate their efforts on growing grain or on raising meat-yielding cattle. Each then exchanges his product for that of another. It is important to comprehend what benefits are accrued by such specialization. By concentrating his efforts, an individual can become knowledgeable about one type of crop—more knowledgeable than anyone who has to divide his efforts among many endeavors. Assuming the specialized farmer chooses the crop best suited to his land, the combination of expertise and proper soil means he can produce more yield per unit of labor than non-specialists. It also means he can take the time to breed the best strain of a particular species. thereby adding quality to quantity.

The cost of specialization is dependence. The expert at growing grain obviously must exchange his surplus produce for the milk of the dairyman, the meat of the cattleman, and the produce of the vegetable farmer. Each specialist needs the other specialists. They are free to specialize only if others do. The complex set of interrelationships arising from specialization and interdependence is called the "division of labor."

Of course, specialists need to exchange their products, otherwise their efforts are futile. Exchange means carrying one's produce to those with whom exchange is intended. Carrying and exchange could be done in an unstructured fashion, that is, one could load a wagon and go to the individual with whom he hopes to exchange at whatever time he likes. This would be a chaotic process, because one could travel to a potential customer and find that he is out, or that he has no goods, or inferior goods, to exchange. The trip was, therefore, a waste of time and labor which could have been spent producing greater yield. Since the first trip was unsuccessful, another equally risky trip is required.

Such haphazard trading would negate the benefits of the division of labor.

Faced with this realization, farmers arranged a time and convenient place for all to bring their produce. Such an exchange, or market, allowed each to choose from the largest number of suppliers, and to offer his own produce to the greatest number of customers.

The location of the market was crucial. It had to be at a spot accessible to all participants. The distance one must travel to the spot must not be so long that the time required spoils milk or produce. More importantly, the time factor must not be so long that its cost, in terms of displaced labor and energy, is greater than the cost of producing the desired produce oneself. In other words, a vegetable farmer goes to the market to exchange a bushel of corn, which took him one hour's labor to produce, for a gallon of milk, which would have taken him, for example, three hours to produce. This leaves him two hours surplus to dedicate to improving the yield and quality of his vegetables. If, however, the market were one and a quarter hours from his farm, the round trip would take two and a half hours, which means he would lose half an hour's labor. In this case, the farmer would not participate in the market. The time it takes to exchange must take less than two hours, otherwise he gains no benefit from participating in the division of labor.

The Spatial Arrangement of Preindustrial Market Centers

The need to be close enough to a market to make the division of labor possible created a spatial arrangement of markets called the "Central Place" pattern (Berry, 1967; Christaller, 1966; Losch, 1941). To understand the forces that led to the central place arrangement, consider an island which is relatively flat and equally fertile throughout. Assume the island is covered by farms roughly equal in size. To gain the benefits of the division of labor, a market is begun in the center of the island. As demonstrated earlier, a market will only draw farmers from a distance at which exchange of goods produces a time surplus. Assume, in this case, the distance is one mile. The result is the formation of a circular service area with a radius of one mile (Fig. 3-1a) around the market. Inside this circle, farmers will travel to the market to exchange the goods they specialize in producing. Because each specialty is likely to be represented by more than one farmer, producers can "shop," compare quality, and work out the exchange they feel is most beneficial to them. The shopping process leads to competition and, therefore, to higher quality and reasonable exchanges.

A second market is established because farmers outside the mile service area also want the benefits of the division of labor. The founders of the second market want to include as many farmers as possible in the division of labor so the new market is established two miles to the east of the old. Following the example of the second market, a third is established two miles to the south of both the existing markets. A fourth is added to the north, again at two miles distance (Fig. 3-1b). Fifth, sixth and seventh markets likewise form to the west of the original, always maintaining a distance of two miles from the existing sites

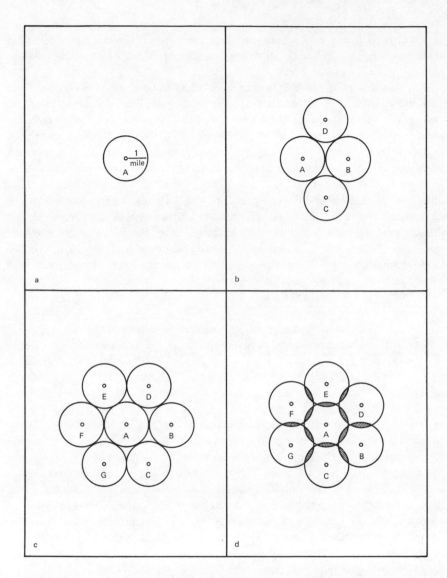

Fig. 3-1. a: Market and service area. b: Original market and three additional markets. c: Original market and six additional markets. d: Overlapping service areas formed to cover interstitial areas.

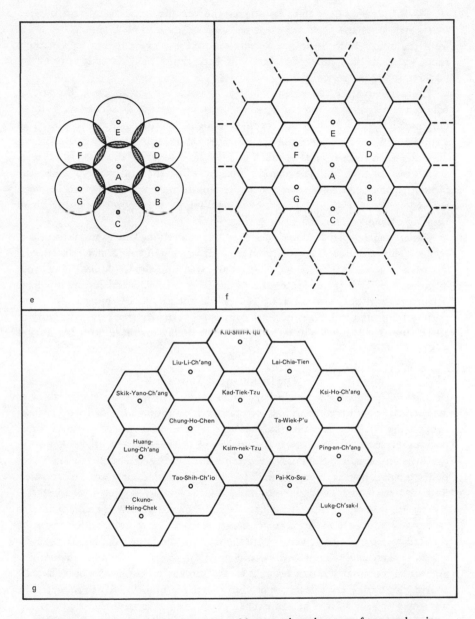

Fig. 3-1 (continued). e: The emergence of hexagonal market areas from overlapping circular areas. f: Honeycomb pattern of markets and service areas. g: An example of central place markets found in a rural area of Szechwan, China.

(Fig. 3-1c). The result is that the original market and service area is surrounded by six new ones and their service areas. Each of the markets is spaced two miles from the other. There is no reason why the formation of evenly spaced markets should stop at this point. Markets will form until our island is covered by markets and their service areas.

The service areas, however, will not remain circular, because the spaces between the circles, or interstitial areas, are not covered. To service these areas, our market centers shift closer together reducing the distance between each to 1.8 miles (Fig. 3-1d). While this seems irrational at first glance, because overlap develops, each market adds as much area by now covering the interstitial areas, as it loses by overlap. The market areas in effect become hexagons because farmers in the overlapping areas go to the closest market, forming lines between the service areas (Fig. 3-1e). These hexagonal service areas cover the entire island forming a honeycomb configuration (Fig. 3-1f).

While "central place theory," as the logic underlying our example is called, seems highly abstract, the orderly or uniform spacing of towns and market areas has been observed in several agricultural areas around the world including those in Germany, Washington State, and China (Fig. 3-1g). Several researchers have performed analyses demonstrating that when the effects of topography, transport systems, and soil differences are considered, central place logic is at work in areas where there appears to be little rhyme or reason to market location (Mayer & Kohn, 1954).

The Hierarchy of Towns

Permanent populations, including facilitators of religious, political, and maintenance functions, as well as non-farming members of the division of labor, convert the equally spaced markets of our example into towns. Among the most obvious of the town dwellers is the trader, who served an essential function in the division of labor. Suppose a vegetable farmer needed milk, but on a particular market day no one with milk to exchange needed, or wanted, vegetables. Rather than going without the milk, the vegetable farmer exchanged his vegetables with the trader who gave him tokens in return. These tokens, or money, usually were made of some scarce substance, like gold, which could be equated to the value of produce. With the money, the farmer could buy the milk from the dairyman, who, in turn, would go to the trader and purchase something he needed, but that was not brought to the market on the day he needed it. Of course, the trader never gave the producer as much money for his product as he was going to sell it for. The difference between what he paid the producer and what he sold the product for was the trader's income. Money became a common denominator with which the relative values of products could be compared. A bushel of corn was worth, for example, one gold piece, a gallon of milk, two, etc. The use of currency revolutionized the division of labor, for it freed it from the barter or pure exchange system.

In addition to the trader, other members of the division of labor resided in the market. If a farmer became very good at making shovels, he could do so on his farm, bring them to market, and sell to other farmers who came to exchange their produce. Unlike the others, however, he did not have to live on a farm to make his product. He could just as well have rented a small piece of land near the market and made his shovels there, avoiding the waste of time of moving back and forth to a farm he did not till. Moreover, he could spend all his time perfecting his skills and selling his product. In fact, if he stayed out on the farm, a competitor near the market devoting all day to shovel making could eventually produce more shovels per unit of labor, and underprice him. Craftsmen not tied to the land moved to the market.

The addition of craftsmen to the towns leads to a phenomenon which can be explained by returning to the island example.

Because different goods have different service areas, some markets will offer more products than others and will have larger service areas. For example, assume there are 100 market towns on the island, each offering milk, vegetables, grain, and shovels. At some point, a farmer who is an especially good carpenter gives up farming to move to town to make and sell fine furniture. He is successful, and other towns begin to attract cabinetmakers, until all 100 have them. Soon the furniture makers find that they have only half the sales they need to make their business more profitable than farming. The result is that half will go back to farming. The remaining carpenters discover that customers are willing to travel twice as far to buy furniture than vegetables, for to make their own furniture would take more time than the longer trip. Only 50 towns keep furniture makers, and these towns are spread at twice the distance than are market towns without furniture makers. It should be noted that the towns with furniture makers continue to sell meat, vegetables, grains and shovels, and that their service areas for those products remain the same.

There would, of course, be products and services that are purchased either less frequently or by fewer people than is furniture. Art, for example, would be available at fewer markets spaced at greater distances. The extension of this logic is that some products require the entire population of the nation to support their production and sale, so they will be available only at one city, which will also offer all the other services and goods down to meat and vegetables. This leads to a "hierarchy" of towns and cities which includes one city offering all goods and services, and subsequent ranks with more cities offering fewer goods. The lowest rank has the most towns offering the most basic array of goods and services.(Berry, 1967).

The Growth of Preindustrial Towns

So far we have seen that preindustrial human communities emerged from the division of labor, and that their location and economic functions were not randomly determined. Before we can move on to draw the increasingly obvious analogy between human communities and the natural ecosystem, however, some very important processes must be understood. These pertain to economic flows, population growth, and migration.

Assume the island we have been using for an example is preindustrial Britain. The social structure of Britain in that period was made up roughly of three types of people, those wealthy enough to live wherever they pleased, those who had to follow the wealthy, and those tied to land. The wealthy were usually property owners whose land was given to them or their ancestors by royalty. Their land was farmed by tenant farmers who paid rent in the form of a percentage of the crops produced. The land owner would sell his share of the crop to the trader for gold or currency. This system encouraged the farmer to work hard, for the absolute value of his share, and that of the landlord, increased as the total crop size increased.

Early observers (Steuart, 1966) of the landed class wrote that the wealthy, who were usually also educated, chose to spend a good portion of their time in town, away from their country estates. The reason, we are told, was mainly that the wealthy classes were ostentatious; that is, they enjoyed exhibiting their wealth and taste to other wealthy, educated people. By moving to town and building a "townhouse," the wealthy could socialize with their peers and indulge their ostentation. Given the choice of all the market towns, they usually chose those close to travel routes or harbors. This allowed them to purchase more goods and services, as well as goods from distant places. London, for example, by virtue of its political and ceremonial role, as well as its harbor, was a very attractive town for the wealthier, more ambitious families. Other cities further down the hierarchy and more widely dispersed also collected their share of lesser gentry.

Once the wealthy began moving to towns to spend money and impress their peers, those craftsmen and merchants who sold goods to the wealthy had to follow. These craftsmen were those whose skill and artistry produced objects or services of little value to, or too highly priced for, those who participated in the smaller markets. If, for example, a blacksmith advanced to the point where he produced elegant wrought iron fixtures, he would not be able to find buyers in small markets, for the price of the time he invested in the product would make it too expensive for the farmer. The only alternative, if the craftsman wanted to progress in developing his skills, was to go to the larger towns where potential customers were. The greatest art and institutions of education emerged from the cities because only there could an artist, poet, or teacher find someone to buy his product, allowing him to devote his time to perfecting his skills.

The third class, or farmers, had to stay on the farms. Some stayed by choice because it was all they knew, others stayed because they had incurred debt to a land owner, and they and their children had to work until it was paid.

As noted earlier, tenant farmers always strove to increase their income by increasing their crop size. This could be achieved by adding labor. When a farmer and his family were working as intensively as possible, but had more land to work, extra hands could be hired. This was rational as long as the value added to the crop by the laborer was greater than his wages. At some point, however, adding another hand would cost more than what his labor produced. The land was being worked as intensively as possible given existing technology. This meant the farmer and his landlord had reached the limit of their profits.

When this point was reached, it influenced the growth of the towns in two important ways. First, any growth in the rural population would mean people would be without work. Since there was no welfare, the surplus population had to do something to live. The most obvious strategy was to lower the price asked for one's labor. This meant the farmer could hire help at reduced costs. The effect, however, was to lower the income of all agricultural laborers, for everyone had to lower his wage demands to compete for jobs. This disenchanted many laborers. The most adventuresome and talented decided to go to the city to try their luck at some craft or service.

A second outgrowth of having reached the point at which land was being worked as intensively as possible was to move the landlords to commission the construction of labor saving devices. Profits for both the farmer and landlord equaled the value of the crop less the cost of production. Since the total crop could no longer be increased because all an owner's land was being worked as productively as possible, the only way to increase profit was to lower production cost. While the oversupply of labor helped to do this by lowering laborer's wages, the advantages of city life were drawing more and more of the most talented help. The only long run solution was to reduce labor costs by replacing men with machines. Improved tools and ploughs had been developed before this time, but there was little demand for them because the cost of increasing crop size by merely cultivating more land was less than that of the tool. Once all an owner's available land was being worked as intensively as possible, however, his and his tenant farmers' only alternative was to reduce labor costs. Landlords, therefore, commissioned craftsmen to make the tools which began to reduce the demand for agricultural labor. The result was to create more surplus labor, much of which moved to town. Each time a landlord's income went up, he would spend more in town. As more was spent in town, more people were attracted to it. The division of labor became amazingly diverse. Jugglers, musicians, jesters, actors, and myriad other roles were devised to earn the money needed to live from day to day. Since demand for unskilled industrial labor had not yet begun, and because the alternative was abject rural poverty, sheer need motivated individuals to create ways to earn cash. One's imagination was the limit. In Paris, for example, one group, called "The 14th's," made its living when a superstitious hostess was troubled to find only 13 of her invited guests arrived for a dinner party. She would send quickly for a "14th" who made a living with his talent as a professional party goer!

Not all roles were officially encouraged. Prostitution, thievery, fraud, and other illegal pursuits produced money for those with the inclination, skills, or lack of alternatives.

The "Cost of Friction" and "Highest and Best Use"

As seen in our example of central place theory, the cost of moving through space has a great impact on the location of markets. While time spent in transit was cited as the principal cost, there are others. In pre-industrial society, other costs included wear and maintenance of animals and wagons. These costs, time and wear, as a class are referred to as the "cost of friction." The cost of friction will vary with distance from market and the type of goods being moved. It costs more to move something ten miles than five miles, and more to move a perishable good than a nonperishable good five miles. The value of milk, for example, depends on its freshness, so the five miles have to be covered more quickly than if hay were being moved. Animals and vehicles moving milk, therefore, must be worked harder. The containers used for moving perishable liquids, moreover, have to be much more complex, and, therefore, more costly, than those for hay.

These variables had a great impact on the use of land around the growing towns. Agricultural economists of the nineteenth century studied these effects and generated theories of land use based on the cost of friction (von Thunen, 1826). To understand these, consider the following example. Assume you inherited a farm eight miles from one of the growing towns described above. You must decide what uses to put your farm to, and, understanding the division of labor, you know one crop will dominate. You spend a few days observing the market activities to find which products are bringing the highest prices. Simplifying our example, assume there are four types of products being exchanged in the market: milk, vegetables, cereal grains, and hay. You note that milk is bringing $20 per wagon load, vegetables $15, cereals $10, and hay $5. You ask the various sellers what their production costs were per wagon, and find they were $10, $7, $4, and $1 respectively. Based on the data, you compute the following:

	Milk	Vegetables	Cereals	Hay
Selling price	$20	$15	$10	$5
Production costs	$10	$ 7	$ 4	$1
Profits	$10	$ 8	$ 6	$4

Given your naivete and computations, you decide to become a dairyman. When your first yield of milk is ready, you call a milk transporter to bring the milk to market. Upon asking his price you are dismayed to find it is $2 per mile. The transporter, to pay for his cooling tanks, ice, wagon, and fast moving animals must charge that much to make a living. Since you are eight miles from market, his bill of $16 will not only wipe out your profit, but put you $6 in debt. You move your milk, take your loss, and decide to look more closely into the cost of friction before converting your land to some other crop.

After some researching you find that vegetables cost $.80 per wagon load per mile to move, cereals $.40 and hay $.20. Subtracting these figures from your profit figures, you generate the following table:

	Milk	Vegetables	Cereals	Hay
Selling price per wagon	$20	$15	$10	$5
Production costs	$10	$ 7	$ 4	$1
Profit before cost of friction	$10	$ 8	$ 6	$4
Cost of friction at 8 miles	$16	$ 6.40	$ 3.20	$1.60
Profit or loss	-$ 6	$ 1.60	$ 2.80	$2.40

Given your new calculations, you decide to become a cereal farmer. The point of the example is that the cost of friction is a crucial consideration in any decision dealing with land use. Over time, all farmers at a distance of eight miles will decide to grow cereals because those crops bring them the highest profit. Someone not perceptive enough to understand the economics underlying the example would soon be brought into line, because his landlord, whose profit is a share of the farmer's profit, would make sure the most lucrative crops are grown. As we will see shortly, someone who owns his own land, and is not using it to produce the most profit, is often brought into line by societal pressure manifested in land taxes.

The effect of each farmer producing the most lucrative crop is the emergence of a predictable pattern of crops around a market. Returning to the costs given in the example, a graph can be constructed which demonstrates the patterning of crops. In Fig. 3-2 the horizontal axis is distance from the market, and the vertical is profit. The four lines represent the profit earned by each crop type at a given distance from market. At the market or "0" on the horizontal axis, a wagon load of milk, for example, brings $10 profit. As you move away from the market, profit drops $2 per mile as the cost of friction increases. At five miles, profit is 0. The line for vegetables starts at $8 at the market and reaches 0 at ten miles. The line for cereals intercepts the vertical axis at $6 (profit at market) and the horizontal axis at 15 miles, or the point at which no profit is returned. The hay intercepts, as shown, are $4 and 20 miles.

Figure 3.2 shows that a farm eight miles from the market could make a profit growing cereals, vegetables, or hay. The obvious choice, however, is the crop whose line is highest on the vertical axis at eight miles. As already calculated,

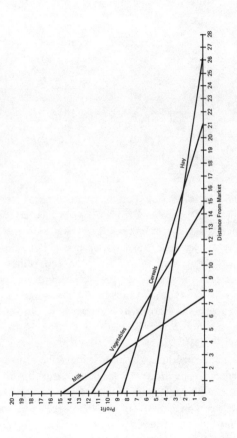

Fig. 3-2. Graph showing relationship between profit and distance from market for milk, vegetables, cereals and hay.

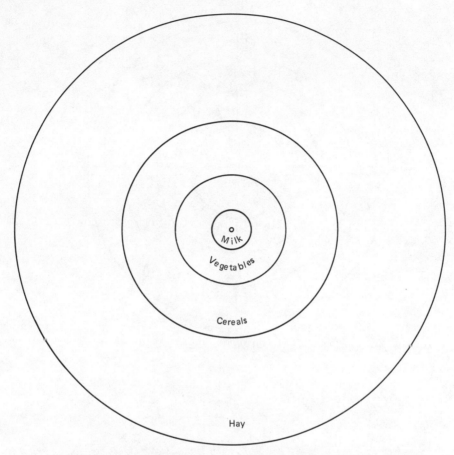

Fig. 3-3. Aerial view of land use pattern emerging from highest and best use of farm land around market.

that line is cereals which, at eight miles, has a value of $2.80 per wagon. An aerial view of the market and surrounding farm land in our example is shown in Fig. 3-3.

The concentric zone pattern shown in Fig. 3-3 reflects the most economically rational use of the land. Each farm is producing the highest profit possible after costs of production and friction are subtracted. When a farm or any piece of land is being used in the most economically rational fashion, economists and planners say it is in its "highest and best use." This is an important concept which will be used several times in subsequent chapters.

The Highest and Best Use of Urban Land

The same economic logic underlying our agricultural land use example also determines the use of land in the town at the center of Fig. 3-3. At the center is

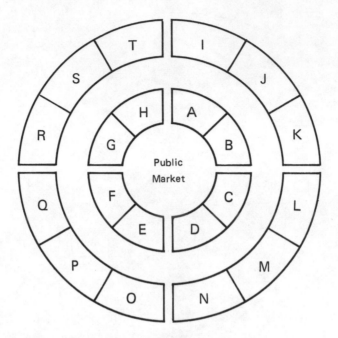

Fig. 3-4. Lots auctioned to craftsmen by landowners.

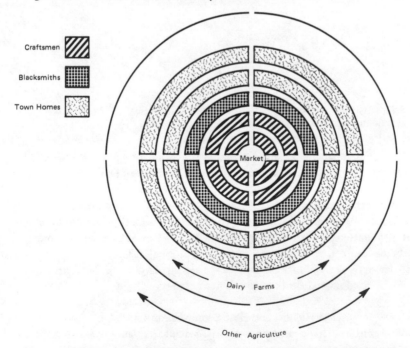

Fig. 3-5. Urban and agricultural land use patterns around central markets.

an open field that was the original market place and remains the spot where farmers come to sell their produce. The market was considered public property, and the farmers were not charged for its use. Each farmer, of course, wanted to get the spot in the market where most people pass, so he could increase his sales. If a farmer knew that about two of every ten persons who look over his produce buy something, he would want to find the spot at which the most people would pass. In time, he learned where that spot was, as did other farmers. Assuming locations are taken by order of arrival, farmers would trade off leaving their farms later in the morning against added sales. If a farmer felt supply was outrunning demand, or that his produce was not the most attractive, he went to the market early to maximize location. On days when demand was likely to exceed supply, or when his produce was so good it would sell regardless of location, he left later.

Assume that as the town's division of labor grew, the circumference of the market became dominated by craftsmen, each trying to sell his goods to the people going to market. As the town's population grows, its demand for food grows, and the central market must expand. This pushes the craftsmen back until they reach land no longer considered public property but rather belonging to a landlord, trader, or other townsman. The owner sees a chance to make money by leasing his land to craftsmen. He divides his land into lots (Fig. 3-4) and each morning holds an auction at which craftsmen bid for the day's use of a lot. Lots will bring varying rents, depending on their location. Lots A to H, for example, because of their position on the market and a street, will bring a higher rent than will lots I to T.

On his first day in the market, an eager craftsman might bid high for stall A because he thinks he can make the most profit there. He finds at the end of the day, however, that his rent was too high. The craftsman in lot J, however, did very well and feels with the added traffic at lot A he could do even better. At the next day's auction, therefore, the craftsmen bid on different lots. Other craftsmen are likewise making adjustments to maximize their profits. In time, when all adjustments are made, and each craftsman is in the lot which leaves him the most profit after rent, the lots are said to be in their highest and best use.

As with agricultural highest and best use patterns, urban patterns become predictable. Craftsmen rent all the lots around the market to make and produce their goods, blacksmiths take the lots behind them, and these might be followed by the townhomes of the landlords. The townhomes give way to the dairy farms (Fig. 3-5).

The Dynamics of Highest and Best Uses

Neither the agricultural or town land use patterns remain static very long. As more wealthy people move to the city, more craftsmen come, as do more surplus agricultural workers. As the division of labor and the population grow, so does the demand for market and lot space. More people need more food, so the

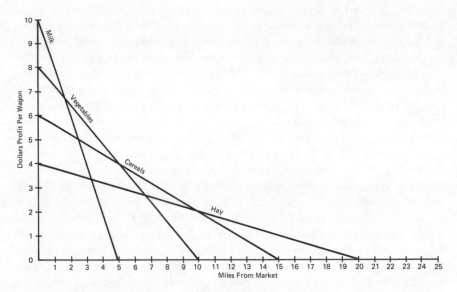

Fig. 3-6. Graph demonstrating expansion of highest and best use zones as a result of growth in division of labor.

farmers' market area must expand, and the craftsmen are moved back. More people also means greater demand for crafted products, so, not only must the craft areas move back, they must also expand.

The result is that, at auction, the lots that usually went to blacksmiths begin to go to craftsmen who bid more. The wealthy, who own the land, increase their profits and see a chance to make even more by converting their homes and yards to blacksmith use. The land owners, in turn, build new homes on land that was formerly dairy farm.

As urban uses begin to spread into the farm areas, the highest and best use of agricultural land begins to change. As dairy farm land is purchased for townhomes, less milk is produced. Since the demand for milk is growing as the population grows, the price for the available milk goes up. Compared to the $20 a wagon it brought in the earlier example, assume milk now brings $25 a wagon. The milk line in Fig. 3-2, therefore, shifts, so that the vertical intercept is $15 (profit if milk did not have to be transported) and the horizontal is 7.5 miles, or the distance at which no profit is made. As Fig. 3-6 shows, this shift means it is now more rational for farmers at a distance of 2.5 miles, who used to grow vegetables, to become dairy farmers. For a brief period, fewer vegetables will be grown as fewer acres are used to produce them. Reduced supply and the increased demand of a larger population drives the cost of vegetables up. An increased selling price shifts the vegetable line and, as in the case of the expansion of the dairy zone, the vegetable zone expands into the cereal zone as the highest and best use of the land changes. The process repeats as cereal supply falls behind demand. Cereal production becomes the highest and best use of former hay producing land. Finally, the hay zone expands into virgin land as the market price of hay increases to the point at which it is economically profitable to grow hay beyond twenty miles.

As long as the population of the town continues to grow, the demand for crafted goods and food will grow. As the demand for these goods grows, the demand for land used to produce them grows. Each of the zones expands, meaning the town and its agricultural hinterland spread over a larger area.

The Concept of Economic Base

In the example of a town's growth, the landlord played a key role. Because he collected relatively large amounts of wealth due to his land holdings, he had the money to buy goods and services beyond the ability of the farmer to purchase. This made it possible for craftsmen, artisans, and artists to find consumers for products which took considerable time and skill to make. Of course, these craftsmen had to buy materials, food, and clothing from other craftsmen and farmers who, in turn, spent their earnings on other goods and services. The money spent by the landlord became the medium of exchange among the entire labor force of a town. For example, assume the population of a town included three landlords whose country estates were in the hinterlands of distant smaller market towns. These landlords would collect, for the sake of the example, 45 percent of the value of their tenant farmer's crops in rent payments. These payments were made in gold because the landlords spent their wealth in the town where they lived most of the year. Transporting "in kind" crop payments would be foolish, since the produce would spoil. Their agents at home converted the landlords' portion of the crop into cash and forwarded it to them.

Assume the three landlords collect $500 each a month which they spend in town. The $1,500 is spent purchasing goods from 15 craftsmen and farmers who receive approximately $100 each. These craftsmen and farmers, in turn, spend their $100 buying goods and services from each other and 20 other participants in the division of labor who receive $5 each. The transfer continues as the landlords' money circulates throughout the labor force which includes, for the sake of the example, a total of 150 butchers, bakers, candlestick makers, barbers, prostitutes, thieves, artists, farmers, etc.

One could say that the three landlords support 50 craftsmen each, and that the per capita wealth of the town and its hinterland is $10. The craftsmen, bankers, farmers, and others who prosper from the division of labor recognize that the best thing that can happen to their town is the arrival of a new landlord, who, assuming his wealth and spending habits are similar to the resident land-lords', will increase the money circulating among the 150 members of the division of labor by $500.

The added money increases demand for products, leading to an increase in prices, which, in turn, motivates craftsmen and farmers to produce more. Added supply may lower prices, but since everyone is selling more, each participant's earnings are increased.

The increase in per capita income occasioned by the arrival of a new landlord usually did not last. Word of higher incomes in town soon attracted more craftsmen desiring to improve their economic condition. The result was that the ratio of craftsmen to landlords returned to the 50-1 relationship existing before the arrival of a new lord.

If a lord left a town, there was less currency per capita to stimulate the division of labor. Spending decreased, and craftsmen left to find a town where the prospects were better. Relative wealth of towns and their agricultural surroundings created a "push-pull" effect in that poorer towns pushed their surplus population out and wealthy towns tended to pull or attract population.

The pull effect was one of the most immediate reasons for the formation of guilds. A guild was an association of craftsmen that determined how long an apprenticeship a new craftsman needed to serve before he could go into business for himself in a town. By restricting the number of craftsmen who could practice, the guilds tended to reduce the influx of new migrants to the city caused by the addition of another landlord.

Landlords were not the only source of gold a town could have. The trader, or merchant, also served the essential function of bringing gold from other towns. He did this by selling to other towns the products that landlords came to his town to buy. Assume landlords chose a town because it had a harbor and could offer imported goods, and because it had a stand of rare hardwood trees in its hinterland which carpenters made into fine furniture. A shrewd trader would realize that these products, furniture and imported goods, were rare enough that landlords came from other towns to buy them. He would, therefore, buy goods from the importers and carpenters, and travel to other towns to sell them for more gold than he paid for them. He would return, and buy more furniture and imported goods with the gold, and sell these in other towns. Like the landlords, the merchant trader is bringing money in from outside the town which circulates among the town's division of labor and increases its per capita wealth.

The assets of the town which attract the landlords and produce goods that are sold in other towns are, in this example, the importing and furniture business. These businesses bring in the gold upon which the division of labor is based, and are called the "economic base" of the town. It is important to note that the amount of money the economic base of a town brings into the economy influences the population size. If the base brings in so much money that the members of the labor force are better off than those in nearby smaller towns, the "pull" effect will mean in-migration. If the economic base does not produce enough money to maintain the population at a level of wealth equal to surrounding towns, the push effect will lead to out-migration.

MERCANTILIST POLICY
AND THE EMERGENCE OF NATIONS

The merchants, craftsmen, and other knowledgeable members of a town's work force understood that the best course of action for a town was to discover what a town and its people did best, or exclusively, and sell that product or products in other towns for gold. The result was an influx of gold, and with effective controls such as guilds, the increase in per capita wealth. Such wealth meant that the workers in the industry which produced the exported, or basic, goods would be well off, and spend their money among all the local craftsmen. The local craftsmen, in turn, spent among themselves and the farmers distributing the wealth throughout the town's population.

Figure 3-7 shows the ideal system in which the raw materials, say the hardwood trees cited earlier, are in the hinterland, the carpenters are in the town, and the merchant sells the furniture in other towns, bringing money back which circulates throughout the local economy.

The example also cites the sale of imported goods as a basic industry. That is, a ship owner sails to foreign nations and buys a product for $5. He returns to town and sells it to a merchant for $7. He keeps $5 to buy more on his next trip, and spends $2 in town. The merchant sells the product in another town for $12. He keeps $7 to buy more from the ship owner, and spends $5 among the local craftsmen. A total of $7 is, therefore, added to the local economy by the importing business.

For the same reasons that merchants from town A are trying to sell goods in other towns, merchants from other towns are trying to sell goods in town A. Suppose there are no iron ore sources in town A or its hinterland, and that the carpenters need nails to make furniture. Merchants from town B, which has iron sources and iron workers, come to town A to sell nails. Assume the carpenters in town A buy $100 worth of nails a month. That $100 has to be subtracted from the per capita wealth of town A because it goes to town B. The goal of those who manage a town's economy, therefore, is to maintain a "balance of payments" which keeps more money coming in than going out of a local economy.

The policy of pursuing a favorable balance of payments was implemented through a number of strategies. Among the most common of these was the tariff, or tax on imported goods. Assume town A begins to spend a great deal of money on goods from other towns so that as much currency goes out of the economy as comes in. This means members of the division of labor begin to earn less money. Those in control decide to produce wood pegs to substitute for nails purchased in town B. The pegs are not as easy to use as nails, and cost as much, so the carpenters do not buy them. To force the purchase of locally produced pegs, a tariff is placed on imported nails. The tariff raises the price of nails so far above the pegs that the carpenters begin to use the latter. The money spent on pegs, therefore, remains in town A and flows through its division of labor.

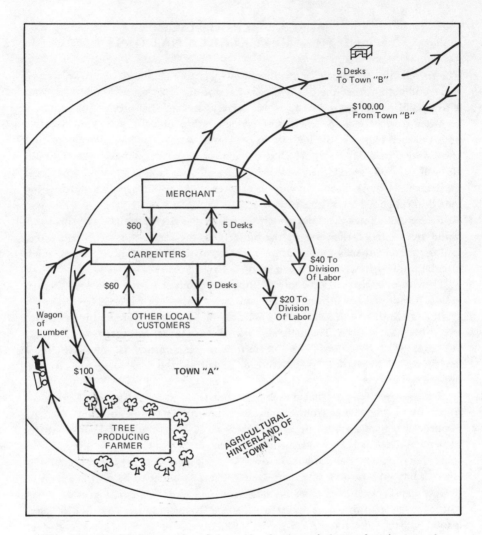

Fig. 3-7. Simplified example of how the furniture industry functions as the "economic base" of town "A" by bringing currency from outside the system. The farmer, carpenter, and merchant each make a profit, which then circulates among the other members of town "A"'s division of labor.

Those in control of town B, however, soon retaliate by placing a tariff on imported furniture. The quality of domestic furniture in town B is not as good as that produced in town A, but the cost added to the latter by the tariff makes town A furniture too expensive. Residents of town B begin to buy furniture made in their own town. The balance of payments improves for B, but worsens for A.

The battle between the two towns continues with tariffs and counter taxes. Town A attempts to produce all it needs locally to preclude dependence on other towns. Every other town does the same. The result is that towns become frustrated in attempts to develop their economic bases. Valuable time and money must be spent building facilities and training people to produce goods previously purchased from other towns, which produced them cheaply as part of their economic base.

Economic struggle turned to armed battle as the rush to include valuable natural resources in the hinterland led to confrontation.

The economic leaders of competing towns soon realized that the policy of independence was self-defeating because it precluded the benefits of a division of labor among towns. Towns began to enter into agreements which allowed each to specialize, and to exchange what they did best, without tariffs. The result was the formation of leagues of cities which attempted to promote specialization and dependence among towns. Under such an arrangement town A could make furniture and town B could make nails. More likely, town A would supply hardwoods and imported raw materials to other towns in the league, while town B supplied the iron ore. Each town gained something through its cooperation in the league. The object in establishing membership was to form as complete an economy as possible, without duplication, so that each city would gain more than it lost.

Leagues began to compete with non-member towns. The league would under-sell non-member producers and place high tariffs on non-member products in member towns. The intent was either to force the town to join or to use it as a captive consumer. Victimized towns formed their own leagues, and the struggle for supremacy among leagues took on the violence of the earlier struggle among towns.

The wastefulness of such competition was recognized by some who realized an even larger union of leagues would prove more beneficial. This realization was one of the prime movers in the nationalist movements that resulted in the formation of nation states. The policy of attempting to become as independent as possible, and of using tariffs to protect domestic producers, was adopted by nations and was called "mercantilism" (Gras, 1922). In the same way that mercantilist competition led to violence among towns and leagues attempting to control raw materials and markets, it eventually led to violence among nation states.

THE NEED FOR INDUSTRIAL ORGANIZATION

One of the objectives of forming a nation state was to include in the boundaries of one political jurisdiction the specialized cities and towns which together formed a complementary system of collection, production and distribution. Political unification meant that trade among towns could be facilitated by standard currencies, weights and measures, and contract procedures. It meant free trade could be pursued without the hindrance of tariffs.

One outgrowth of the formation of nation states was that each nation that successfully encompassed the leagues and cities needed to form a complementary economy became relatively self-sufficient in terms of the goods and services perviously produced by town and league economies. Yet, each sought to develop new products or ways to make old products more cheaply, so that they could export goods and drain gold from their competitors. Each also attempted to become as self-sufficient as possible to avoid having to use gold to buy things from competitors. This mercantilist policy led to the rise of industrialism by creating two phenomena. The first were the wars of imperialism. These struggles grew out of the drive to exploit raw materials in foreign lands which could be made part of a nation's territory. For example, both France and England struggled to control America, because each realized that if one became dominant, the other would have to pay gold to its competitor for any raw materials gotten there. Moreover, any finished products sold to Americans would be subject to high tariffs. In fact, one of the principal motivations for the American revolution was the realization by American merchants that their economy was being sapped by England, and their independence could mean the emergence of America as a successful mercantilist nation. The Boston Tea Party was occasioned by the fact that England not only took America's raw material without paying for it, but required Americans to pay a tax on products sold back to them. America, as a supplying nation, was being treated as if she were a part of England, in that English firms controlled the extraction and pricing of her raw materials; yet, as a consuming nation she was being treated as a competitor, for she was forced to pay higher prices for English products than Englishmen.

Recurring wars brought on by the struggle to control sources of raw materials and markets meant that nation states had to produce increasingly sophisticated weapons. Such weapons required steel and other products not easily produced in one town. Iron ore had to be supplied from one town, coal from another, and craftsmen from yet another. This need to collect raw materials, energy, and labor from disparate sources led, as will be demonstrated shortly, to the emergence of systems of industrial cities.

Mercantilist competition also hastened the emergence of industrial urban systems by motivating merchants and craftsmen to constantly devise new products which could be sold to other nation states for gold. This meant products became increasingly sophisticated and costly to produce—so much so that no one town had the raw materials, labor, and money needed to produce the new products. Entrepreneurs had to collect the raw materials, labor, money, and knowledge from many places to make the increasingly complex products.

Both military and industrial needs of mercantilist nations created a new attitude among mercantilists toward cities and towns. The production of more sophisticated goods required that the contributions of, for example, three towns be collected in a fourth. This meant merchantilists could no longer be loyal to one town or region. Such places had to be seen as specialized members of a nation of towns and regions. It was the balance of payments of the nation that was crucial, not of towns. Each town had to be discouraged from attempting to be independent, and encouraged to specialize, and to depend on other towns to supply needed goods in return for its specialty.

The Logic of Industrial Location

Once mercantilists and political leaders of a nation understood the need to produce complex goods, such as weapons and machines, individuals were encouraged to establish the physical facilities needed to collect raw materials and labor, and to produce the products. These individuals, or entrepreneurs, devised a new logic of urban location and growth which greatly influenced the human community as we know it.

To understand this logic, assume you are an entrepreneur who has developed a new process which makes steel production economically possible. The first task you are faced with is to choose a location for your factory. Understanding the costs of friction, you want to be very careful to place your factory where the costs of assembling iron ore, coal, water, and labor, and of shipping the finished product to market will be lowest. Figure 3-8 shows that the location of iron ore, coal, and market form an equilateral triangle with sides of ten miles.

Collecting data on the production of steel and on the costs of moving materials, you find that one ton of steel requires 1.5 tons of ore and 1.5 tons of coal to produce, and that it costs $1 per ton mile to move bulky products such as coal, ore, and steel. Based on this data, you devise the chart shown in Table 3-1 which shows the costs of friction for producing one ton of steel at several plant locations. As the chart shows, locating at the market would be the most expensive alternative, while the cost of locating at either the coal or ore source would be equal. It is obvious that it costs much more to move the raw materials than the finished product, so you test options that reduce moving coal and ore at the expense of moving steel. Location X in Fig. 3-8, for example, reduces the cost by $1.40 per ton to $23.60. After experimenting, you find that the optimal location is location Y, which reduces cost to $23.20. The process of finding the point of lowest production cost is called the "geometry of industrial location," and becomes quite complex given that most products involve more inputs in more varying proportions than does the example (Weber, 1968).

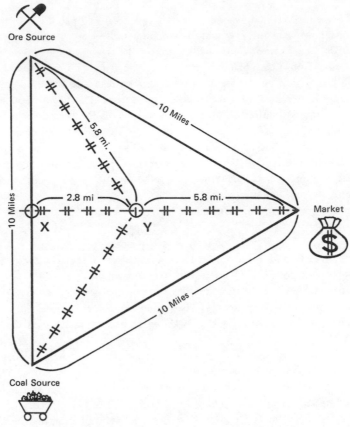

Fig. 3-8. The geometry of industrial location; an idealized spatial distribution of raw materials, production sites, and markets for the steel industry.

Once you have found the point of lowest production cost, you visit the site to find what is there. If you are lucky, it will be close to a river or near one of the towns that emerged from central place forces. You would, therefore, have water, labor, and existing roads to work with. If you are unlucky, and your computed location is not very near a river or existing town, you would have to compute the cost of moving water and building roads, as well as paying employees enough to attract them from nearby towns. If these costs are more than the added cost of friction of locating your factory in the nearest town with a water source, you locate in that town. If they are less, you invest in the roads and water supply, and pay the higher salaries. In either case, you have found the spot where the cost of producing steel is lowest. This means no one can produce steel, given the same technology, at a lower cost than you. It, therefore, means that all new steel producers will locate near you, for they also understand the costs of friction, and will come to the same conclusion you did. The geometry of location for steel production, therefore, will make the town a steel producing center.

Table 3-1. Costs of Friction for Producing
One ton of Coal at Differing Locations

| Plant Location Choices | Cost of Friction at $1 per ton mile | | | Total Cost of Friction for Location Choices |
	Ore (1.5 tons)	Coal (1.5 tons)	Finished Product (1 ton)	
Market	$15.00	$15.00	0	$30.00
Ore Source	0	$15.00	$10.00	$25.00
Coal Source	$15.00	0	$10.00	$25.00
Location X	$ 7.50	$ 7.50	$ 8.60	$23.60
Location Y	$ 8.70	$ 8.70	$ 5.80	$23.20

In the same way that the steel industry used the geometry of location to find its most economically rational location, other industries found theirs. Soon a pattern of industrial centers began to overlay the central place pattern of markets that served pre-industrial economies. The central place markets do not disappear but, as we shall see, they became less important as the population of industrial nations became urbanized.

Before describing the logic of the urbanization process more fully, two concepts must be introduced. The geometry of industrial location finds a point in space which is the most rational place to build facilities. The quality a place has when it is singled out by such computations is called "situs." Pittsburgh, for example, is the point of primary situs for the steel industry. It must be realized, however, that situs for an industry can shift. If the west coast consumes more steel than the northeast, or if a new source of high quality ore is found far from the Mesabi Range, Pittsburgh would no longer be the point of primary situs. New computations would have to be made to find the most rational site. Situs, therefore, is not a tangible quality inherent in a particular location.

The same way that the furniture industry and importing were the economic bases of the town in the earlier example, steel becomes the economic base of Pittsburgh. The industry which locates in a place because it has situs, or is the point of lowest production cost, becomes part of that city's economic base. The economic base serves the important function of bringing currency into a town from the larger regional or national economy.

ROBERT M. HAIG AND THE ECOLOGISTS

Much of the logic summarized thus far in this chapter had been formulated by the time the first human ecologists began their work. None of these men,

however, were economists, and, therefore, had not been exposed to the seminal
works of urban economics. What economics they did know came from the work
of Robert Murray Haigh (1926), whose "Understanding the Metropolis"
appeared early in human ecology's development.

Haig was a Columbia University professor who was hired in 1922 by the New
York Regional Plan Association to prepare an economically sound guide to land
use decisions in New York and its environs. The Regional Plan Association was a
privately funded organization created to investigate the development of the New
York region and to recommend action to the political jurisdictions in the region
which were planning on a much smaller basis without regard for the economic
well being of the area as a whole. Most planning decisions at that time were
made on the basis of aesthetics or arbitrary values. This situation worried the
business and financial community, which understood the economic implications
of location, and had the most to lose from economically irrational zoning codes.

Haig was asked to summarize the economic theories of location, and to
demonstrate how they could be applied to the New York region. Haig's report
was an incisive synthesis of location theory, and a clear exposition of its usefulness to planning decisions. Because Haig's report supplied much of the economic
rationalization of human ecology, it will be summarized below.

The Force of Agglomeration

"Understanding the Metropolis" was divided into two sections, the first of which
dealt with the economic forces leading to industrial urbanism. "To explain the
emergence of the modern city," Haig rhetorically asked, "how would the distribution of people and land uses in the U.S. be different had a super-rational
economist developed the nation?" The conditions were that the amount of
capital available was limited, and that the industrial system to be developed had
to provide a standard of living comparable to that enjoyed by a population equal
to that of the United States in 1920.

Haig asserted that the economist's first chore would have been to identify
sources of raw materials, and find the points of lowest production costs for
heavy industries, such as steel. Since there would not yet be any markets, the
computations need only have considered raw materials and energy. Once determined, these locations would have been connected by railroads to the sources of
raw materials.

After the factory sites had been determined, the economist would have
located housing for the laborers needed to build and work in the facilities. The
most rational location for such homes would have been around the factory sites.
The further away from the factories the workers lived, the more it would have
cost to move them back and forth between home and work. Since capital was
assumed to be limited, such costs had to be minimized.

Another reason for concentrating population around production sites was to
reduce the cost of consumption by minimizing the cost of friction of retail

shopping. Retail outlets would have been located as close to the railway and factory as possible, since to move them further away would have required raising the price of goods to cover the cost of friction. A store away from the railway must charge more than one near the railway in order to make the same profit, assuming other variables, such as rent, are equal.

Secondary factories which used the products of heavy industries also would be located as close as possible to the railway and factory. If the basic industry were steel, tin can factories, for example, would have been located in the town as close to the steel producers and railway as possible to reduce the cost of friction.

The economist would have continued to locate activities as close to the center as possible to lower the cost of friction. This would hold true for all the locations with situs for heavy industry. In addition to these primary centers, there would, of course, have been people who manned the farms, fishing ports, lumbering operations, and mining sites which supplied the raw materials for industry. Haig argued that the economist would have strived to keep the number of people living away from the cities to a minimum. The reason is that farmers, miners, lumberjacks, etc., want to consume roughly the same goods available to the city dweller. Because these goods would have to be carried from the city to the outlying community, they would cost the farmer more than they would his city cousin. The cost of living in distant communities would, therefore, be higher than in the cities. If this were allowed to happen, no one would want to live on the farms and distant areas. They would flock to the cities where the cost of consumption is lowest. In order to avoid this, the people in outlying areas must be subsidized by the remainder of the population, either in the form of higher wages or in the form of lower prices on goods shipped to them. In order to keep this subsidy at a minimum, the economist would have made every effort to keep the rural work force small. Automation would have been encouraged, so that such workers could have come to the city where the cost of consumption was lowest.

At the core of Haig's example is the axiom that given limited capital, every effort should be made to reduce the cost of friction through centralizing population around sites of lowest production costs. In response to his own question, "What difference would it have made in the location of cities and distribution of population if economic rationality had been followed in developing North America?," Haig answered, "Very little." He asserted that each firm, in order to compete in a free market, must keep all costs, including the cost of friction, at a minimum. Since labor and raw material costs remain fairly constant for all producers, the cost of friction becomes a crucial variable in the economic viability of all firms. If a firm is improperly located, it will, assuming a competitive market, be at a disadvantage.

Households, Haig claimed, make the same location decisions on their own as the economist would make for them. The reason is that most families have a limited amount of money to spend on food, housing, clothing, and all the other goods they consume. Reducing the cost of friction leaves them more to spend on other more tangible goods, or the inverse, little is left to spend to overcome friction after other goods have been purchased.

Haig argued that there is a force of "agglomeration" based on the desire to lower costs, which attracts people and activities to urban areas. His reasoning was correct in that the United States, and in fact the world, continues to become increasingly urbanized. It is sometimes difficult for us, living in an era of relatively cheap transportation and high incomes, to understand how strong the force of agglomeration can be. In the early industrial era, however, being near the central city and its railway was a significant cost advantage for industry. Once on the railroad, bulky materials could be moved at high speeds for low cost. But to move goods from the factory to the railway meant using horse and wagon, a time consuming method requiring a great deal of manual labor to load and unload small capacity vehicles. It might take ten wagon trips to fill one box car, making the cost of friction between factory and railway very high. The laborer could rarely afford the carriage prerequisite to living any great distance from the factories. Public transportation, moreover, was slow and limited in range, reducing residential choice to the core areas.

The effect of agglomeration was to produce extremely high densities in the core areas, which often were made even more unpleasant by noise and air pollution, as well as by water and sewer systems. The American experience with high-density, poorly serviced, early industrial cities must have been very traumatic, for it has left us with a cultural antiurbanism which persists to this day. The human costs of industrial urbanization were higher than many of its early proponents suspected. Not high enough, however, to deter the masses of rural and foreign migrants moved by the force of agglomeration.

Deviations from the Economically Rational Pattern

Haig's assertion, that the force of agglomeration was concentrating the population and economic activity into urban centers located at points of lowest production costs, was apparently contradicted by the fact that some factories were located in rural areas and small towns. He attributed these anomalies to several factors, which strengthened his assertion that the drive to lower costs, and, thereby, increase profits is at the base of all rational location decisions.

Product perishability was the first reason Haig cited to explain the location of industrial activity away from the city. Some products, such as fish and several vegetables, have to be frozen or canned immediately at the harvest site. These sites, therefore, will have packing, canning, and freezing plants.

A second class of exceptions to agglomeration are those industrial processes which reduce products in bulk and/or weight at the extraction site. Haig cites copper, which requires 100 tons of ore to produce one ton of usable metal, as an example of a product which will be preliminarily processed at the extraction site. It would be foolish to incur the cost of friction of moving one hundred tons of ore to the city to smelt it. Although keeping industrial workers at the extraction site requires subsidy, the cost is less than that of moving huge amounts of unsmelted ore to the city.

A third reason why some industrial activity is found outside the city is that labor is often cheaper there. Such labor is usually the wives and teenaged children of the workers who man the extractive industries. Labor unions in the cities often increase the cost of production to the point where the cost of friction incurred by moving to a rural site is less than the difference between the wages of cheap rural labor and those of unionized urban workers.

A fourth reason for some industries locating outside of urban areas is the availability of free energy in the form of water. While there are very few factories left that use water wheels for power, they were numerous enough in Haig's time to cite as an exception.

Haig realized that some industrial facilities are irrationally located. These, he claimed, would be constantly undersold by rationally located firms. The long range effect of competition, therefore, was to reinforce rational patterning of industrial facilities.

The Benefits of Highest and Best Use Patterns

Haig's article was divided into two sections. The first, briefly summarized above, was essentially a synthesis of existing theories of urban growth. The second half of the work dealt with the economically rational use of urban land. Haig updated the concept of highest and best use of land, and cited empirical data describing its manifestation in New York.

Haig began by explaining that the force of agglomeration created heated competition for the most central locations in the city. In a process similar to the bidding for lots near the market, cited in an earlier example, industries and businesses bid for the locations they felt would leave them the most profit after the cost of friction. Haig claimed that experience leads to adjustment and, eventually, to an industry finding the site for which it has the highest and best use. Those uses which make the most profit after rent by locating at the center compete for central locations. The result is high rents at the center of the city, and gradual decline as distance from the center increases.

Haig emphasized that the maintenance of a highest and best use pattern is as important to society as a whole as it is to the businessman. When a parcel of land is not in its highest and best use, society loses in several quantifiable ways. Capital that could be used to stimulate new jobs is being wasted. The price of the product being produced by the improperly located firm is probably too high. The taxes paid by the firm are lower than they would be if it were properly located. These losses are compounded by the fact that the firm that should be using the parcel but cannot (because the present user owns, or holds a long term lease on, the land) is also forced to locate improperly.

The primary function of planning, in Haig's opinion, is to make sure that as much of the city is in its highest and best use as possible. This is not an easy task because of the complexity of highest and best use computations becomes immense as the rate of change in the division of labor accelerates.

Haig's Analysis of New York

Haig believed that the best way to begin to determine the highest and best use of a city's land is to observe the bidding process, for it tends to reflect economic reality. Haig's analysis involved gathering all the available information on land use in the New York region for the years 1900 to 1922, and determining which uses had been winning and which losing in the bidding process for central land. By charting the changes in land use over the 22 years, Haig hoped to get an indication as to the trends in highest and best use patterns.

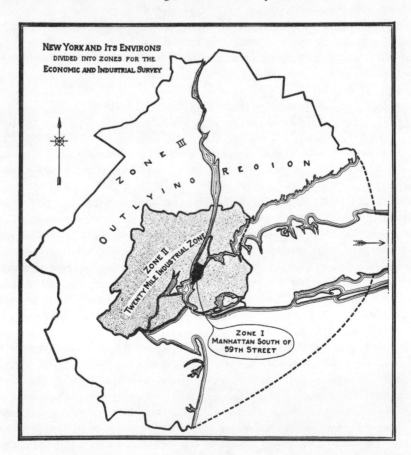

Fig. 3-9. Haig's division of the New York region. (From Haig, 1927. Reproduced by permission.)

Haig began the study by dividing New York and its region into three zones. The central zone included Manhattan south of 59th street. Zone II included the area outside zone I circumscribed by a circle with a 20 mile radius drawn around central Manhattan. Zone III included all the area outside zone II and within the area considered part of New York's hinterland (Fig. 3-9).

To devise an empirical description of the shifts in land uses, Haig computed how many persons were employed by the region's nine largest industries, and an "all-others" category, in each of the zones for the years 1900, 1912, 1917, and 1922. The results are shown in tabular form in Table 3-2.

The total of industrial workers in Zone I decreased from 1917 to 1922. In fact, only printing and textiles increased in Zone I during those five years. Industrial uses in Zone I were clearly losing in the bidding for land, indicating that the highest and best use of the most central land was shifting.

What uses were winning? During that five year period, bank employees increased by 58 percent, insurance brokers by 90 percent, lawyers by 108 percent, jewelry wholesalers by 165 percent, and forwarding agents by 236 percent. The number of the following types of *firms* (not employees) were also increasing from 1917 to 1922: buyers for out of town wholesalers 435 percent, accounting firms 1,588 percent, and corporation headquarters 726 percent. During the same period, retailing floor space in Zone I increased by 73 percent.

These figures clearly indicated that the highest and best use of central New York was changing from manufacturing uses to those characterized as management and service. As New York became the financial and corporate center for the western hemisphere, corporate headquarters, brokerage firms, banks, accounting firms, law firms, and other management services entered the bidding for central land. These uses needed to agglomerate for several reasons. Corporate headquarters concentrated at the center to facilitate the exchange of information. Executives of large corporations must meet to negotiate and complete agreements. By locating in physical proximity, executives earning, for example, $400 a day can meet with many business contacts. If they were dispersed, the number of contacts would be reduced as the time spent in transit increased. Paying an executive $50 an hour to ride in a taxi when he could be working on new business is a very real cost of friction. Corporations obviously strive to minimize this cost by locating as close to each other as possible.

The professionals and businesses that service corporate managers also want to be as close to their customers as possible. A lawyer, broker, accountant, or consultant wants to maximize the number of business contacts he can make per working day. This is best done by locating near customers.

Sales representatives for firms must also be centralized, because a purchasing agent wants to "shop around" to see as many possible product lines as possible in a work day. By concentrating in one area, sellers for clothes manufacturers, for example, attract more buyers than they would if they were dispersed. The buyers for the clothes manufacturers, in turn, want to see as many lines of raw

Table 3-2. Haig's data describing shifts in land use
in the New York region from 1900 to 1922.
(From Haig, 1926. Reproduced by permission.)

Industry	Number of employes			
	1900	1912	1917	1922
Zone I—Manhattan South of 59th Street				
Chemicals	5,400	6,262	7,775	7,523
Men's clothing	35,471	63,189	70,119	52,670
Women's clothing	59,181	112,756	128,108	114,061
Metals	37,623	44,940	42,870	42,065
Printing	35,946	50,648	52,868	53,873
Food	22,361	·25,393	27,457	24,197
Textiles	9,774	11.437	10,325	11,417
Wood	21,701	20,774	17,058	14,872
Tobacco	10,515	11,740	6,658	5,423
All others	51,931	62,996	96,225	93,683
Total	289,903	410,135	460,463	419,784
Zone II—Twenty-mile Industrial Zone				
Chemicals	21,336	36,560	38,914	56,882
Men's clothing	10,045	37,024	36,516	43,110
Women's clothing	6,911	20,510	26,364	28,210
Metals	89,200	147,973	164,161	182,814
Printing	5,374	9,871	13,233	16,601
Food	23,201	39,553	38,516	53,177
Textiles	55,255	87,520	82,940	96,420
Wood	18,804	40,731	31,280	36,393
Tobacco	12,319	17,595	13,147	19,946
All others	59,301	106,255	94,488	128,407
Total	301,746	543,592	539,559	661,960
Zone III—Outlying Area				
Chemicals	1,284	2,185	15,722	6,096
Men's clothing	4,580	7,015	8,545	12,119
Women's clothing	4,220	3,931	7,662	7,924
Metals	23,638	36,177	63,881	44,200
Printing	983	1,738	2,132	2,870
Food	2,760	2,586	3,899	5,098
Textiles	8,380	11,672	12,944	15,924
Wood	2,494	2,469	2,773	4,298
Tobacco	1,005	1,010	1,486	1,126
All others	15,994	35,737	24,593	24,724
Total	65,338	104,520	143,637	124,379

textiles as possible in a day, so textile sellers also concentrate. The buyers for the textile producers also want to minimize the cost of friction, so the cotton and wool sellers concentrate.

The managers, bankers, financiers, buyers, sellers, and service professionals all experience the economic imperative to agglomerate. The bidding for central space drives the cost of land very high. The high price of land leads to the construction of skyscrapers, for the cost of building up is less than that of buying more land to spread out on ground level. The higher the building the greater the ratio of leasable space to land area covered.

As the bidding intensifies, the price per square foot of central space becomes too high for manufacturing enterprises, which need a great deal of space. The factory, therefore, must move out of Manhattan to a place where the rent is low enough so that the difference offsets the added cost of friction incurred by moving goods back and forth to Manhattan.

The factory owner, however, cannot afford to move all his operations from Manhattan. The sales and purchasing offices must remain at the center. The result is that firms "decentralize" their functions. The management functions which require little space remain in the center, while the manufacturing function which needs a great deal of space is moved further from the center to find cheaper land.

As the bidding for central land becomes more intense, even the management functions decentralize to save space. Inactive files, for example, are sent to warehouses in New Jersey to lessen space consumption in Manhattan. The telephone company moves its equipment from Manhattan, but maintains its offices there.

Haig found that the result of decentralization and introduction of new central area consumers was the dominance of Zone I by management and service functions. The displacement of manufacturing uses from Zone I meant their relocation in Zone II. As Table 3-2 shows, Zone II experienced an increase in all categories of industrial employment from 1917 to 1922.

Former Zone I uses enter the bidding for Zone II land and outbid their competitors. Former Zone II uses, in turn, begin to move to Zone III. Table 3-2 shows Zone III increased its industrial employment in all categories except chemicals and metals, which apparently were agglomerating in Zone II. What the listings in Table 3-2 do not show is the conversion of agricultural land in Zone III to residential use in progress during the first quarter of the century.

The dynamics of land use changes Haig found in New York are similar to those described earlier in our example of pre-industrial towns. As the economy becomes more diverse, central land uses expand, driving the cost of land up so that other users must relocate farther from the center. These displaced uses, in turn, increase rents in the area they move to, meaning a displacement of previously existing uses. This displacement continues until urban uses replace agricultural use, and the latter displaces virgin land. The result is the emergence of a pattern of highest and best uses which, in the abstract, takes the form of concentric zones.

Social Costs in Highest and Best Use Computations

One of the questions raised by Haig's analysis is, if the bidding process and economic rationality tend to produce the highest and best use of land, why should the planner meddle at all? Haig answers that there are two reasons why the planner, representing the public, should interfere in the bidding process. The first is that increasingly rapid changes in the number and complexity of products and services offered by the division of labor makes it difficult for individual entrepreneurs to keep abreast of highest and best use computations. Someone has to become a specialist at monitoring changes and projecting their impact on land use if the costs of improper location are to be avoided.

The second, and most important, reason why planners are needed to facilitate the assignment of land uses is that some costs of production are not added into a firm's computations, because the producer does not have to pay them. For example, a producer of asbestos may, using the most sophisticated techniques available, find that the location of lowest production costs and highest profits is near the center of a large city. The calculations would have included all the costs the company has to pay directly to suppliers, labor, financiers, taxing jurisdictions, etc. There is, however, one important cost the entrepreneur has not included in his calculations: the cost incurred by persons who live and work around his factory and develop lung cancer due to asbestos poisoning. These people, besides the pain and misery caused them and their families by the illness, must pay physician's bills and leave their jobs. These are costs the asbestos producer does not have to pay. If these were added to his rent, the location would not be as attractive. The factory would have to locate somewhere away from populated areas. If such a factory were located where the calculation of only direct costs dictated, it would not be the highest and best ust of the land, because the costs to the entire economy would be more than the benefits.

Costs that are not directly paid by the producer of a product are called "social" or "external" costs (Kapp, 1950). Haig argues that the planner should calculate the social costs of all location decisions, and insure that they are included in highest and best use calculations.

FROM ECONOMICS TO ECOLOGY

It is intentional that the chapter ends with Haig's concept of "social cost," for it was the social costs of enlarging and changing the division of labor which most concerned the early ecologists. Their work followed logically from contemporary economics, which had described the benefits and rationality of an expanding division of labor functioning in a series of highly interdependent urban areas.

The benefit was the increased physical security of the species. The larger and more diverse the division of labor, the greater were the chances of survival of its members. Economic theory, moreover, logically demonstrated the inevitability of concentrating the population into rationally located urban areas. Concentration lowered the cost of friction, thereby increasing the resources and time available to stimulate more production. Economists, such as Haig, had also recognized the fact that not all costs were considered in the market economy, and that these must be accounted for if the benefit of increased security was to be realized. Economists, however, were not equipped to estimate the social costs of a growing and changing division of labor, and the increasing urbanization of the population.

4 The Ecological Paradigm

INTRODUCTION

The need to understand the health and behavioral costs of change in the physical and social environment was recognized at least as early as the 1920s. Haig, for example, demonstrated that highest and best use calculations were rational only when the social costs of change were added to the market assigned costs. The need for social cost accounting was painfully obvious to many of Haig's contemporaries including several sociologists. Robert Park, Ernest Burgess, Roderick McKenzie and several of their colleagues and students formed a research group interested in the human implications of change in the industrializing societies. Their efforts led to the founding of human ecology, or the use of the ecosystem concept to explain change in the size, diversity, spatial distribution and well-being of human communities. While justifiably criticized for reasons discussed in subsequent chapters, human ecology was unique among modern disciplines in its attempt to relate illness and abnormal behavior to the dynamics of community change. Human ecology is *not* the primary subject of this book, but its proposition that illness and abnormal behavior are adaptation-related disorders has greatly influenced the volume.

The behavioral propositions of the early human ecologists are the foci of this chapter. The intellectual history of the propositions is traced to three works representative of earlier research on the human impact of urbanization. The first is Adna Weber's *The Growth of the City in the Nineteenth Century* which described the process by which succeeding generations of urban dwellers improved their status. The second is Georg Simmel's "The Metropolis and Mental Life" which offered influential, though untested, hypotheses concerning the psychological impact of urban life. The most important aspect of Simmel's work is its suggestion that migrants to the city must make difficult psychological adaptations. Thomas and Znaniecki's *Polish Peasant in Europe and America* is the third work discussed. This classic of American social science should be remembered for documenting the problems immigrants had in adjusting to the behavioral expectations of urban society.

The human ecologists synthesized the works alluded to above with the economic theories discussed in the previous chapter. The synthesis produced several spatial and behavioral propositions which are summarized in this chapter. These propositions provide the basis for the ecological perspective on ill-health and abnormal behavior presented in Chapters 5, 6, and 7. When considering the propositions, the student should remember that one of the causes of human ecology's dissipation was its preoccupation with spatial analyses. While the spatial propositions are important they are not as important to this book as are the behavioral propositions.

THE PREPARADIGMATIC STAGE OF HUMAN ECOLOGY

Normal science, or the accumulation of knowledge made possible by the adoption of a paradigm, is preceded by a period of uncoordinated research. During this preparadigmatic period, researchers investigate a common subject but do not synthesize their findings into an organized body of knowledge with common terminology, measurements, or assumptions. In the case of human ecology, the subject was the effect of the growing organization of collection, production, and distribution on man. While there were numerous preparadigmatic works concerned with this subject that influenced the first human ecologists, three stand out as the precursors of the ecological paradigm. These are Georg Simmel's "Metropolis and Mental Life" (1950), Adna Weber's *The Growth of the City in the Nineteenth Century* (1963), and William Thomas' and Florian Znaniecki's *The Polish Peasant in Europe and America* (1920).

Simmel: Adjusting to Urban Life

Georg Simmel, a German sociologist in the last quarter of the nineteenth century, was concerned with how organization affected interaction among individuals. This interest led him to a consideration of industrial urbanism.

Simmel produced very few formal publications, and most of his work has been preserved in the form of lecture notes. One of his most famous lectures described the impact of urban environments on behavior.

In the "Metropolis and Mental Life," Simmel asserted that urban residents had to make several adjustments which included assuming a "detached" or "blasé" attitude, learning to compute the money value as well as the personal utility of things, and balancing the tension between the desire for anonymity and the need for recognition.

The need for a detached attitude arose, according to Simmel, from man's inability to become familiar with all the phenomena he was exposed to in the city. Simmel claimed that man had a limited capability to identify and store information about things which stimulated the senses. The more capacity one dedicated to identifying stimuli, the less capacity one had to store detailed information about each stimulus identified.

In rural areas, the number, as well as spatial and temporal pattern of stimuli, remained relatively constant. Changes in the stimuli themselves were supposedly highly predictable because they were governed by life cycle and season. Rural residents had to dedicate less capacity to identifying new stimuli, and could, therefore, become more familiar with each individual stimulus.

Simmel claimed that the urban environment bombarded man's senses with a huge number of seemingly unrelated stimuli. The urbanite could not identify and store detailed information about each stimulus impinging on his senses, simply because it was beyond his mental capacity. The alternative—to devise abstract classes of stimuli such as "people," "buildings," "autos," etc.—allowed the urbanite to simplify the identification process. For example, the urbanite does not look carefully at each individual passed on the street and store the person's visual characteristics. The person is simply, perhaps subconsciously, identified as being of the class "people." The use of abstract classes supposedly allows the urbanite to cope with urban complexity, and maintain enough capacity to store details about the people, places, and things of immediate importance to his life. The result of this strategy, according to Simmel, is that the urbanite becomes detached from, or indifferent toward, many stimuli with which he comes in close proximity. Simmel (1950, pp. 409-10) writes:

Man is a differentiating creature. His mind is stimulated by the differences between a momentary impression and the one which preceded it. Lasting impressions, impressions which differ only slightly from one another, impressions which take a regular and habitual course and show regular and habitual contrasts—all these things use up, so to speak, less consciousness than does the rapid crowding of changing images, the sharp discontinuity in the grasp of a single glance, and the unexpectedness of onrushing impressions . . . thus the metropolitan type of man . . . develops an organ protecting him against the threatening currents and discrepancies of his external environment which would uproot him. He reacts with his head instead of his heart.

Simmel claimed that the second adjustment required of man by urban life, learning to recognize the money value as well as the personal utility of objects, grew from the city's function as a market place. At some point in his economic development man had to turn from a barter economy to one in which some medium of exchange was used to represent the relative worth of goods. Simmel claimed that this shift had a subtle effect on the way man thought about reality. In the barter system, people viewed the worth of goods in a personal way. One who needed shoes equated their worth to the effort he had to make to produce the milk exchanged for them. One's labor and time determined worth.

In the cash economy, the addition of the abstract value of money often made computing worth more complex. If one borrowed money from a lender to buy shoes for which he had no milk to exchange, he found that interest charges meant the shoes cost more of his labor when he had milk to exchange. While the money system reflected the same forces of supply and demand that determined barter transactions, the former required a much higher level of abstract equations and considerations. The merchants and craftsmen had to become preoccupied with the cash value of his work and the products he desired. Money became a value, or end, in itself, rather than a means of measuring value. Simmel (1950, pp. 414) wrote:

> By being the equivalent to all the manifold things in one and the same way, money becomes the most frightful leveler. For money expresses all qualitative differences of things in terms of "how much?" Money, with all its colorlessness and indifference, becomes the common denominator of all values; irreparably it hollows out the core of things, their individuality, their specific value, and their incomparability. All things float with equal specific gravity in the constantly moving stream of money.

Simmel claimed that the third adjustment—balancing the tension between the desire for anonymity and the need for recognition—stemmed from the city's size and division of labor. Many rurals came to the city to escape social pressure and role expectations. Amid the detachment and size of the urban population, one could act in any fashion he chose, short of violating the law, without suffering social stigmatism. Furthermore, the division of labor encouraged people to pursue whatever role they chose. Opportunities were limited only by one's imagination, skills, and willingness to work.

While anonymity did provide freedom, the cost, according to Simmel, was the loss of individual recognition. The migrant was just another of the mass of people drawn to the city by the hope of improving his lot.

Not everyone, moreover, could be an actor, poet, or captain of industry. Because the migrant was usually unskilled and poorly educated, opportunities offered by the division of labor shrank to one—industrial laborer. Assembly line work, designed to be simple and non-challenging, could be assumed by nearly anyone. The result was that workers gained little individual identity through their roles in the labor force. Simmel claimed that the anonymity of the urban population, and the depersonalizing effect of industrial work drove many to seek ways to assert their individuality. Bizarre fashions and mannerisms, and the drive to achieve notoriety through politics, business, or crime were outgrowths of the need to be recognized.

Simmel saw the tension between the desire for anonymity and the need for recognition as an inevitable product of modern civilization. Urbanites had to learn to cope with this tension, and to live with the problems growing from the fact that not everyone would be able to cope.

Simmel recognized that the three adaptations required by urban living—the detached attitude, economic rationality, and the balancing of tension between anonymity and the need for recognition—were not easily made. He never explicitly predicted who would or would not be able to make the adjustments. His emphasis on the differences between rural and urban environments leads, however, to the inference that migrants from the latter to the former would be the most severely tested.

Weber: Social Mobility

Very little of the work done by nineteenth century commentators on urbanism was based on empirical data. No one had attempted to collect the few measurements of urban growth and social problems available. The lack of such information hampered attempts to test the theories concerned with the effects of urban living on people. Recognizing this void, an American statistician, Adna Weber, decided in the mid-1890s to gather global census data for a volume describing urban growth during the previous century. *The Growth of the City in the Nineteenth Century* appeared in 1899 and marked the beginning of serious research into the effects of urbanization on man.

In his book, Weber suggested how to test popular theories on the condition of urbanites. As an example, Weber demonstrated that three popular beliefs about urban populations were inaccurate. These were (Weber, 1963, p. 370):

1. The city-born reside in the poorest quarters of the city; the country-born in the wealthiest.

2. The city-born predominate in the lowest occupations and the lowest social classes.

3. The city-born contribute an unduly large proportion to the class of degenerates (criminals, lunatics, suicides, etc.).

Concerning these assertions Weber (1963, p. 372) wrote:

. . . the main reason why the city-born predominate in the poorest quarters of Berlin, London, New York, etc., is that the poorest classes of immigrants have so many children, who, of course, are classed as natives of the city. The slums of the cities were originally created by the flooding in of the most degraded peasant classes, who have married and propagated their kind until they now figure in the statistics as natives of the city, the product of urban conditions, the urban proletariat. The fact is amply demonstrated by the Vienna statistics, which show that the central and wealthy districts contain a larger percentage of immigrants than the outer districts when the children of the immigrants are credited to Vienna, but when the children are credited to the father's birthplace . . . it appears that the immigrants predominate in the older and poorer districts of the city.

Weber's empirical finding that the rural migrant and his children concentrate in the poorest sections of the city was to be confirmed by the human ecologists. More importantly, Weber found that, over time, many children and grandchildren of rural migrants improved their social and economic status and moved into better city districts. Weber (1963, p. 389) described this upward social mobility as follows:

. . . The countryman coming to the city begins a slow ascent, rather than a descent; his children . . . advance to a higher rank on the industrial and social ladder while the third generation . . . is still more capable and efficient . . . the country immigrants do not at once assume the higher positions in the economic organism, but enter the unskilled occupations where muscular strength and vigor are in demand . . . And just as the newcomers work their way up from the unskilled into the skilled industries, so do they rise from the ranks of employees into those of undertakers and employers.

Weber's description of social mobility became, as we shall see, a central element of the ecological paradigm.

Thomas and Znaniecki: The "Disorganization" of the Urban Migrant

The third pre-paradigmatic work—William Thomas and Florian Znaniecki's *The Polish Peasant in Europe and America*—was published in 1920. The authors were familiar with the work of Simmel and several others who had asserted that urbanization changed the human condition. Thomas and Znaniecki, recognizing that much of this earlier work, aside from Weber's, had been based on limited observations, decided to carefully analyze facts collected and organized in scientific fashion. They proceeded to collect data describing the lives of migrants moving from Polish towns to Polish cities and then to American cities. These data included personal letters, court records, diaries, newspapers, and personal interviews.

The resulting two-volume *Polish Peasant in Europe and America* is one of the seminal works of American social science. While the work drew several conclusions concerning the effect of urbanization on the migrant, the most important was that the move left him without behavior guidance formerly received from the social intimacy typical of rural areas. Because the rural community was small with a closely knit division of labor, little information could be kept from becoming common knowledge. Social indiscretions were highly visible, and the guilty party quickly became stigmatized or ostracized. Those experiencing grief or "hard times" through no fault of their own were consoled and given moral or material support. Achievement was quickly recognized and rewarded by community respect. Mores were enforced by community pressure, and personal misfortune assuaged by community support.

In the city, however, the division of labor was large and impersonal, and very often separate from friendship and family networks. Little attention was given to the behavior or to the problems of the urbanite. Thomas and Znaniecki (1920, p. 1821) described the impact of moving from the intimate organization of rural areas in Poland to the impersonal environment of the industrial American city as follows:

> 1. The peasant has adapted to the life of a permanent agricultural community, settled for many hundreds of years in the same locality and changing so slowly that each generation adapted itself to the changes with very little effort of abstract reflection.

> 2. The peasant was not accustomed to expect unfamiliar happenings in the course of his life within his community, and if they came, relied upon his group, which not only gave him assistance, but helped him regain mental balance and recover the feeling that life in general was normal in spite of the unexpected disturbances.

> 3. The peasant drew all social stimulation, checks, and suggestions from direct social contact with his milieu, and the steadiness and efficiency of his life organization depended on the continuity of his social intercourse with his own group.

> 4. He was until quite recently a member of a politically and culturally passive class, and did not participate consciously, even in the slightest measure, in any impersonal institutions that existed in his country.

> In view of all this, it is not strange that in the different conditions in which he found himself in this country he becomes more or less disorganized.

One manifestation of disorganization preoccupied Thomas and Znaniecki: criminal behavior. They claimed the migrant population would commit more than its proportional share of crime because mores and norms, including public laws, were enforced in small towns and rural areas through primary group monitoring. One did not steal a coat, for example, because he could not use it without immediately acknowledging guilt and suffering ostracism, as well as punishment. Indiscretions involving personal conduct, drunkenness, promiscuity, etc. were avoided because everyone knew everyone else's "business," and social stigmatism was unavoidable. In the city, however, the mere size of population allowed anonymity and myriad opportunities for vice and crime. The division of labor itself often included illegal or unsavory means to material success. The law-abiding urban citizen was motivated by the realization of interdependence central to the social contract concept. This realization led to compliance, supposedly because most individuals believed the maintenance of order was in their long-run benefit. Thomas and Znaniecki claimed that the migrant population, not yet cognizant of the social contract, or not yet well off enough to accept it, would produce more than its share of criminals. Some would feel released from the constant peer group reinforcement of norms, and pursue the material goods genuinely needed or desired for status. Promiscuity and vice also could be expected to increase as the primary group pressure lifted, leaving the migrant without behavior guidance, or exposed to several conflicting codes leading to Durkheim's "anomie" or normless malaise.

Thomas and Znaniecki did see the vast majority of migrants as reorganizing and joining the stable, productive population dedicated to the social contract and to middle class values. The disorganization of migrant populations, and the tolerance and treatment of those unable to cope were the price society paid for the benefits of industrial progress.

THE NORMAL SCIENCE STAGE OF HUMAN ECOLOGY

The Chicago School

In the early 1890s, Robert Park, an American journalist, studied sociology in Germany under Georg Simmel. Greatly influenced by Simmel, Park became interested in the effects of social organization on behavior. Upon returning to America, Park accepted Booker T. Washington's invitation to teach at Tuskegee Institute. On a visit to Tuskegee in 1913, William Thomas, co-author of *The Polish Peasant in Europe and America* and professor of sociology at the University of Chicago, was impressed by Park and asked him to visit Chicago. Park's visit led to a permanent teaching position at Chicago.

Three years later, Ernest Burgess joined the sociology faculty at Chicago, Burgess, whose research dealt with the spatial arrangement of social problems, interested Park in his work.

Another sociologist, Roderick McKenzie, was engaged in graduate work at the University of Chicago in the early 1920s. His background included training at an agricultural college where he learned basic biology. As a graduate student he was influenced by Park and also became interested in Burgess' work.

Chicago was experiencing a rapid influx of migrants in the early 1920s. The migrants seemed to account for more than their proportional share of crime and other social problems. Chicago provided an ideal laboratory for the study of the effects of urbanization on people, and Park, Burgess and McKenzie took full advantage of it. In 1926, several of the papers prepared by Park, Burgess and McKenzie describing the findings of their work in Chicago were published in a volume entitled *The City*. The book, especially the papers of McKenzie and Burgess, provided the paradigm that elevated the study of the impact of urbanism on man from preparadigmatic to normal science.

The Ecosystem/Metropolis Analogy

The ecological paradigm emerged from an analogy drawn between the ecosystem concept discussed in Chapter 2 and the metropolis described in Chapter 3. The analogy was drawn by McKenzie (1926) in his "The Ecological Approach to the Study of the Human Community." In his article McKenzie posited that the ecosystem of the human community was the metropolis and its hinterland. The abiotic elements of the metropolitan area included climatic and geologic conditions, as did those of the natural ecosystem. The most important of the metropolis' abiotic elements, however, was its "economic base," or role played in the regional or national system of collection, production, and distribution.

As in the natural ecosystem, the abiotic elements of the metropolis controlled, according to McKenzie, the characteristics of the biotic elements. Climate and natural amenities attract or repel people with common likes and dislikes, but, more important, the economic base attracts people with particular skills and discourages those with others. If the economic base were lumbering, for example, people not wishing to be, or capable of being, lumberjacks would go elsewhere. A small town can take on the image of the type of people attracted by its economic base. One will often hear such cities referred to as "college towns" or "lumbering towns." This labeling is based on the fact that professors and students behave differently than lumberjacks. The labels themselves tend to attract and repel people.

The most obvious parallel of the analogy is the homeostatic relationship between the size of the biotic element and the fertility of the abiotic elements. In the natural ecosystem, as the amount of water and fertility of the soil increase, the trophic organization becomes larger and more complex. If, on the other hand, the abiotic elements become less supportive, the biotic population decreases in complexity and size. A similar homeostatic relationship exists between the economic base and population size of the metropolis. When the regional or national demand for the products of a city's economic base increases, more people are employed by the basic industries. This creates a demand for more laborers in the service sector. People desiring to increase their income and consumer choices respond to this demand by moving to the city. If demand for the basic product remains constant, young people entering the division of labor can be absorbed only as quickly as older members retire. The excess of indigenous new labor will migrate to other areas with expanding bases. When the demand for the basic product decreases, the cash flow into the community shrinks, and people must be laid off. The displaced workers, and those entering the work force, must go elsewhere to find work. In systems terminology, the population size seeks equilibrium with the economic base. Equilibrium, according to the ecologists, is reached when the economic base grows just fast enough to employ increases in indigenous population.

It should be noted that the size of the economic base, like the abiotic elements of the natural ecosystem, is controlled by forces beyond local control.

Demand for the basic product is controlled by the vagaries of the regional or national economy. The early ecologists cited technological advances as the chief causes for change in economic bases. A city whose base was processing natural rubber, for example, would be severely affected by introduction of synthetic rubber. The introduction of trucks, as another example, completely changed the situs computations of many industries previously tied to the railroad. The result was the gradual phasing out of older, improperly located facilities. The towns and cities based on these facilities suffered serious population declines.

THE SPATIAL PROPOSITIONS
OF THE ECOLOGICAL PARADIGM

Economics tends to sort land uses into a predictable pattern, which in the ideal case is a series of concentric circular zones. Haig had found these forces at work in New York, and the early ecologists, Ernest Burgess in particular, found them in Chicago. The similarity between the circular array of plants around moisture sources (Fig. 2-2) and the arrangement of land uses around the point of highest accessibility in the city reinforced the metropolis/ecosystem analogy. In the same way that specific plant species were best suited to particular areas of the ecosystem, specific uses were best suited to areas of the city.

The similarity in the processes by which plant species and land uses became dominant in well-defined areas fascinated the ecologists. In the case of plants, any given location in an ecosystem has a combination of environmental characteristics which can support life. Over time, the plant type that uses the combination most efficiently will become dominant there. For each location in the city, there is a use which returns the most profits after rent and transport costs. In effect, that use is making the most efficient use of the environmental characteristics of the site.

In "The Growth of the City: An Introduction to a Research Project," Ernest Burgess (1926) described how highest and best use calculations led to distinct zones of human activities. He and his students mapped Chicago's land uses, distribution of migrants and incidence of crime, and health and other social problems. After several years of such mapping, Burgess concluded that the metropolis develops five distinct zones of human activity (Fig. 4-1).

As Haig demonstrated, the central business district, or CBD, became dominated by corporate, professional, and retail users which paid high rents for the land area they occupied (in Burgess' charts the CBD is labeled "the loop" after the name given Chicago's central area by her citizens). Few people actually lived in the CBD because the rents were very high, yet the area, especially during the day, bustled with people and activity. Shoppers, businessmen, professional people, and working men and women of all sorts conducted their affairs in the central district.

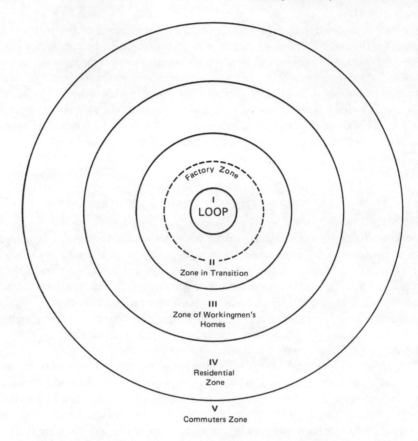

Fig. 4-1. Burgess' concentric zone model. (From Park & Burgess, 1926. Reproduced by permission.)

When Burgess wrote, the CBD also contained the cultural and entertainment facilities which kept the area busy through the evening. The central business district was the focus of the metropolis' economic, political, and social functions.

Burgess' second zone, or zone in transition, has become the area most associated with his work. This zone, as indicated in Fig. 4-1, consisted of two very different uses. The first were the factories and industrial activities being forced out of the central district by increasing rents. As Haig had found in New York, new corporate and professional uses drove up CBD rents forcing large-space consumers, such as factories, farther from the center. These factories relocated just outside the central area replacing older homes which were sold to industry for more money than could be made through continued residential use.

The second use found in the zone in transition was the low rent residence. These residences were of two kinds. The first were old structures allowed to decay while their owners waited for industry to purchase the land at high price. To invest in a structure that would be torn down by its next owner, who was interested only in the land it stood on, was irrational. The renters were usually unskilled laborers who worked in nearby factories and could not afford higher rents that would come with better maintenance. The second type of residence was the high density tenement. A tenement was an economically rational use of zone in transition land not likely to be converted to factories in the near future. Industrial workers could not afford to buy homes in better districts and commute, so a high density tenement near the factories could be filled, despite its unattractive environment. The owner, in order to make profit on expansive land with low rents, often increased the ratio of units to covered land surface to the technological or legal limit.

The zone in transition was the area occupied by most new migrants to the city. This led ecologists, given their familiarity with Simmel, Weber, and Thomas and Znaniecki, to conclude that the zone in transition would exhibit the most social problems. As we shall see shortly, this was indeed the case.

Burgess' third zone, the zone of workingmen's homes, consisted of modest homes owned by workingmen who originally migrated to the city's zone in transition, found work in the factories, and prospered enough to buy their own homes.

Burgess called his fourth zone the "residential zone" which was inhabited by the children of migrants who, because of better education, became "middle class."

Burgess' last zone, a "commuter zone," was inhabited by those wealthy enough to incur the cost of moving to and from the CBD.

According to Burgess, the size and location of the zones were not static. As the economic base increased, and more cash became available to stimulate the local economy, each zone increased its size by expanding its circumference. As in the case of the natural ecosystem, the zones "shifted" outward through "invasion and succession." While the terms "invasion and succession" are descriptive of the changes in spatial patterning, they can be misleading. The shift is brought about by changes in highest and best use calculations, as described by Haig, not by the use of force.

Burgess' description of land uses in the city provided a spatial context for the behavioral propositions of the human ecologists. These propositions are important. They explain the relationship between change in the system of collection, production, and distribution and the incidence of crime, mental illness, and, to a degree, poor health.

THE BEHAVIORAL PROPOSITIONS
OF THE ECOLOGICAL PARADIGM

The early human ecologists knew that the behavior of the biotic elements of a natural ecosystem became less predictable when the abiotic elements changed quickly. They saw in this fact a close analogue to what happened in the metropolis when its economic base changed quickly. By placing the work of Simmel, Weber, and Thomas and Znaniecki in the context of the metropolis/ecosystem analogy, they derived the behavioral propositions of the ecological paradigm. The propositions, preceded by the ecologist's assumptions concerning the determinants of behavior and perception of normalcy, are described below.

I. Assumptions concerning the determinants of behavior.

Given their biological preoccupation, the early human ecologists saw the division of labor as analogous to the trophic organization of natural ecosystems. This led them to believe that the division of labor required participants to behave in predictable fashion nonthreatening to, if not supportive of, organizational maintenance. That is, in order to benefit from the system of collection, production, and distribution, individuals performed specific tasks and did not interfere with the performance of others. Supportive behavior was rewarded by greater security, while threatening or nonsupportive behavior was punished by denying or lessening security. "Security" usually was seen as economic power to obtain the things necessary to maintaining an acceptable standard of living. More specifically, the ecologists believed most of any individual's behavior could be predicted by three variables:

A. *Trophic Role.* The role one played in the productive system determined, they claimed, a great deal of his behavior. In order to keep their jobs, lumberjacks had to cut trees, professors had to teach, and factory workers had to perform repetitive tasks on the assembly line. Trophic role also determined much behavior not essential to maintaining role, but highly associated with it.

B. *Mores, ethical codes, and laws.* In order to insure the maintenance of the system of collection, production, and distribution, society establishes mores and ethical systems which foster supportive, and discourage nonsupportive behavior. These mores and ethical codes are transmitted to new members through institutional means, such as schools and religious or fraternal organizations. Some behavior is considered so potentially destructive of, or essential to, the trophic organization that the threat of force is used to preclude or insure its performance. These proscriptions and requirements are embodied in formal laws. The concept of "general welfare" is used by society to legitimize the coercion needed to insure compliance to laws.

C. *Place.* Man, like all organisms, must function in real space. Survival in a given place depends on one's ability to assess proximate threats and opportunities, and behave accordingly.

II. Assumptions concerning society's perception of normalcy.

The early ecologists believed that society considered an individual's behavior "normal" when it was congruent with, or predicted by, the above three variables. Normal behavior is that which is intended to promote one's own well-being, as well as that of the trophic organization. If, however, someone's behavior were not predicted by the determinants listed, he could be labeled "abnormal." Which type of abnormalcy is ascribed depends on the violated determinant and the degree of the behavior's deviance from the norm.

A. *Behavior not predicted by role.* If someone performs the function central to his role but does not assume the attendant behavioral characteristics, he could be labeled "eccentric" or "strange," as might a chess-playing lumberjack. If he does not perform the central function, he can be labeled "incompetent" and forced to seek another role in the division of labor. If his behavior is not predicted by any of the roles he assumes, he can be labeled "marginal" or "mentally ill."

B. *Behavior not predicted by mores, ethical systems, and laws.* If someone's behavior is not predicted by mores, ethical systems, or laws, the labeling process can be more serious. Deviation from mores or ethical systems may lead to being labeled "heretic," "sinner," or the like. Variation from formal laws, however, may lead to much more serious labels such as "criminal," or those more descriptive of the ecological perspective, such as "public enemy" or "menace to the commonwealth." These labels make the deviant liable to punishment rendered on behalf of the general welfare.

C. *Behavior not predicted by place.* Behavior not predicted by, or incongruous with, place usually leads to less disdainful labeling than that caused by deviations from role expectations, and less punitive than those arising from deviations from law. This is probably due to the fact that behavior not predicted by place is usually immediately costly only to the individual, and harms the trophic organization only when it leads to a loss of an individual's labor. The individual's over- or under-reaction to threats proximate to him can lead to his being labeled "daring," or "insane" depending on the risk involved. Someone who walks through New York's Central Park after midnight could be called "daring," while one who refuses to enter at noon may be called "eccentric." Someone who walks about the park clad in swimwear during a January storm could well be suspected of "mental illness."

III. The behavioral proposition of human ecology.

The most important contribution of the early ecologists to behavioral science was the hypothesis that changes in the incidence of abnormal behavior in a metropolitan area could be explained by changes in its economic base. Placing the assumptions listed in I and II above in the context of the metropolis/ecosystem analogy produced the following propositions:

A. *Abnormal behavior caused by an increasing economic base.* When economic base increases, the trophic organization or division of labor will expand through in-migration and internal role mobility. The early ecologists claimed that under such conditions the following could be expected:

1. The impact of an increasing economic base on role-determined behavior. Migrants from rural areas or small towns have to learn the skills and behavior expectations of new roles. During the transitionary period, they can exhibit behavior not predicted by their new roles. If they do not learn quickly, they may be labeled "incompetent" and assume the behavior pattern expected of the unemployed.

2. The impact of an increasing economic base on behavior determined by mores, ethical systems and laws. According to the ecologists, migrants to the city could be expected to exhibit proportionately more criminal behavior than the established population. This was due, supposedly, to the lifting of community pressure as described by Thomas and Znaniecki (1920), and to the fact that the sheer physical needs of migrants would often override any restraint arising from dedication to the social contract. An important corollary added by the early ecologists to this axiom (borrowed from Thomas and Znaniecki) was that "norm clash" between dominant populations and migrants to the city could explain the high crime rates among the latter. An Irishman arriving in Boston before 1900, for example, might be labeled criminal for publicly drinking to excess, a behavior not formally proscribed in his previous ecosystem.

3. The impact of an increasing economic base on place-determined behavior. An expanding economic base means a portion of the population will experience changes in its immediate location through both in-migration and internal residential mobility. These shifts in place create a population assessing and adapting to new physical environments. For some, the adaptation process may be easy, because the expanding base means they have the money to choose an environment they perceive as amenable. Others will be economically limited to environments which seem overwhelmingly complex and threatening compared to the place to which they had previously adapted. The latter population could be expected, claimed the ecologists, to produce more than its proportional share of behavior considered "abnormal" than those more familiar with the environment.

B. *Abnormal behavior caused by a decreasing economic base.* A shrinking economic base, or one not expanding quickly enough to provide roles for indigenous population increases, means out-migration of some of the population and the loss of role security for others. This leads, according to the ecologists, to the following behavioral problems:

1. The impact of a decreasing economic base on role-determined behavior. When the economic base decreases, the division of labor shifts downward, in the sense that formerly highly paid job holders must take

lower paying positions and many other workers simply go unemployed. Behavior required to maintain old roles and behavior highly associated with those roles must be terminated. The behavior required and associated by new downshifted roles must be learned and exhibited. During the period of transition, the chances of exhibiting behavior incongruous with role are greatly increased.

Some behavior, such as that associated with the role of unemployed laborer, becomes predictable. This behavior is nonsupportive of the trophic organization and accelerates the economic downturn.

2. The impact of a decreasing economic base on behavior determined by mores, ethical system, and laws. The early ecologists believed that the effect of economic downturn or stagnation was to lead the affected population to moral dilemmas between individual security and formal law. Under those circumstances, a portion of the population may feel that former compliance to law did not increase security, and that continued compliance will decrease security. This portion of the population will be larger in times of economic downturn, meaning a larger absolute number will take the chance of punishment for noncompliance given the lack of reward for compliance.

3. The impact of a decreasing economic base on place-determined behavior. Decreased economic well being means many will not be able to remain in, or choose new, residential environments they perceive as amenable. Given the increase in criminal behavior likely to accompany economic instability, moreover, environments formerly perceived as amenable may become threatening. Changing from one environment to another, or being in a changing environment, means one must change behavior patterns. The population adapting to new places will, therefore, exhibit proportionately more behavior incongruent with place.

C. *Abormal behavior caused by an economic base changing in composition.* As Haig described in his work, new industries constantly emerge as new products are introduced. These industries locate in existing metropolitan areas and become part of the economic bases. At the same time, older industries may decline, the natural rubber industry for example, or phase out old facilities made obsolete by changes in the geometry of location. The result of such cycles is that most metropolitan areas experience a shifting economic base rather than simply an increasing or decreasing base. Under such circumstances, the problems are compounded. The population associated with the growing industries experiences the problems listed in "A" above, while those trained to function in, or who were dependent on, the shrinking industries experience the problems described in "B".

The Ecological Gradient

A synthesis of the spatial and behavioral axioms led the early ecologists to conclude that in a hypothetical metropolitan area, the rate of abnormal behavior would be highest in the zone in transition, and would decrease as distance from that zone increased. Graphing this hypothesized relationship between rates of abnormal behavior and distance from the zone in transition produced what the ecologists called an "ecological gradient" (Fig. 4-2).

The rates in the zone in transition were expected to be highest for two principal reasons, both based on the fact that low rent residences were found there. The first reason was that migrants to the city, who, for reasons described above, exhibited the highest rates of abnormal behavior, had to settle where rents were low. The second reason why abnormal behavior was highest in the zone in transition was that the area housed the derelict or "misfit." As Thomas and Znaniecki and Weber had shown, most immigrants adapted to their new

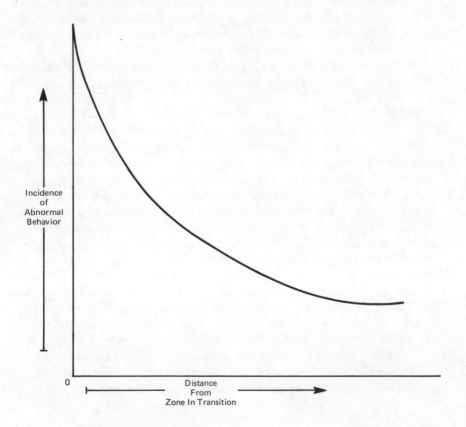

Fig. 4-2. Idealized ecological gradient.

roles, social settings, and environments, and eventually moved from the zone in transition. Some, however, never made the adjustment and became labeled "derelict," "misfit," or "defective." These individuals, along with the outcasts and dropouts from established society, were forced by economics to exist in the zone in transition. The zone was a place of tremendous variety and juxtaposition which fascinated the early ecologists. It housed not only the adapting migrant and those who had adapted and longed to move to "better" neighborhoods, but also the derelicts, artists, and bohemians who took advantage of low rents. The zone also attracted enterprises close to, and on both sides of, the line between legal and illegal. And because of its reputation as the home of "lost souls," it also attracted the religious rescue missions.

As the zone in transition gave way to the workingmen's and residential zones, the rates of abnormal behavior decreased. The ecological explanations for these declining rates can be best understood by remembering that behavior supportive of the trophic organization or system of collection, production, and distribution is rewarded by increased security in the form of money. Behavior threatening to, or not supportive of, the trophic organization is discouraged or punished by lowering economic security, and by labeling such behavior as abnormal, criminal, deranged, marginal, lazy, and anti-social.

The physical environments of the areas near the industrial zone were often unpleasant. Most people wanted to move away from these areas, but, because moving away from the center meant incurring the cost of friction, how far away one got depended on his economic power. Those whose behavior was most predictable, most supportive, that is most "normal," had the most economic power and could move further away. "Abnormal" behavior, therefore, decreased as distance from the zone in transition increased.

It must be noted, of course, that the rates never dropped to zero, reflecting the fact that upward social mobility meant changes in role, place, and mores, and the population experiencing such mobility could be expected to exhibit abnormal behavior.

Variations in the Spatial Patterns

It must be understood that the concentric zone pattern and the ecological gradient of abnormal behavior assume a flat, unbounded area with no geologic features which might affect building patterns. The ecologists knew that such conditions did not exist and that the peculiarities of each metropolitan area's natural abiotic elements would distort the hypothetical pattern and gradient. Their first test case was, of course, Chicago, which is located on a flat plain. The zonal pattern in Chicago, therefore, was easily discerned and distorted only by the lakefront. The desirable waterfront location elongated the CBD. and high-income central residences to form Chicago's famous "Gold Coast." The ecological gradient, therefore, did not apply to the eastern sector, because no zone in transition formed between the center and lakefront (Fig. 4-3). The

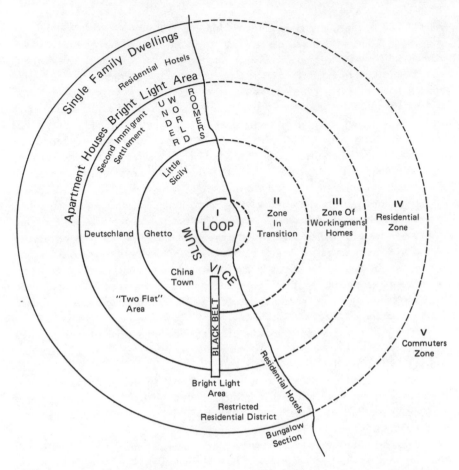

Fig. 4-3. Concentric zone model applied to Chicago. (From Park & Burgess, 1926. Reproduced by permission.)

gradient, however, was evident in the inland sectors. Similar distortions have been noted where topography creates desirable residential areas near the CBD, such as the Beacon Hill district of Boston where affluent persons will "bid up" rents (Firey, 1936). Such populations will, of course, exhibit fewer of the behavioral characteristics considered nonsupportive of the trophic organization, and will, therefore, distort the ecological gradient.

Since the first human ecologists posited the concentric zone pattern, a very important phenomenon has accelerated and distorted the supersession of land uses in metropolitan areas: the slashing of the cost of friction. Cheap mobility—precipitated by the auto, interstate highway system, and increases in disposable income—has slowed the succession of zone in transition land into CBD uses. The cost of buying, clearing, and building in the zone in transition has now become greater than the cost of friction incurred by building in areas beyond the zone. As a result, CBD land uses have leap-frogged over the zone in transition, creating an area of chronic slums.

The reduction in the cost of friction has also led to expansion of residential areas beyond central city boundaries. The implications of this expansion will also be covered in subsequent chapters.

The Elements of the Ecological Paradigm

The Chicago School used the ecosystem/metropolis analogy and the attendant spatial and behavioral axioms as its first paradigm. This "ecological paradigm" can be divided into the four components suggested by Kuhn and described in Chapter 1.

I. *Basic Assumptions*

These are the basic propositions about a discipline's subject from which the members develop testable hypotheses. A brief list of such propositions imbedded in the ecological paradigm would include:

A. The economic system of collection, production, and distribution consists of rationally located urban centers each of which performs a particular, but not necessarily exclusive, function.

B. The function an urban area performs, or its economic base, determines the size, composition, and spatial arrangement of the population.

C. The relationship between economic base and the population is homeostatic. As the base grows or changes, the population size, composition, and spatial arrangement adjusts, or seeks "equilibrium."

D. Behavior is perceived as "normal" when it is predicted by one's functional role, physical surroundings, and societal mores and laws.

E. Fluctuations in economic base lead to increased rates of abnormal behavior by changing the roles and physical surroundings of the population, and by increasing moral dilemmas.

F. The closer the population and economic base of an urban area are to equilibrium, the lower the rates of abnormal behavior; the further from equilibrium, the greater the rates.

II. *Analogies*

The analogy drawn by the early human ecologists between the metropolis and the natural ecosystem is a classic example of the use of analogy to explain newly perceived phenomena.

III. *Conventions*

The Chicago School's conventions reflecting its roots in economics, biology, and sociology are as follows:

A. Epistemology. Park, Burgess, and McKenzie considered themselves to be empiricists, and emphasized the need to collect as much descriptive data as possible. *The City*, in fact, was intended as a stimulus to further research. Park's contribution to the Volume, *The City*, "Suggestions for the

Table 4-1. Disciplinary Matrix of the ecological paradigm.

PARADIGM	BASIC ASSUMPTIONS	ANALOGIES	CONVENTIONS	EXEMPLARS
ECOLOGICAL	1. The economic system of collection, production, and distribution consists of rationally located urban centers, each of which performs a particular, but not necessarily exclusive, function.	1. The metropolis is analogous to the ecosystem.	1. Empirical epistemology.	1. Burgess' concentric zone model.
	2. The function an urban area performs, or its economic base, determines the size, composition, and spatial arrangement of the population.		2. Qualitative description.	2. McKenzie's "The Ecological Approach to the Study of the Human Community."
	3. The relationship between economic base and the population is homeostatic. As the base grows or changes the population size, composition, and spatial arrangement adjust or seek equilibrium.		3. Naturalistic research.	
	4. Behavior is perceived as "normal" when it is predicted by one's functional role, physical surroundings, and societal mores and laws.		4. Community as unit of analysis.	
	5. Fluctuations in economic base lead to increased rates of abnormal behavior by changing the roles and physical surroundings of the population, and by increasing moral dilemmas.			
	6. The closer the population and economic base of an urban area are to equilibrium, the lower the rates of abnormal behavior; the further from equilibrium, the greater the rates.			

Investigation of Human Behavior in the Urban Environment," for example, lists 100 questions which he urges sociologists to pursue through field research.

B. Descriptive Mode. While the Chicago School was concerned with empirical justification of its proposition, early ecological studies were qualitative, as opposed to quantitative, in their descriptions. Park's journalism background led not only to a concern for the collection of facts to substantiate conclusions, but also to the use of reporting as a means of communicating findings.

C. Research Setting. The most distinctive aspect of the ecological paradigm is its emphasis on gathering knowledge by observing phenomena in their natural setting over extended periods of time. This "naturalistic, longitudinal research," as field observation is often called, departed radically from the traditional methods of studying human behavior. Laboratory research, as will be discussed in subsequent chapters, was, and probably remains, the dominant research method in the behavioral sciences.

D. Unit of analysis. Due to its roots in sociology, economics, and biology, the ecological paradigm emphasizes collective or aggregate, rather than individual, behavior. It is assumed that there are common influences acting on groups of people, such as families, organizations, and societies, and that these forces are adapted to through collective action.

IV. *Exemplar.*

The fourth component of Kuhn's disciplinary matrix is "exemplar," or the presentation of the discipline's symbolic generalizations most often used to initiate students to the field. In the case of the ecological paradigm, human ecologists have used the concentric zone analysis of Chicago found in Burgess' "Growth of the City: An Introduction to a Research Project."

As Kuhn suggested, the four components of a paradigm can be arrayed in a "disciplinary matrix" to facilitate the comparison of paradigms. A disciplinary matrix of human ecology is shown in Table 4-1.

THE NORMAL SCIENCE PHASE
OF THE ECOLOGICAL PARADIGM

Some students of the Chicago School felt that man's behavior was much more complex than that of lower species and could not be understood simply by extrapolating from animal studies. These ecologists split intellectually from their colleagues, and their work became known as "social ecology." Those who maintained the more biological approach maintained the title, "human ecologists." The dichotomy remains to this day, and is reflected in the fact that human ecology is more associated with the biological sciences and social ecology with the social sciences.

Research conducted by both social and human ecologists into vice, crime, gangs, and mental disorders inevitably involved them with other disciplines, such as anthropology, psychology, and geography. This involvement led to their association, either in fact or by reputation, with those disciplines. The few ecologists who pursued research into the effects of economic organization on human populations became recognized as demographers or sociologists. This diversification of interests meant that until very recently, few if any schools or departments of human or social ecology could be found on university campuses. Those who considered themselves human or social ecologists usually were found on sociology or biology faculties.

The result of intellectual splits and diversification of interests has been that the normal science made possible by the ecological paradigm has contributed to several disciplines. This has been beneficial in that those disciplines have added to their storehouse of knowledge by using the paradigm. Its disjointed use, however, has precluded the orderly collection and synthesis of knowledge generated through ecological analysis. More unfortunate is the fact that, unlike the Chicago School, the other disciplines have shown little interest in coalescing their findings into statements useful in solving human problems.

The remaining chapters of this book will reflect the Chicago School's assumption that many of the health and behavioral problems of the contemporary community can be understood as outcomes of adaptation to change in the system of collection, production, and distribution. The book should not, however, be considered an endorsement of all the inferences drawn by the students of the ecological paradigm. A half century of hindsight indicates that the paradigm's original analogy (the human community is *like* a natural ecosystem) has often been confused with identity (the human community *is* a natural ecosystem). This error has led to the contention that the spatial and socio-economic structure of the contemporary community is "natural" in the Social Darwinistic sense. That is, if left alone the community would "evolve" into a system which uses its abiotic resources most efficiently. Progress is seen as secured through economic competition among individuals and organizations mistakenly equated to the species of natural ecosystems.

This volume rejects the ecosystem *identity* as logically unsound (the human community is *not* a multi-species natural ecosystem) and ethically dangerous. As Haig readily acknowledged a half century ago, uncontrolled economic competition generates social costs. The assignment and regulation of these costs are political acts which define what will be considered efficient performance by a firm or community. Economic efficiency, therefore, is not literally equivalent to the equilibrium between biotic and abiotic elements produced by natural selection. Any explanation of the contemporary community which contends that economic efficiency is *identical* to ecological efficiency is ethically invidious, because it implies that those who bear the costs of change are the victims of nature rather than of politics.

5 Paradigm Succession in the Study of Public Health

As noted at the outset, the chapters of this book form three clusters, each of which serves a different end. The second cluster includes Chapters 5, 6, and 7, which are historical overviews of the intellectual development of public health, abnormal psychology, and criminology. These overviews are organized by the disciplinary matrix device in that they describe a succession of paradigms. The three chapters are held together by the demonstration that ecological concepts have influenced the development of each of the considered disciplines. This ecological convergence is presented as a precedent for pursuing comprehensive accounting of the health and behavioral costs of community change.

Each chapter in this second cluster ends with a disciplinary matrix for the subject discipline. While these matrices emphasize differences in a discipline paradigm progression, the reader is urged to note the similarities across disciplines.

The following chapter overviews paradigm succession in the study of public health. The chapter precedes those dealing with abnormal behavior and crime for two reasons. First, public health had an ecological perspective on illness before the time of Christ. *Airs, Waters, and Places*, a book of medical instruction written in ancient Greece, offered explanations of health problems which are remarkably similar to contemporary theories based on ecological principles. Public health has come full circle from an ancient ecological perspective, through periods of non-science and the germ paradigm, to what appears to be an emerging modern ecological paradigm.

A second and more important reason for beginning with public health is that many of the assumptions and conventions of its germ paradigm were borrowed by abnormal psychology and criminology. The discovery that several dreaded diseases were caused by virulent microbes so impressed the scientific world of the nineteenth century that all sorts of maladies were attributed to germs and biological processes. Identifying the biological differences between the healthy and the sick became the object of psychology and criminology despite the fact that the analogy between physiological and behavioral disorders was usually erroneously drawn. The legacy of the erroneous analogy is still with us today.

Among the most important topics in the next chapter is the logic inherent in the experiment Jacob Henle suggested as the test of the germ theory. The experiment, later carried out by Henle's student Robert Koch, requires symptom classification, microbe identification and isolation, and the use of controlled laboratory experiments. These concepts and techniques are important in the history of public health and of abnormal psychology and criminology.

Another important concept described in the chapter is "necessary but insufficient" cause. The concept refers to the fact that while a whole population may be exposed to a virulent microbe, not everyone develops the illness associated with the germ. The presence of the germ is necessary to become ill but not sufficient.

Other concepts in the chapter which should be remembered are "general adaptation syndrome" and "stressor." Both concepts are central to understanding adaptation related disorders.

The paradigms discussed in this chapter will not be those of medicine (the analysis and treatment of individual health problems), but rather of public health, or the study of health problems in communities of individuals. While medicine and public health may share several exemplars, the disciplines vary paradigmatically in their conventions and, most importantly, in their prescriptive foci. Medicine is concerned with individual, usually remedial, treatment, while public health attempts to prevent health problems through monitoring and controlling environmental factors which affect whole communities.

A BASIC MODEL OF HEALTH PROBLEMS

Illness can be parsimoniously explained as a function of the interaction among an organism's adaptive capacity and infectious agents, non-biological toxins, or safety hazards. Adaptive capacity refers to the individual's ability to resist infectious agents, and to avoid non-biological toxins and safety hazards. The concept of adaptive capacity also includes genetic predispositions to certain symptom syndromes. Infectious agents include the bacteria and viruses responsible for such dreaded diseases as smallpox, bubonic plague, polio, hepatitis, typhoid fever, and diphtheria. Non-biological toxins are naturally occurring and man-made phenomena, which destroy tissue or disturb the systemic balance of the organism. Such phenomena include natural and man-made radiation, ambient air and water pollutants, and harmful substances in the home and work environment. Safety hazards include problems such as automobile, occupational, and recreational accidents, as well as floods, tornadoes, earthquakes, and fires.

Each factor listed has been of concern to public health through its historical development. At different times, however, one or another has become the principal focus of the discipline, reflecting the dominance of a paradigm which underestimated the importance of other factors. While public health's ancient paradigm assumed the importance of all four factors, and stressed a precociously ecological perspective, the breakdown of the Roman Empire's economic and political system left the discipline in dormant condition. Not until the eighteenth century and the advent of germ theory did public health resume normal science. The acceptance of the germ paradigm, however, led to underestimation of the importance of adaptive capacity, non-biological toxins, and safety hazards. As the major epidemic diseases came under control, emphasis shifted to toxic agents in the form of environmental pollutants. Most recently, ecological analyses of human communities appear to be leading to a renewed interest in the adaptive capacity factor, bringing public health full circle back to an ecological paradigm which replaces the precocious, but crude, observations of the ancient Greeks with twentieth century empiricism.

THE PREPARADIGMATIC PERIOD OF PUBLIC HEALTH

Most public health treatises portray the pre-Greco-Roman period as horrendously ignorant of the causes of disease. Perhaps because we know more of ancient man's ceremonial life and monumental works than of his everyday life, we are tempted to view ancient man as attributing all events he did not control to the gods. While the myths of antiquity are replete with references to illness as the work of supernatural forces, ancient civilizations were not totally ignorant of the natural etiologies of disease. This evidence has been found in cities where the division of labor was diverse enough to support the study of human existence. The early civilizations of the Indus Valley (Northern India), for example, knew enough about sanitation to equip their communities with paved streets complete with covered sanitary and storm sewers. In Mohenjo-Daro, and Indus community dating to at least 2000 B.C., the rationally planned city blocks were serviced by covered sewers, baths, and running water. The finer homes had interior plumbing including baths and drains to the public sewers (Piggott, 1950). In the Egyptian city of Kahum, archaeologists have found sewer systems dating to 1700 B.C. The ancient city of Tel-el-Amarna, dating to 1400 B.C., also had sewers, and bathrooms in private homes. Knossos, on Crete, not only had sophisticated public bathing facilities 2,000 years before Christ, but also what appears to have been flush toilets (Varron, 1945). Personal hygiene also appears to have been highly valued in several ancient civilizations. Egyptians, Mesopotamians, and Hebrews all portrayed cleanliness as a virtue. The Incas of the Western Hemisphere held a feast each September in which all homes were cleaned to help avoid diseases which increased with the rainy season (Ackertnecht, 1949).

Because so little written material from these early civilizations has survived, it is impossible to reconstruct the theoretical bases for their early concern with sanitation. It is safe to assume, however, that the ancient Greeks' explanation of disease was rooted in the knowledge of earlier civilizations which must be characterized as preparadigmatic.

THE ANCIENT ECOLOGICAL PARADIGM

Western man's study of early civilization has been preoccupied with the Greek city states. This interest is due in part to the Greeks' sophisticated search for knowledge, and to their immense influence on the development of Western thought. In few fields were the Greeks more advanced and more influential than in the study of human illness. The first paradigm, in the Kuhnian sense, of public health was devised by a school of Greek physicians approximately 400 years before Christ. That paradigm was the first in the progression which has eventually come full circle to the advent of the modern ecological paradigm.

Hippocrates and the School at Cos

The origins of the ancient ecological paradigm are difficult to describe with certainty, despite the considerable amount of lore that has passed down from the second century A.D. Its basic assumptions are usually attributed to Hippocrates, a fifth century B.C. physician who taught at a medical school on the island of Cos. The school library contained volumes on anatomy, surgery, prognosis, public health, and other medical topics. One volume on public health, entitled *Airs, Waters, and Places*, and traditionally attributed to Hippocrates (Jones, 1923), is commonly cited as the exemplar of the ancient ecological paradigm.

Airs, Waters, and Places was based on the early Greek assumption that bodily functions were a means to maintain balance among four fluids or humors—blood, phlegm, black bile, and yellow bile. As long as these bodily fluids were in equilibrium, the individual was healthy. The relative proportions of these fluids was determined by environmental variables and an individual's life style. Environmental variables affecting the balance of humors included temperature, humidity, and ventilation. Life style characteristics included eating and drinking habits, sexual activity, work and recreation behavior, and dress. In the classic Hellenic tradition, it was believed that moderation in each environmental and life style variable should be striven for to avoid disturbing the balance among the bodily fluids. Too hot or cold, wet or dry, windy or closed an environment or immoderate or stoic a life style could cause imbalance and illness.

The Precocious Advice of the Hippocratic Tradition

The most important contribution of *Airs, Waters, and Places* was not its assumption of environmental life style influences on health, but rather its recommendations for predicting and controlling a community's health problems. As the author, or authors, of the volume noted, some diseases—referred to as "endemic" were always present in a given community at seasonally predictable rates. Other health problems, however, appeared unexpectedly, swept through a large proportion of the population, and disappeared equally mysteriously. These occasional, rapidly spreading diseases were referred to as "epidemic." Writing for physicians of their day who traveled from community to community to offer services, the authors of *Airs, Waters, and Places* suggested how to predict what types of endemic diseases would be found in a town or city. Based on their belief in environmental and life style influence on humor balance, the authors wrote (Jones, 1923):

> . . . when one comes into a city to which he is a stranger he ought to consider its situation, how it lies as to the winds and the rising of the sun . . . and concerning the waters which the inhabitants use, whether they be marshy and soft, or hard and running from elevated rocky situations . . . and the ground whether it be naked and deficient in water or wooded and well watered, and whether it lies in a hollow and confined situation or is elevated and cold; and the mode in which the inhabitants live and what are their pursuits . . . for if one knows all these things well . . . he cannot miss knowing when he comes to a strange city either the disease peculiar to the place or the particular nature of common diseases . . .

In surprisingly ecological fashion, *Airs, Waters, and Places* assumed that the health problems of a community could be predicted best by understanding the natural setting and economic functions of a city—the abiotic elements of the human ecosystem. The authors were the first ecologists. They were concerned with measuring the relationship between social and environmental factors and human health.

Another characteristic of the ancient ecological paradigm of public health which presaged human ecology was its emphasis on prescription. *Airs, Waters, and Places* recommended how new Greek colonies should be sited. When locating new communities, the authors recommended avoiding marshes, damp valleys, or unprotected hilltops. They urged, instead, the selection of sites with running rather than standing water, moderate temperature, and gentle winds for ventilation. Stagnant water and still, moist air were considered serious health threats because they supposedly stimulated the production of biles which led to the onset of malaria. While the prescription of avoiding such sites helped reduce malaria, its effectiveness was due to a reduced exposure to mosquitoes, not to the preservation of humor balance.

The Roman Variant of the Ancient Ecological Paradigm

To ensure a favorable balance of payments, the Romans learned to expand and control their trading area by military force. The communities ringing the Mediterranean became extensions of the Roman political and economic system. By the time of Christ, most of the scientific and technical knowledge accumulated by the Greeks had been absorbed by the Romans, and used to enhance the wealth and order of the empire. Included in this assimilated knowledge were the Hippocratic tradition and the principles of the ancient ecological paradigm.

The Roman genius was not for the creative or abstract arts and science, but for the applied and functional. Roman physicians, for example, expended little energy in augmenting the conceptual bases of Greek clinical practice. They chose, rather, to fuse existing medical knowledge with their engineering and organizational talent to lift the limits on how large the human community could grow without poisoning itself. The ancient Romans may not have surpassed the Greeks as clinicians or researchers, but they far outstripped all previous civilizations in finding ways to translate medical knowledge into public health policies and procedures. The best example of this ability is the water and sewer systems of Rome. The availability of potable water severely limited the growth of ancient cities, and, therefore, the division of labor. It appears that few ancient cities ever reached 50,000 people, and that Athens may never have reached the 130,000 persons some have estimated (Hawley, 1971). Rome was the giant of early cities reaching an estimated 350,000 at its zenith. The ability to establish and sustain a community more than twice the size of any previous city accounted for Rome's dominance of the known world. No other state could produce the diversity of human skills and specialties made possible by such a relatively huge division of labor. One of the crucial factors in Rome's growth was her system of aqueducts, which delivered clean water from the surrounding hills. In the third century A.D., there were at least 11 aqueducts supposedly capable of carrying 40 million gallons of water per day (Robins, 1946).

In addition to clean water, another public health prerequisite was disposal of waste. Roman engineers were as talented in removing stagnant and foul water as in bringing in clean. The main sewer serving ancient capitoline hill, for example, still functions and has never been used to capacity. Public latrines and toilets in the private homes were connected to the sewers. Many multiple-story dwellings that housed the hordes of unskilled rurals who flocked to Rome also had inside toilets. The areas where these tenement-like structures were built eventually became sources of disease, because the migrants never learned how to use the toilets and dumped their waste in the streets (Reid, 1913).

Besides water and sewer systems, the Roman government provided many public baths and encouraged personal hygiene as a means to reduce disease in the city. By the first century A.D., a thousand public baths made it possible, though not probable, for all Romans to bathe daily. The cleanliness and operation of the baths were supervised by a special branch of the government which also regulated the public markets. While the policy of *Caveat emptor* or "buyer beware" has been attributed to the Romans, the public supervisors of the markets could prohibit the sale of merchandise or food which posed a public health or safety threat.

Roman concern for healthy environments, learned from the Greeks, influenced the planning of colonies and outposts. Ruins of Roman aqueducts, baths, and sewers can be found throughout Europe and North Africa. Even before their assimilation of the Hippocratic tradition, Roman planners sought out well-ventilated sites, away from marshes and swamps, to build their communities. Vitruvius, the most famous Roman city planner, inspected the livers of animals inhabiting potential new town sites to determine if the environment was healthful. In refining Greek warnings against building near marshes, Vitruvius also noted that the chances of illness could be greatly reduced if sea water could be added to the marsh. While he did not explain why this would reduce malaria, we know today that salt destroys mosquito larvae.

Rome had a highly organized medical care system which administered treatments borrowed from the Hippocratic tradition. In the second century A.D. the public medical service assigned physicians to outlying cities and towns in numbers determined by population size (Gossen, 1939). Physicians' salaries were fixed and paid by the state. Although they could accept fees, public physicians were constantly monitored to assure no one was turned away due to lack of money. Each public physician was also expected to choose and train students to serve in the public service. In addition to the free public medical service, Rome also had private practitioners who formed groups which attended families for yearly fees. Evidence also exists that in addition to private institutions analogous to hospitals, the state maintained free facilities for the poor who needed intensive care.

Roman physicians expanded on the Hippocratic observation that certain occupations produced characteristic diseases. Mine workers were commonly cited as having "pallor" or a pale and wan appearance due to work in dark, moist mines. This pallor and the presence of dust and caustic materials was believed responsible for the miners' short lifespan. Other workers noted as having peculiar health hazards included blacksmiths among whom varicose veins were common, and those working with copper who were often burned by vitriolic by-products, such as copper sulphate (Rosen, 1943).

The Elements of the Ancient Ecological Paradigm

The paradigm devised by the physicians at Cos in the fourth century B.C., and operationalized by the Romans through the fifth century A.D., had the following elements:

I. *Basic Assumptions.*

Given their belief in the humor balance model of health and the effect of environmental factors on that balance, the adherents to the ancient ecological paradigm assumed:

A. Illness was a manifestation of systemic imbalance among blood, phlegm, and bile.

B. Environmental factors such as temperature, humidity, and ventilation affect the production of bodily fluids.

C. Life style variables such as eating, drinking, and sexual habits, as well as types of work and recreation affect the balance of bodily fluids.

D. Individuals should avoid extremes in life styles and should be concerned with personal hygiene.

E. Those responsible for public health and planning should avoid placing populations at risk by situating communities in extreme environments.

F. The health problems of an existing community can be predicted by knowing its environmental characteristics, its economic base, and the dominant life style of its inhabitants.

II. *Analogies.*

While the ancient ecological paradigm drew no explicit analogies to demonstrate its assumptions, the humor balance model served the analogy function.

III. *Conventions.*

It is difficult to determine how formal the Greek and Roman medical schools were, but the fact that physicians were expected to teach and were monitored for competence indicates medicine was recognized as a discipline. The conventions of that discipline can be characterized as follows:

A. Empirical epistemology. The epistemology of the Greeks and Romans cannot be characterized as empirical in the modern sense, yet it is closer to empiricism in spirit than to the intuitive epistemology of, for example, the Freudian paradigm discussed in the next chapter. For the sake of the discussion, the paradigm's epistemology will be described as empirical.

B. Qualitative description. While quantitative measurement was used commonly by Greek and Roman engineers, the Hippocratic tradition maintained its preference for qualitative description.

C. Naturalistic research. Given the paradigm's assumption of environmental influence, its mode of collecting data must be characterized as naturalistic.

D. Community as unit of analysis. While public health is, by definition, primarily concerned with affecting the health of the community, its paradigms have differed in the choice of variables to be analyzed and manipulated. While the ancient ecological paradigm was concerned with such community level variables as climate and economic base, the germ paradigm, as will be discussed, was primarily focused on the characteristics of individuals.

IV. *Exemplars.*

The work most commonly cited as exemplary of the ancient ecological paradigm is *Airs, Waters, and Places*, attributed to Hippocrates. It should be noted, however, that *Airs, Waters, and Places* in only one volume of an estimated 70 which were produced by the students of the school at Cos over several centuries. Together these volumes are referred to as the Hippocratic Collection and are more representative of the ancient ecological paradigm than *Airs, Waters, and Places* alone.

RETREAT TO MAGIC AND MIASMAS

By the third century A.D., the Roman system of organized markets and colonies maintained by military power began to disintegrate. While speculation on the reasons for this decline abound, little agreement has emerged. Most theorists cite the combination of Christianity, with its emphasis on pacifistic anti-materialism, and the inability of the principal cities to educate and productively utilize the numerous migrants attracted by the wealth accumulated through exploitation of colonial markets. Faced with the advance of Germanic tribes desirous of recovering their wealth from the empire, the Roman emperor and bureaucracy moved to Byzantium (Istanbul) in 330 A.D. The military and civil organization of the western empire crumbled, leaving Rome without the economic base of taxes from her colonies. Unable to hire mercenaries, and lacking the military and administrative experts who had migrated to Byzantium, the defenseless city was sacked by Alaric the Goth in 410. Rome was reduced to a minor city, important mostly for its religious function. The Popes and Church assumed the administration of civil services, but were not able to restore the destroyed aqueducts, health facilities, or, perhaps more importantly, health service delivery systems. The collapse of Roman organization also reduced the division of labor. Without the wealth and stability of the empire, few laymen could take time from survival tasks to study medicine, science, art, or engineering. Only the religious orders were sufficiently organized to free enough time and energy to support the arts and sciences. The study of illness, as a result, regressed from normal science to a pre- or non-paradigmatic state.

The Dark Ages

The period from 500 to 1000 A.D. has been referred to as the Dark Ages because of the apparent stagnation of scientific and economic progress in Western Europe. While some historians argue that social and economic evolution was far from suspended during this period, all would agree that to characterize the study of health as stagnant would be to enhance what was a regression to supernaturalism. While the eastern empire, centered in Byzantium, continued the Hippocratic tradition, Western European medicine was little more than a combination of pagan myth and Christian spiritualism in which incantations, exorcism, penance, and saintly invocations were considered the best prophylaxis. As a result, the effectiveness of public health practices fell below those of the Roman Empire. Water supply, limited to wells and springs, severely restricted city size. Existing sewer systems were not repaired, nor were new ones built. Animals ran in the unpaved town streets, adding to the problem of garbage and waste removal, which acted to limit urban growth.

The exception to the general breakdown of public health services between the fall of Rome and the year 1000 was the work of the religious orders. Heirs to the Greco-Roman intellectual tradition, the monks of the dark ages built their monasteries and communities in the fashion dictated by *Airs, Waters, and Places*. These self-contained settlements of well-ventilated and heated buildings often had their own pure water supply and means of waste disposal. The monastic centers served as hospitals in times of need, and administered a brand of medicine combining Greek clinical procedure and Christian admonition. While monastic orders eventually influenced the reemergence of medical science in the twelfth and thirteenth centuries, they apparently had little impact on the communities of their lay brethren before the eleventh century.

Very little is known with certainty of the diseases which plagued Western Europe in the Dark Ages. Records and descriptions of the period have led historians to conclude that at least diphtheria, measles, influenza, ergotism, anthrax, trachoma, and tuberculosis were regular problems. The most feared health problems were bubonic plague and leprosy. The probability of plague becoming epidemic increased dramatically with urbanization and commerce. Rodents thrive in urban areas which are not properly sanitized, and the indigenous rat population can be easily infected by rats or rodent fleas carried on merchant ships moving from one port to another. As public health systems broke down in the Roman Empire in the sixth century, the urban centers became increasingly susceptible to plague, and in 543 the plague of Justinian swept through the population. While the death toll is unknown, the plague reduced the cities to towns, hastening the Empire's fall. As the urban population decreased, and trade with central Asia (where the bubonic plague is generally considered to have originated) fell off, the incidence of plague was reduced.

Another health problem dreaded by medieval society, leprosy, appeared to be a major problem as early as the sixth century. The Council of Lyons in 583 empowered local officials to control the activities of lepers and to prohibit their mingling with the healthy population. Leper houses were reported in Paris as early as the sixth century. In the seventh century the King of Lombardy decreed that lepers must be isolated to avoid the spread of the disease. Towns established committees consisting of a bishop, local clerics, the local barber, and a known leper to determine if suspected victims actually had leprosy. If the determination were positive, the victim was banished to the nearest leper colony. The need for isolation was considered so great that those found to have the disease were considered dead upon their banishment. In a ceremony preceding his delivery to the leprosarium, the afflicted was clothed in a shroud and covered with dirt while a solemn mass for the dead was read (Simon, 1959). Such isolation, however, did not help decrease the incidence of leprosy which continued to be a major problem through the Dark Ages and the Renaissance.

The Late Medieval Period

By the thirteenth century, urban society began to reemerge in southern Europe. Towns and villages spilled over the walls and fortifications which had bound them during the previous six centuries. As towns pursued mercantilist policy, their populations grew, and the division of labor expanded. As lay expertise reemerged, civil engineering and medicine improved. The Dark Ages had ended; the political and economic forces which shaped the Renaissance were in motion. The clear break between the early and late medieval periods is demonstrated by the fact that, despite having only one cleric/physician in the year 1000, Florence had both a physician's guild and standard fee schedule by the year 1250. Also indicative of the increasing organizational ability was the appearance of numerous hospitals. While the Eastern Empire had maintained the Greco-Roman tradition of providing institutions for the infirm, such facilities were not common in the west, with the exception of leper colonies, before the eleventh century. In 1198 the Pope founded the Order of the Holy Ghost to build hospitals in Europe. Soon thereafter, the civic pride of the merchant class, which prospered through town mercantilism, led to a spate of hospital building in the more wealthy cities. Florence, for example, had 30 hospitals by 1300, and Paris, with a much larger population, had 40. In England, 750 facilities were opened by the early fifteenth century.

Cities of the late medieval period expanded with the ability of civil authorities to provide water and sanitary conditions. The private water systems devised by monasteries and nobles were assumed by city governments and paid for by taxes. Basel, Bruges, Dublin, Florence, and scores of other communities had publicly-owned systems by the fourteenth century. Codes prohibited the washing of clothes, and the dumping of waste or dead animals in rivers, streams, or other water sources.

To improve city sanitation, ordinances prohibited the presence of animals in streets. The major cities also began paving their streets to facilitate runoff and cleaning. Paris began paving her streets around 1180. By the early fourteenth century other cities including Florence, Nurnberg, Prague, Basel, Augsburg, and Milan began to pave streets. London, Paris, Milan, and Florence began to reconstruct sewer systems, and trash collectors were hired to clean public places.

In addition to improving water, sewer, and street cleaning systems, the strengthened public sector began to monitor the sanitation of markets and wholesomeness of food. The marketplaces of Florence, for example, had to be swept and washed every evening. No refuse could be disposed of within a thousand paces of any market. Meat could not be held in the market more than two days. In Zurich, fish could not be held in the market more than one day. Augsburg sent inspectors to the market to collect objectionable meat which was then sold at a special stand to those passing through the city (Rosen, 1958).

Despite these improvements in the sanitary conditions and health services during the tenth through fourteenth centuries, Western Europe continued to be racked by serious health problems. Outbreaks of smallpox and measles were common. Epidemics of diphtheria struck the city of Rome in 1039, Holland in 1337, and many European cities in 1382. Influenza epidemics were common in Germany, Holland, and France, and Leprosy continued to be a major problem.

The epidemic which most shook Europe, the Black Death, is generally believed to have originated in Central Asia where wild rodents were chronic bubonic carriers. About 1346 the disease is believed to have reached the Black Sea where merchant ships and sailors came into contact with infected rodent fleas and victims. These ships then sailed to Constantinople, Venice, Genoa, and other ports. By April of 1348 the disease appeared in Florence and northern Italy, and by May in Avignon, Valencia, and Barcelona. In the next three years the disease swept over the entire continent. While mortality estimates vary widely, it appears safe to say that the Black Death was the worst epidemic experienced by western civilization.

The Black Death and the persistence of leprosy led the officials and physicians of Europe's city states to devise the "quarantine" (from the Italian *quarantenaria* or 40 day period). While it is not clear that isolation actually reduced the incidence of leprosy, many officials believed that separating diseased from healthy populations would control epidemics. The eventual response to the Black Death, therefore, was the quarantine system. In Venice, all ships from plague-stricken areas had to wait outside the port for 40 days to determine if the plague were aboard. Any stricken household was isolated, and food was passed in through windows. Corpses were likewise passed out the windows and immediately buried away from the city. Anyone in contact with the stricken family before the appearance of the disease was similarly isolated.

Miasmas

Besides inspiring quarantine and other health measures, the horrors of the plague prompted pre-Renaissance society to theorize about the etiology of disease. Normal science had not been pursued in public health since the Roman period, but by the thirteenth century a corrupted form of the ancient ecological paradigm replaced the supernatural explanations of the Dark Ages. The Hippocratic tradition had cited stagnant foul air as an indicator of environmental conditions which could disturb the balance of the four humors. Roman physicians also warned that bad air, or "miasma," brought on disease. By associating the stench of death and disease of the Black Death with the miasma concept, the late medieval physicians theorized that corrupt air was the primary cause of disease and was to be avoided. One physician, Johannes de Tornamiera, wrote (Rosen, 1958, p. 70):

> In times of epidemic, you must first of all avoid corrupted air which may come from marshy, muddy and fetid places, from stagnant water and ditches, from burial places, from stables of draught animals—avoid completely such places.

Astrology was somehow added to this miasmic explanation to produce the theory that under certain celestial arrays, miasmas were more likely to be present and would affect those whose constitutions were weakened by the alignment of stars. This combination of simplified Hippocratic principles and astrology persisted through the Renaissance until the advent of the Germ Theory.

The Renaissance and the Rise of the Nation State
The alignment of city states and smaller towns into leagues for trade advantages eventually led to the emergence of nation states. This evolution from city to nation states was paralleled by the emergence of a division of labor diverse enough to support artists, scholars, and researchers. The resulting increase in creative expression and intellectual pursuit is referred to as the *Renaissance* or "re-birth" of western culture. While many advances may have been made during the two centuries (1300-1700) usually attributed to the Renaissance, the Miasmic theory continued to dominate the study of ill health.

Epidemics continued to ravage the cities and their hinterlands. The same urban centers which spawned and supported the grandeur of the Renaissance were scenes of horror when struck by disease. The epidemic of 1629 to 1631 took one million lives in northern Italy alone. Epidemics of smallpox, syphilis, scurvy, the "English Sweat," and scarlet fever also ravaged the continent during its "re-birth." For some reason, amid the breakthroughs in art and technology, this huge loss of human life did not motivate western man to suggest new theories of disease. Physicians who theorized about disease inevitably resorted to the Hippocratic tradition for inspiration. Guillaume de Baillou (1640), for example, attributed disease to atmospheric conditions and local miasmas. Thomas Sydenham (1685), an English contemporary of Baillou, published several treatises which expanded on the notion of atmospheric miasmas. He claimed that illness could be separated into two classes differentiated by the degree to which they were atmospherically precipitated. Outbreaks of the epidemic diseases of plague, smallpox, and dysentery were supposedly controlled by the "epidemic constitution" of the atmosphere. The lesser diseases, such as pleurisy and rheumatism, were attributed to individual weaknesses aggravated by local miasmas. While Sydenham did not describe the "epidemic constitutions" of the atmosphere, he did say they were produced by miasmas rising from the earth and fluctuated with celestial alignments. The notion of atmospheric miasmas perpetuated by Renaissance physicians lingered until at least the early nineteenth century, when the advent of the germ paradigm returned public health to normal science.

Precursors of the Germ Paradigm

While variants of the miasma theory dominated the Renaissance period, important works presaging germ theory appeared as early as mid-sixteenth century. The most widely cited of these, Fracastoro's *On Contagion, Contagious Diseases and their Treatment*, was published in 1546. The three volumes dealt with the theory of contagion, the diagnosis of diseases, and the treatment of specific diseases. The volume on contagion was advanced in its use of empirical data and rigorous logic to draw conclusions concerning the spread of epidemic diseases. Using information gathered while treating plague, typhus fever, syphilis, and other diseases, Fracastoro reasoned that disease must be caused by infectious agents which pass from one person to another. He claimed these agents had to be particles which were transmitted through direct contact between infected and uninfected persons, common use of utensils, clothing or other objects, and, under certain conditions, through the air. He analogized these particles to tiny seeds, or *seminaria*, which differed for each disease, and which germinated in the bodily humors of the host. When the larger organism sprang from the seed it supposedly upset the balance of humors producing external symptoms. Using these concepts, Fracastoro could parsimoniously explain the spread of epidemic diseases without resorting to astrological or atmospheric conditions, which were impossible to classify. His explanation, however, had one serious problem—no one had ever seen a seminaria. Fracastoro's theory on contagion remained a curiosity scoffed by those positing the miasmic explanation of disease.

Instruments devised by lensmakers in Holland caught the fancy of scientists in the mid-seventeenth century. The telescope, for example, made Galileo's work possible; and improvements in the microscope revealed the existence of the microcosm. The microcosm was at first considered more a curiosity than a source of new knowledge, but in 1658 a Jesuit, Athonasius Kircher, claimed to have observed the seminaria which caused the plague. His claim was reinforced in 1676, when Leeuwenhoeck reported observing through his microscope "little animals" on several common substances. These reports led several intellectuals to convert the microscope from a parlor toy to a scientific instrument, and to catalogue their observations. The "microscopists" hoped that the data would eventually help substantiate, or refute, hypotheses relating not just to the study of illness, but to all the natural sciences. Their hopes would not be realized in the case of medicine and public health until 1830. Most physicians of the eighteenth century preferred to theorize about miasmas than to observe seminaria.

THE GERM PARADIGM

The late eighteenth and early nineteenth centuries are often referred to as the Age of Enlightenment. During this period, the economic, social, and political structure of western civilization changed radically. As the economic organization of the medieval period accelerated, nation states emerged to forge independent cities into systems of collection, production, and distribution which finally surpassed the Roman Empire in complexity. The explosion of economic functions inherent in this growth led to the emergence of the middle class, or those who accumulated wealth through entrepreneurial ability rather than blood line. The freedom of the marketplace, and the relative stability of national monetary systems allowed the risk taker with business talent to become wealthy without the protection, or blessing, of royal families or established churches. The increasingly powerful middle class, viewing the inertia and backwardness of religiously based civil authority as a hindrance to economic and social progress, championed and financed the work of secular scientists and thinkers. The secular intellectuals were convinced that reason and the scientific method would free human society from ignorance, disease, starvation, and war. Revolutions in America and France, which rejected Divine Right Monarchy, dramatically demonstrated the confidence of the new middle classes in the power of reason and man's perfectability. Science and education, it was believed, would replace divine right and dogma as the means to orderly humane society.

Miasmic Theory and Sanitary Reform

The increasing economic productivity of the late eighteenth century triggered a population boom across Europe. Given that most of the increased economic opportunities were in the cities and towns, urban centers grew even faster than the general population. While the population of Prussia, for example, doubled between 1750 and 1800, Berlin's population increased fivefold. The urban infrastructure (water supply, sewers, streets and housing) was not able to assimilate these increases. The result was a breakdown of the sanitary and health service systems. The problem of overwhelmed health systems was most dramatically demonstrated by the infant mortality rate in England in the mid-eighteenth century. Records indicate that in some sections of London only 10 percent of newborns survived the first year of life (Rosen, 1958).

The enlightened classes reacted strongly to the suffering they witnessed about them. Spontaneous movements began throughout Europe to reverse the trend of degenerating public health. These efforts, which marked the beginning of the Sanitary Reform Movement, were based entirely on miasmic theory and the Roman tradition of providing basic health services. In London, for example, dispensaries for the treatment of infants began to appear around 1770. Hospitals specializing in obstetrics were also opened, and campaigns begun to educate the poor in child care. Educational treatises such as Cadogan's *An Essay upon*

Nursing and the Management of Children (1748) became increasingly common in Western Europe, adding to the knowledge of physicians as well as reformers. As the spirit of enlightenment grew, the zeal of the sanitary reformers increased, and their push to reduce suffering achieved some success. Scurvy was eliminated as physicians recognized that citrus fruits greatly reduced individual susceptibility to the disease. Occupational hazards of miners, factory workers, and of several crafts were identified and steps taken to reduce them. The appalling conditions of prisons were publicized, and reforms enacted. Pinel, whose work will be described in the next chapter, reformed the mental institutions of France. Hospitals for the general public appeared throughout Europe and America. Water and sewer systems were improved. Street paving became common. Boards of Health were established in several English cities. By the first decade of the nineteenth century, the infant mortality rates had decreased, the plague had disappeared, leprosy was rare, and occupational hazards were coming under control. For a brief period before the onset of the huge population dislocations engendered by the industrial revolution, it appeared that sanitary reform, based on miasmic principles and medical procedures dating to the Roman period, would stabilize the trend of increasing suffering.

The high point of miasmic medicine was marked by Frank's six volume work *System of a Complete Medical Policy*. This ambitious series of books published from 1774 to 1821 synthesized the knowledge that western man had added to the Hippocratic tradition between 500 and 1800 A.D. Reflecting the mercantilist spirit of his day, Frank organized his material as advice to political leaders wishing to maximize the productive capacity and well-being of their nation's population. The volumes cover such diverse topics as: means to encourage population growth, the education of midwives and new mothers, the care of infants and new mothers, the environment of schools, controlling miasmas, personal hygiene, monitoring the wholesomeness of food, proper diet, water and sewer systems, municipal sanitation, vital statistics, accident prevention, and hospital administration. While Frank's work was a thorough compilation of facts, advice, and useful instructions, his unquestioning acceptance of miasmic theory demonstrated that the study of human diseases had made little progress since 1000 A.D.

While plague and leprosy were no longer major threats to the population, other infectious diseases continued to vex western civilization. Miasmic theory and sanitary reforms had not lessened the incidence of smallpox, for example, which had become endemic in most urban areas. By 1760 smallpox was reported to be the principal cause of infant mortality in Europe. Because of its horrific impact on the most helpless and innocent segment of the population, the humanist reformers made smallpox the principal target of their attempts to understand and control disease. One of the earlier methods devised for dealing with smallpox, in fact, initiated the line of research from which the germ paradigm was to emerge.

It had been noted since the tenth century that those who survived an attack of smallpox rarely contracted the disease again. Physicians in the Eastern Empire, apparently as early as the tenth century, had attempted to preclude children from contracting serious cases of smallpox by infecting them with the blood of another who had a very mild case. By precipitating the immunization process with a mild case, it was hoped that a more severe attack would be avoided. The process of "variolation," as it was called, apparently worked well enough to be widely practiced in Istanbul in the early eighteenth century. The process was reported to English physicians around 1720, and in 1722 the children of the royal family were inoculated. Many citizens followed the royal example, despite controversy over its wisdom. The virulency of the induced infection was difficult to control, however, and often proved fatal. The inoculation campaigns precipitated outbreaks among people who might not otherwise be at risk. The lack of statistical sophistication precluded determining when the risk of variolation was less than that of allowing an epidemic to run its course. Controversy over the wisdom of inoculation continued to flare through most of the eighteenth century. The risk of death remained high enough to convince many competent physicians that mass inoculation would take more lives than it would save. The need for a strain which produced a consistently mild infection capable of eliciting immunization was widely recognized.

Edward Jenner, an English physician, practiced in a rural area where he was often called upon to treat "cowpox," a mild illness common among those who dealt with dairy cattle. Jenner noticed that those children who had cowpox very rarely contracted smallpox. To test if the cowpox infection could elicit immunization, Jenner, in 1746, infected a young boy with the mild cowpox disease. After recovery, the boy was then inoculated with a smallpox strain used for variolation. No signs of smallpox were observed.

Jenner's experiment, replicated several times with the same results, confirmed that the mild cowpox infection would lead to smallpox immunization. The term "vaccination," based on the Latin *vacca* or "cow," replaced variolation, and has become the generic term to describe the process of eliciting immunization through mild infection. Jenner's vaccination process was widely reported and practiced throughout the western world.

The immunization discovery was immense in impact, but little understood. Why did vaccination work? What had it to do with miasmas? Would the same process help control other diseases? These questions vexed physicians and researchers during the first quarter of the nineteenth century. One effect of their increasing interest in work such as Jenner's was the relegation of the Sanitary Reform Movement to nonphysicians. Physicans and public health experts began to drift apart as the former moved closer to the germ theory and the latter continued to argue for better environmental conditions as a means to reduce miasma.

The Sanitary Reform Movement became increasingly concerned with the problems arising from the immense migration to the emerging industrial centers of Britain and Western Europe. Britain, given her early leadership among industrializing nations, was the first to experience the overwhelming demographic shift that marked a new era in human organization. Not only did the economic advantages described in Chapter 3 tend to draw populations to English cities, but the state, convinced that industrialization was the key to progress, intentionally accelerated the migration. Understanding that a mobile labor force was crucial to an efficient industrial system, those believing in unrestrained capitalism passed the Poor Law Reform Act of 1834 which cut off welfare payments to able-bodied or seasonally unemployed laborers living in small towns. The intent, and the effect, was to force these men to move to the industrial centers. The human costs of such policies were displayed in Manchester, which the geometry of industrial location had made the prototypical industrial city. Block after block of tenements were constructed to house the migrants who had been forced to move there. These slums had no running water or sanitary facilities. Those unable to find a tenement lived in unlit, dirt-floored cellars where a survey, conducted in the 1840s, found 281 instances of five persons sleeping in one bed, 738 cases of four persons in a bed, and 1,500 where three shared a bed. Excrement was dumped in tiny alleys between tenements causing frequent cholera outbreaks. Manchester, in short, was a hellish example of what unfettered, economic greed could produce.

The sanitary reformers of the mid-nineteenth century believed that government had to step in. Southwood Smith (1856), a noted reformer, wrote of the lives that were lost during an epidemic: "For every one of the lives of these 15,000 persons who have perished . . . those are responsible whose proper office is to interfere and endeavor to stay the calamity—who have the power to save but who will not use it." Pressure brought by reformers, such as Smith, eventually led to such legislation as Britain's Public Health Acts of 1848 and 1875, which established the public sector's right to enforce codes requiring sewers, plumbing, clean streets, and other sanitary reforms.

Despite the continued action of reformers in America, Europe, and England, the industrializing west continued to suffer from epidemics of cholera, yellow fever, diphtheria, and other contagious diseases. The inability of the urban system to assimilate the onslought, and the general increase in mobility made possible by the steam engine, led to diseases sweeping through the western world with frightening rapidity. The inability to control disease through sanitary reform based on miasma theory added impetus to research pursued by physicians into the phenomenon of contagion.

Following the work done by Jenner, a number of physicians became interested in contagion and the process by which humans developed immunity. Peter Panum (1847) was among the several researchers who argued that contagion was a more parsimonious explanation than miasma. During his research on the transmission of measles in the Faroe Islands, Panum observed that the disease was transmitted by personal contact, and that symptoms appeared after two weeks of incubation. He also noted that those who contacted a victim in the disease's early stages contracted the illness, while those who did so later in its course did not. Having had the disease, moreover, apparently immunized the victim. Based on these observations, Panum concluded that measles was not caused or transmitted by miasmas but by the transmission of a "poison" which reproduced itself once in the body. He recommended that quarantine, not sanitation, was the best way to halt the disease.

Two English physicians, John Snow (1855) and William Budd (1849) working independently, concluded that cholera also was best explained and treated as a disease spread by contact with infectious agents, rather than by exposure to miasmas. Snow carefully monitored the 1848 cholera epidemic in London, and noted that the illness could be traced to water drawn from a section of the Thames polluted with excrement. He concluded that the disease was transmitted through contact with the excrement of victims and through sewer water which mixed with water used for drinking and washing clothes, dishes, and utensils. While he did not identify the infectious agent, he described it as a "poison." Budd concluded much the same after tracing cholera in rural areas back to wells polluted with excrement. Unlike Panum and Snow, Budd attributed the disease to a living organism which entered the system through the mouth, multiplied in the intestines, and passed to other persons exposed to the victim's excrement.

By 1850 several investigators, included Panum, Snow, and Budd, had parsimoniously explained epidemics without resorting to miasmas; but public health represented by the sanitary reformers, was so rooted in miasmic theory that it would take the dramatic breakthroughs of Koch and Pasteur to precipitate a return to normal science.

The Emergence of the Germ Paradigm

While research such as Panum's, Budd's, and Snow's demonstrated the need for a reformulation of public health's understanding of disease, it was a conceptual, rather than investigatory, work which prepared the way for the advent of the germ paradigm. Jacob Henle, a German anatomist, published a volume in 1840 which cogently argued that living microscopic organisms, not miasmas or astrological arrays, caused disease. Synthesizing the findings of research conducted by others, Henle presented data demonstrating that the particles which cause disease must be organic, because they multiply during an incubation period after entering the body, and before symptoms appear. He further argued, citing data from sources as diverse as veterinary medicine and volumes describing beer brewing, that these organisms were plants rather than animals. Henle also described the logic researchers would have to follow to test his hypothesis. This logic is very important because it structured the research procedures which made the germ paradigm possible. As will be discussed in the next chapter, Henle's logic was also later adopted by those studying abnormal behavior. Henle listed the following steps as essential to testing germ theory:

1. *Cataloging of Symptom Syndromes.*

   Before illness could be attributed to micro-organisms, researchers first had to establish that there were identifiable diseases which could be reliably differentiated from each other. This meant observing and classifying the symptoms of people judged "sick." Measles, for example, should be associated with a distinct group of symptoms which occur in a regular temporal pattern. This group of symptoms would be measurably different from the group associated with smallpox. Identifying these symptom "syndromes" was important, because, if germ theory were correct, each would be associated with a different micro-organism.

2. *Identifying the Micro-organism Peculiar to Each Syndrome.*

   Henle's next step was to inspect tissue and waste from persons manifesting different syndromes and from those who were healthy. If germ theory were correct, sick people should have micro-organisms not found in healthy persons. The peculiar micro-organisms found in sick persons should, moreover, be specific to each symptom syndrome. The germ found to be peculiar to smallpox victims, for example, would become the suspected causal agent.

3. *Isolating the Suspected Micro-organism.*

   In order to devise an experiment which would prove that the suspected germ actually caused a syndrome, the researcher would need a pure strain of the microbe. This required removing the germ from a victim and cultivating it in some medium uncontaminated by other microbes.

4. *Devising a Controlled Experiment to Determine Causation.*

   Once a pure strain of the suspected agent was cultivated, the researcher had to establish that it could produce symptoms in a healthy subject. This involved more than just exposing a laboratory animal to the microbe. The experiment required that other possible causal agents, such as miasmas, be controlled. Henle suggested this be done by having two similar groups of animals which would experience the same environment. One group would be infected with the suspected microbe. If that group developed the symptoms while the other, or "control" group, did not, the researcher would have compelling evidence that the suspected microbe was causal.

5. *Determining if the Disease is Transmitted Through Contact.*

   Henle's last step was intended to demonstrate that the causal agent could be transmitted through interaction between ill and healthy subjects. To do this, similar groups of healthy animals would be placed in the cages with the control and sick groups. If the new animals exposed to the sick group became ill, but those placed with the control group did not, Henle claimed the researcher would have established that disease could be caused by germs and transmitted through contact.

Henle's arguments failed to produce the response they deserved, mainly because experimental technology was not advanced enough to allow his ideas to be tested. Since physicians were using procedures devised by the Romans, and since the sanitary reformers were motivated by miasmic theory, the chore of developing experimental procedures and technology fell, for the most part, to chemists. Perhaps the most widely known of these chemists was Louis Pasteur.

Pasteur's interest in contagious disease evolved from his early study of crystal structures, which established him as an accomplished scientist. While studying crystals, Pasteur became interested in the light distorting quality of such organic compounds as amyl alcohol which was a product of fermentation. In the course of this work he became very familiar with fermentation processes and means of controlling them through environmental factors such as light and heat. This familiarity led to his being asked by French wine and beer producers to help explain the frequent spoiling of their products during fermentation. Pasteur investigated the problem, and, in the 1860s, discovered that the fermentation process was due to the action of microorganisms, some of which produced the desired results and others of which spoiled the product. After identifying the unwanted organisms, he began to test ways of destroying them without harming the desired microbes. Pasteur found that carefully heating the wine to a particular temperature would produce the desired results. The process of heating fluids to destroy harmful bacteria took the name of its inventor, Pasteurization.

From his work with fermentation, Pasteur learned that microorganisms were ubiquitous and would contaminate anything left open to the air. He deduced that these microorganisms were responsible not only for fermentation, but for all processes traditionally attributed to putrefaction and spontaneous generation. Pasteur demonstrated that maggots did not arise spontaneously from decaying matter, as had been theorized for over a century, but rather from microscopic larvae which fed on exposed organic material.

Pasteur suspected, as early as 1863, that the microorganisms he had discovered were responsible for contagious diseases. To test his theory he studied the diseases of silkworms which threatened to destroy the French silk industry. He carefully observed the worms and delineated two separate syndromes which, in 1868, he traced to two different microorganisms. In the same year, Pasteur suffered a stroke and had to put his work aside. His discoveries, however, had generated great interest in germ theory, and other researchers maintained the line of research which was to culminate in Koch's experiment.

Jean Villemin, a French surgeon, published a volume on tuberculosis in 1868 which described his research demonstrating that the disease was not caused by miasmas but by germs. While he was not able to isolate the microorganism, Villemin increased interest among physicians in Henle's and Pasteur's work. Casimir Devaine also accelerated the rush to germ theory by demonstrating that anthrax was transmitted from sheep to sheep by a rod-shaped microorganism.

Ferdinand Cohn, a German botanist, brought order to the field by carefully classifying the microorganisms that were being discovered by dozens of researchers. By 1875, Cohn and his students at Breslau developed laboratory procedures and materials which allowed the systematic identification, isolation, cultivation, and classification of bacteria. The only element of the paradigm lacking was the definitive experiment described by Henle. That was supplied in 1870 in Cohn's laboratory by, appropriately enough, a student of Henle's.

Robert Koch practiced in a small town near Breslau. Koch, interested in Devaine's work with anthrax, hoped to use Henle's logic to prove that the strange rod-shaped microbes caused the disease. Koch observed mice he had infected with blood from cattle sick with anthrax and, as expected, found Devaine's rods in the blood of all the ill mice, and not in the healthy control group. He succeeded in the difficult tasks of isolating the bacteria, and cultivating them in hanging droplets of fluid which allowed him to observe their development. When the isolated bacteria were introduced to healthy animals, the mice developed the symptoms and transmitted the disease to other mice. Koch knew he had proven Henle's germ theory, and immediately went to nearby Breslau to replicate his experiment for Cohn, then the most respected man in the field. On April 30, 1876, the obscure country doctor began the experiment in the laboratory of the famous professor. Over the next three days, Cohn and his associates observed as Koch painstakingly repeated his experiment. When the mice infected with the isolated, cultivated bacteria exhibited the symptoms, all present knew that science had finally replaced magic and miasma in the study of human illness.

The Normal Science Phase of the Germ Paradigm

Henle's method, as operationalized by Koch, was adopted by researchers as quickly as word of Koch's experiment could travel. Bacteriologists soon identified the microbes responsible for many dreaded diseases. By 1898 at least 20 pathogenic microbes were identified (see Table 5-1) by 18 different researchers. The last quarter of the nineteenth century was truly, as Rosen (1958) describes it, the "Golden Age of Bacteriological Discovery."

The findings of the bacteriologists were not lost on those desiring to improve public health. Pasteur, recovered from his stroke, again demonstrated his ability to use basic research to solve pressing problems. Synthesizing Koch and Jenner's work, Pasteur literally founded immunology by developing mild strains of infectious microbes which could be used for vaccinations. Between 1880 and 1889, Pasteur devised vaccines for both rabies and cholera, and began the public health immunization movement.

Lister, an English physician, recognized the importance of Henle's and Pasteur's work in explaining infections developing from wounds and surgery. He attributed infection to exposure to ubiquitous microbes which settled on open wounds and incisions. He recommended the use of "disinfectants" such as

Table 5-1. Discoveries of Pathogenic Organisms
(from Rosen, 1958. Reproduced by permission.)

Year	Disease Organism	Investigator
1880	Typhoid (basillus found in tissues)	Eberth
	Leprosy	Hansen
	Malaria	Laveran
1882	Tuberculosis	Koch
	Glanders	Loeffler and Schutz
1883	Cholera	Koch
	Streptococcus (erysipelas)	Fehleisen
1884	Diphtheria	Klebs and Loeffler
	Typhoid (bacillus isolated)	Gaffky
	Staphylococcus/Streptococcus	Rosenbach
	Tetanus	Nicolaier
1885	Coli	Escherich
1886	Pneumococcus	A. Fraenkel
1887	Malta fever	Bruce
	Soft chancre	Ducrey
1892	Gas gangrene	Welch and Nuttall
1894	Plague	Yersin, Kitasato
	Botulism	van Ermengem
1898	Dysentery bacillus	Shiga

carbolic acid. Lister's principles eventually led to sterilization of operating rooms and hospitals.

By 1890, researchers had begun to investigate how germs actually passed from victim to victim. Koch furthered knowledge of how diseases were transmitted by clarifying the carrier phenomenon. Carriers were people who transmitted contagious diseases without exhibiting symptoms themselves. The communication of disease by insects and animals also became a subject of intense study at the turn of the century. The tracing of malaria to the Anopheles mosquito is a classic example of how parasitological research was combined with study of insect carriers to free man of a dreaded disease. The protozoa responsible for malaria was isolated in 1880 by Alphonse Laverne, a French army officer, but the means by which it was transmitted remained a mystery. Several physicians had observed that the disease was most prevalent in mosquito infested areas, and suggested a possible connection. The proof of the relationship came in

1898 when an English army physician in India, Ronald Ross, infected healthy birds with malaria by exposing them to mosquitoes who had fed on birds infected with malaria. The stomach wall of the Anopheles mosquito was found to be an ideal medium for the malaria parasite.

Yellow fever, a disease which had raked the Americas on several occasions, was traced to the mosquito in an especially dramatic experiment conducted by Walter Reed in Cuba. Because no laboratory animals were known to be susceptible to the disease, several members of a special commission sent to Cuba in 1900 exposed themselves to the mosquito suspected of carrying the disease. One member died of the disease before the commission could report its finding that the mosquito was the carrier.

Another important breakthrough involving insect carriers also involved the dreaded bubonic plague which had not been a major problem for several decades. The organism responsible for the plague was isolated in 1894 in Hong Kong. In 1897, M. Ogata, a Japanese researcher, found the bacilli in rat fleas, and suggested that the disease was transmitted by the fleas. Ogata's theory was substantiated in 1898 by Frenchman P. L. Simond, who demonstrated that the plague was essentially a disease of rats which is passed to man via the flea.

The great strides made by bacteriologists, and those who converted basic research into useful prescriptive knowledge, completely dominated public health in the United States from 1900 to mid-century. In 1895 public health laboratories had been established in New York, Boston, Philadelphia, Washington, Lansing, and Providence. By 1900 nearly all states and major cities had laboratories responsible for testing food and water, diagnosing communicable diseases, producing vaccines and antitoxins, and dispensing information. Each succeeding decade brought new discoveries and new means of making the discoveries useful. While fewer dramatic breakthroughs occurred, there were still exciting discoveries, such as the Salk vaccine which eliminated polio as a threat. Death rates dropped dramatically, as did infant mortality rates. Most Americans came to assume freedom from dreaded infectious diseases was the norm, not the exception.

In a period of 80 years the germ paradigm freed mankind from diseases which had caused centuries of suffering. This astonishing progress produced, however, at least one avoidable cost. Total preoccupation with germ theory led public health to overlook the fact that other phenomena besides infectious agents cause physical suffering.

The Elements of the Germ Paradigm

The Germ Paradigm, rooted in the work of Jacob Henle and that of bacteriologists such as Cohn, Koch, and Pasteur, has the following elements:

I. *Basic Assumptions*.

The realization that the environment is permeated with microorganisms, some of which are pathogenic, led the bacteriologists to assume:

A. Disease symptoms are produced by microorganisms which invade the human body and multiply to the point that they, or their toxic by-products, interfere with normal functioning.
B. Each disease has a specific causal bacteria which can be identified.
C. Disease is spread by:
  1. Contact with persons who are infected or carry the disease without manifesting the symptoms.
  2. Contact with water, clothing, utensils, and other media which can transport microbes from person to person.
  3. Contact with insect vectors which can carry diseases from animals to man or man to man.
D. Disease can be controlled by:
  1. Isolating those who are infected by it.
  2. Eliciting immunity by vaccinating with mild strains of diseases.
  3. Administering anti-toxins which inhibit the multiplying of certain microbes.
  4. Destroying insect vectors which can carry pathogenic microbes.

II. *Analogies.*

Over the century that bacteriology has pursued the identification, isolation, and control of pathogenic bacteria, many analogies ranging from "seminaria," "little animals," "tiny plants," etc. have been used to explain microbes. The most pervasive analogy or metaphor, however, has been the description of bacteriological infection as an attack on healthy bodies by invisible pathogens which, once in the system, wage some sort of battle with protective agents.

III. *Conventions.*

Growing from Jacob Henle's recommendations for testing his hypotheses, the conventions of the germ paradigm are:

A. Empirical Epistemology. The demand for replicable, empirical demonstrations of the validity of explanations has become an essential characteristic of bacteriological research.
B. Quantitative Description. The emphasis on replication of experiments assumes exact quantitative measurement.
C. Laboratory Research. Even before Henle, the laboratory experiment, with its emphasis on controlled environments, was the bacteriologist's chief means of gathering data and testing hypotheses. As a result, public health, despite its obvious need to monitor its client population, became under the germ paradigm, more concerned with laboratory than with naturalistic research.
D. Individual as Unit of Analysis. Given the fact that the most serious health problem facing the western world was contagious disease, public health naturally focused its attention on infectious agents and means of controlling their impact on individuals. This approach was clearly the most efficient method to reduce suffering and death. The emphasis on the

individual-germ interaction, however, precluded public health from recognizing that some health problems were more parsimoniously understood, and more efficiently controlled, by viewing them as products of community dynamics.

IV. *Exemplars.*

The assumptions underlying the germ paradigm were first posited as an alternative to miasma theory by Jacob Henle, in his *Pathologische Untersuchungen* which appeared in 1840. The exemplary demonstration of those assumptions, however, did not occur until Koch, Henle's student, replicated his anthrax experiment for Cohn in 1876. While it would be misleading to cite Henle's book as the sole exemplar of the germ paradigm, his contribution to Koch's work was considerable enough to list the teacher's work with the student's as the examplars of the germ paradigm.

The Current Crisis in Public Health

The germ paradigm's domination of public health has clearly weakened and may have passed. This has occurred for two closely related reasons. First, while the germ paradigm has enabled public health to understand the nature of contagious disease, several important phenomena have remained unexplained, despite two decades of attempting to make them coherent with germ theory. The unexplained observation which has most vexed germ theorists is the fact that while exposure to bacteria is a necessary precondition to becoming ill, it is not sufficient. Not everyone in a population exposed to a harmful bacteria becomes ill. In fact, microbes known to produce illness are present in our bodies most of the time. Yet, illness occurs in only a subset of the population at unpredictable times.

Among the better attempts to explain this phenomenon is Rene Dubos' (1955) article, "Second Thoughts on the Germ Theory." Dubos claimed (p. 31) that the germ explanation:

> . . . rarely fits the facts of disease. Indeed it corresponds almost to a cult—generated by a few miracles, undisturbed by inconsistencies and not too exacting about evidence.

Dubos lists several examples of disease associated with ubiquitous microbes and those most humans harbor continuously, and comments (p. 34):

> There are many situations in which the microbe is a constant and ubiquitous component of the environment but causes disease only when some weakening of the patient by another factor allows infection to proceed unrestrained, at least for a while. Theories of disease must account for the surprising fact that, in any community, a large percentage of healthy and normal individuals continually harbor potentially pathogenic microbes without suffering any symptoms . . .

Performing a function resembling that served by Henle a century earlier, Dubos cites research findings which indicate the need for a new paradigm. Like Henle, Dubos also suggests what that new paradigm might assume. Preparing the way for the emergence of an ecological alternative to the germ paradigm, Dubos writes (p. 35):

> During the first phase of the germ theory the property of virulence was regarded as lying solely within the microbes themselves. Now virulence is coming to be thought of as ecological. Whether man lives in equilibrium with microbes or becomes their victim depends upon the circumstances under which he encounters them. This ecological concept is not merely an intellectual game: It is essential to a proper formulation of the problem of microbial diseases and even to their control.

Dubos' criticism helped precipitate crisis by asserting that the germ paradigm no longer answered important questions about contagious disease—the phenomenon it was intended to explain. The current crisis in public health is also due to the fact that phenomena apparently unrelated to microorganisms had become health problems. By mid-century, public health had to concern itself with health problems not traceable to germs but to man-made pollutants, safety hazards, and individual resistance. Unable to further old lines of research and inappropriate to the analysis of new problems, the germ paradigm began to lose favor among those interested in community health.

THE ECOLOGICAL ALTERNATIVE

Any explanation of community health problems offered as a replacement for the germ paradigm must meet the following criteria:

1. It should explain why diseases associated with ubiquitous microbes do not cause everyone to be ill all the time. That is, it must explain why, at any point in time, some members of the community are ill and others not; and over time, why the rate of illness in the community varies.
2. It should offer some explanation of why pollution-caused problems vary from community to community, and in one community over time.
3. It should offer some explanation of why safety hazards vary from community to community, and in one community over time.
4. The explanations it offers for the above problems should be testable.
5. It should suggest some means for reducing the problems.

The remainder of this chapter will suggest that a new paradigm, not unlike the ancient ecological paradigm, is emerging and appears to satisfy the above criteria. This modern ecological paradigm uses an understanding of community dynamics devised by the Chicago School, and, therefore, assumes that the health problems of any community can be parsimoniously predicted by understanding its abiotic elements—that is, its economic base and natural setting.

Indications That Ecological Factors Affect Community Health

Any effort to develop an ecological paradigm for public health must be justified by at least preliminary indications that the incidence of health problems is influenced by ecological factors. That justification has been supplied by research dealing with the spatial distribution of contagious disease and other health problems.

The spatial distribution of health problems has been a subject of interest to geographers and public health experts for some time (May, 1958; Rodenwaldt and Jusatz, 1952-1961). One of the principal reasons for this interest was the desire to understand and predict the spread of contagious disease. It has been widely recognized that as modern commerce and improved transportation increase interaction between population centers, the difficulty of predicting or containing the spread of disease also increases. This truism has led several researchers to recognize the importance of understanding the economic bases of the ecological paradigm.

Urban centers become increasingly interdependent as the system of collection, production, and distribution matures. Based on this fact, Pyle (1968) hypothesized that epidemics introduced into a mature system of cities would spread more quickly than in a less interdependent system. He also hypothesized that the pattern of contagion could be predicted by understanding the interactions among the cities. To test his hypotheses, Pyle collected data describing the spread of cholera epidemics in the United States in 1832, 1848, and 1866. He found that in the epidemic of 1832 the disease tended to spread from a large city to communities in that city's economic hinterland before it spread from one large city to another. Distance from the point of origin was the best predictor of when the disease would reach a community. In the 1848 outbreak, however, the disease spread from a large city to other large cities nearly as fast as from large cities to their surrounding communities. The disease was first reported on December 1, 1848, in New York, and had spread 600 miles to Buffalo by May 30, 1849. It did not appear in Newark, New Jersey, less than 100 miles from New York, however, until June 4, 1849. In the epidemic of 1866, the disease spread from large city to large city before it appeared in their hinterlands. In each epidemic, moreover, the "path" of the disease was predictable from trade routes. The disease spread from New York along the eastern seaboard, and inland along waterways, to the great lakes and down the Mississippi. Each succeeding epidemic also spread further west as the "frontier" gave way to economic integration.

Pyle's tracing of cholera epidemics clearly demonstrated the public health implications of increasingly complex and interrelated systems of cities. Given that ecological theory helped explain the spread of contagion in the system of cities, Pyle suspected that ecological forces might produce a pattern of illness in the human community which resembled the ecological gradient. To test for this pattern, Pyle divided Chicago into areas which were aggregates of census tracts.

Each area was then characterized by the rates of the following problems:
1. Chickenpox
2. Diarrhea
3. Measles
4. Infectious Hepatitis
5. German Measles
6. Mumps
7. Whooping Cough
8. Scarlet Fever
9. Syphilis
10. Gonorrhea
11. Tuberculosis
12. Pneumonia
13. Congenital Malformations
14. Poison Cases
15. Premature Births
16. Illegitimate Births
17. Infant Deaths within 28 days of birth
18. Rheumatic Fever

The community areas were also characterized by density and economic status. Through a statistical routine, referred to as "factor analysis," Pyle was able to measure the degree to which the above problems were associated with each other across areas. He found four groups, or clusters, of problems which tended to appear together. The first cluster included gonorrhea, illegitimate births, diarrhea, premature births, syphilis, measles, poisonings, tuberculosis, and infant mortality. This group was highly associated with poverty, and appeared most frequently in the areas surrounding the CBD and decreased sharply as distance from the CBD increased. A second cluster included mumps, whooping cough, and chickenpox. These diseases were highly associated with density. While this cluster was most common in poverty areas, it also affected densely populated, moderate income areas. A third cluster included rheumatic fever, scarlet fever, and pneumonia. These diseases exhibited an ecological gradient similar to those formed by mental health problems and crime. Rates of these diseases were highest near the CBD and decreased as distance from the central point increased. The fourth cluster included measles (rubella) and congenital malformation. While these problems were most pronounced in the poverty areas south of the CBD, rates throughout the remainder of the city exhibited no discernable pattern.

Findings such as Pyle's indicated that the economic dynamics which produce ecological gradients of behavioral problems also affected the distribution of health problems. This indication inevitably led ecologists to attempt to explain contagious diseases, man-made pollutants, and safety hazards in the context of the ecological paradigm.

The Adaptation Syndrome and Stress Related Diseases

As previously suggested, any replacement for the germ paradigm would have to offer an explanation of why everyone exposed to, or carrying, potentially pathogenic microbes does not become ill. As Dubos observed in 1955, such an explanation would have to center on the concept of individual resistance. If microbe exposure is held constant across the population, the reason why some individuals become ill and others do not must be that not all individuals are equally susceptible to the microbe. The ecologists, therefore, must construct a causal path between variations in individual susceptibility and the economic factors which spatially distribute populations. Tracing the path is best begun by describing Hans Selye's (1946) work dealing with adaptation and resistance.

Selye, a physical and medical researcher, observed that while each pathogenic microbe produced a unique set of symptoms, all diseases, or sets of symptoms, had common components which appeared in predictable patterns. Selye referred to the common pattern of components that could be factored by symptom syndromes as the General Adaptation Syndrome. GAS, as described by Selye, has three phases. The first is the alarm stage which Selye analogizes to a bodily "call to arms." In this phase the body becomes aware of some threat to its systemic balance, and begins an involuntary series of adjustments intended to maintain, or restore, equilibrium. These adjustments include changes in such measurable dimensions as blood pressure, muscular tension, and glandular flows. Selye noted that these measurable changes, or "stress reactions" as he refers to them, are similar for such stressors as microbes, poisons, or, more importantly, rapid changes in such environmental factors as temperature.

Selye describes the second phase of GAS as the "resistance" stage which emerges if the organism survives the alarm stage and if the stressor remains. During the resistance phase, the body restores the secretory capacity of the glandular system expended during the alarm stage, and maintains those systemic adjustments which allow it to return, at least temporarily, to equilibrium.

If the stressor is not mitigated during the resistance stage, the third phase, or exhaustion, sets in. While the physiological nature of exhaustion remains unclear, it has become obvious that the body's ability to maintain resistance against severe stressors, or against mild pathogens over extended periods of time, is limited. Selye compares the resistance capacity to a machine which inevitably wears down, leaving the organism defenseless against the stressor which precipitated the GAS, and against other pathogens previously resisted.

The discovery of GAS has led to a novel hypotheses concerning the etiologies of two classes of health problems. The first class includes those disorders Selye refers to as the "diseases of adaptation," or those diseases which are direct outgrowths of the alarm mechanism and resistive adjustments. One of the alarm reactions precipitated across stressors is the stimulation of the hypothalamus which, in turn, increases the secretion of hormone (adrenocorticotrophic hormone) from the pituitary gland. The hormone secreted by the pituitary stimulates the adrenal cortex to produce corticoids, including cortisone, which, in turn, affect the thymus and lead to atrophy of the lymph nodes and reduction of inflammation reactions. These changes affect the metabolic process and are highly associated with stomach ulcers, hypertension, certain allergies, and several cardiovascular and kidney diseases. These "diseases of adaptation" are not specific to a particular stressor or pathogen, but appear to be the products of the alarm and resistance mechanisms set in action by all serious stressors.

The GAS construct also offers a parsimonious explanation of the incidence of a second class of health problems which are specific to particular pathogens. While these problems are traceable to particular infectious agents, they are considered pluricausal, in that exposure to the agent is a necessary, but not sufficient, precondition to the disease. Not all people exposed to a microbe, as Dubos noted, become ill. Individual resistance plays an important role in determining who will or will not contract the disease. Selye's assertion that resistive capacity is limited leads to two inferences concerning the resistive capabilities of an individual over time. First, during the phase of resistance, the body may cope successfully with the stressor which precipitated the GAS, but as the findings of studies cited shortly indicate, the adjustment apparently leaves the body vulnerable to microbes which had been previously resisted, or are introduced subsequent to the GAS precipitating stress. A second inference is that as the organism approaches exhaustion, it becomes increasingly vulnerable to all microbes, including that which precipitated the GAS. It is important to note that Selye claims GAS can be precipitated by many factors. In addition to stressors such as wounds or poisons, environmental factors such as temperature changes or radiation can trigger GAS. Equally important is Selye's claim that psychosocial factors, such as unexpected good or bad news and demands the individual feels he cannot meet, can precipitate the syndrome.

GAS theory applies not only to microbe based health problems but to other health problems which the common man, as well as physicians, often attribute to stress or anxiety. The incidence of such non-microbial health problems as heart disease can be explained by the adaptation syndrome.

Two hypotheses of interest to public health can be formulated from Selye's GAS concept. First, that portion of a population experiencing more frequent or more severe stress will exhibit a higher rate of adaptation and pluricausal disease than the less often, or less severely, stressed portion. Second, the rate of adaptation and pluricausal diseases exhibited by a population will vary longitudinally with the number and severity of stressors experienced.

Evidence Supporting the GAS Theory

The literature reviewed below is representative of research not originally intended to test the stress hypotheses, but which has led to recent interest in identifying stressful life events and measuring their impact. Typical of such work are the investigations conducted by Hinkle and his colleagues (Hinkle, Pinsky,

Bross, and Plummer, 1956) into the health consequences of changes in an individual's social milieu. The study population for the initial investigation was a group of career telephone operators and a group of telephone workmen, all of whom had been employed by the telephone company for at least 20 years prior to the study. Using extensive company medical records, the investigators rank ordered the subjects according to the total number of days of disability during a 20 year period. The 20 telephone operators with the greatest number of disability days, and the 20 operators with the fewest number of disability days were selected for more extensive examination. An analysis of the data obtained from the employee medical files, physical examinations, and interviews revealed that there was a marked variation among each group in the amount of illness experienced by the individual employees. Further, the investigators detected a clustering of illnesses. That is, subjects tended to experience years marked by many episodes of minor and major illness, involving several organ systems, and arising from several different primary causes. This clustering phenomenon was observed for subjects with high, moderate, and low overall illness rates.

An analysis of the retrospective life histories obtained from the subjects led the investigators to conclude that " . . . a cluster of illnesses (usually) coincided with many demands or frustrations arising from his social environment or his interpersonal relations. These histories suggested that significant changes in the relations of ill people to their social group and in their relations to other important people in their lives were significantly associated with changes in their health" (Hinkle, 1974).

The conclusions drawn by Hinkle were supported by subsequent research including immunization studies conducted at military training facilities (Steward and Voos, 1968). Outbreaks of upper respiratory infection among recruits in such facilities had commonly been attributed to crowded conditions facilitating the spread of the infectious agent. After the infectious agent had been identified, immunization experiments were carried out. While the immunized companies showed a reduction of infection caused by the identified virus, they exhibited the same rate of upper respiratory infection as the non-immunized companies, but traceable to another virus. When the pattern of these outbreaks was investigated, it was observed that the rate of infection increased from the first to the fourth week of training, decreased during the fifth and sixth weeks, and increased again during the final two weeks of training. Further, sick calls from all causes, including musculo-skeletal, skin infections, trauma, and all other causes, displayed a similar pattern. The researchers concluded that adaptation to the military regimen required during the initial weeks, and the stress accompanying anticipation of post-training assignment (especially to Southeast Asian combat areas) were primarily responsible for the observed pattern.

Other studies supportive of the stress hypotheses involved testing the validity of the observation that those with prior understanding of the demands and expectations of their occupation suffer fewer illnesses than those who assume similar positions without preparation. Christensen and Hinkle (1961) compared two groups of managers, one of which had completed college and another which had not. Both groups were engaged in the same job for the same pay in the same company. The latter group, presumably that which experienced the greatest amount of change in assuming a managerial position, exhibited a significantly higher rate of illness of all types than did the college educated group.

The research of Cassel and Tyroler (1961) led to similar conclusions. The study population consisted of one group of individuals who were the first in their families to engage in industrial work, and a second group made up of children of industrial workers. It was assumed that the former group would experience more change because of the lack of previous familial exposure to industrial work. The researchers hypothesized that the less well-prepared group, that is the group that would experience the greatest amount of change, would exhibit a greater number of health problems. As expected, the workers with prior familial experience with industrial work had fewer symptoms of ill health and lower rates of absenteeism due to sickness than did the workers from families with no industrial experience.

Another study supportive of the stress hypotheses sought to document the effects of improved housing on health and performance (Wilner and Walkley, 1963). The health status of a test group of individuals, who had recently moved from the zone in transition to a new housing project, was compared to that of a control group of persons, who remained in the slum. While, in the long run, families who received improved housing exhibited fewer health problems, rates of illness and disability among those less than 20 years of age were significantly higher, during the initial five months after the move, for the test group than for the control group. One explanation for the higher illness rates exhibited during the five months immediately following the change of residence was that the adaptation required during this period acted to lower the individual's resistance to infectious agents.

The Stressful Life Events Research

Findings such as those described above have led to the operationalizing of stressors as discrete life events. Adolf Meyer (1951) was the first to suggest a formalized instrument for the collection of stressful life event information. Meyer suggested that a "life chart"—including such data as changes in residence, school entrances, graduations, changes (or failures) in various jobs, the date of important births and deaths in the family, and other fundamentally important environmental influences —be maintained for individuals under medical treatment. Beginning in 1949, research conducted at the University of Washington School of Medicine utilized the life-chart device to collect information on life events which preceded the onset of disease. One product of this research was the development of a list of 43 life events which required change in the ongoing life pattern of the individual. The 43 items eventually became the basis for the

Social Readjustment Rating Scale developed by Holmes and Rahe (1967). The SRRS was developed by asking respondents to rate the 43 life events by the intensity of effort and length of time required to adjust to each event, regardless of its desirability. The event "Marriage" was assigned an arbitrary value of 500, and the respondents were instructed to assign proportionately larger, or smaller, values to the other 42 events.

The final values for each event were devised by dividing the mean score of each event by ten. Table 5-2 lists the 43 events and their associated readjustment scores which have been validated by several other researchers (Coddington, 1972; Harmon, Masuda and Holmes, 1970; Komaroff, Masuda and Holmes, 1967; Masuda and Holmes, 1967; Ruch and Holmes, 1971).

The Social Readjustment Rating Scale and its variations have been used in a large number of studies investigating the role of stressful life events in the epidemiology and etiology of physical and psychological disorders (Coddington, 1972; Dohrenwend, 1973; Dohrenwend & Dohrenwend, 1974; Theorell, 1974). Rahe and his associates (Rahe & Paasikivi, 1971, Theorell & Rahe, 1971) conducted two studies in Sweden which sought to retrospectively determine whether the onset of heart attacks had been preceded by significant changes in the patient's life. In both studies it was found that the patients reported stress levels (as measured by the SRRS) were twice as high during the six months prior to the onset than during the preceding 18 months, and two times higher than the year following the episode.

Theorell (1974) supplements these findings with clinical research demonstrating a relationship between stress and the production of catecholamines, hormones which facilitate blood clot formation and elevate pulse rates and blood pressure. Theorell was interested in the relationship as a potential causal path between the experience of stressful life events and the onset of heart attack. A week to week prospective study was conducted using 21 male subjects who had suffered heart attacks during the previous year. For each week, life event data and a urine specimen were collected. Instructions regarding smoking, alcohol consumption, diet, and physical activity were given to minimize the presence of extraneous factors influencing the variation of catecholamine output.

Theorell's analysis revealed a significant intrasubject correlation between stress and catecholamine production. When events which occurred on the day that the urine samples were collected were excluded from the analysis, intrasubject correlations remained significant. This suggests that stressful life events had psychoendocrinal effects lasting several days. Theorell's research indicated that a 200 percent increase in stress scores corresponds roughly to a 100 percent increase in catecholamines secreted.

Table 5-2. Social Readjustment Rating Scale

Rank	Life Event	Change Score
1	Death of spouse	100
2	Divorce	73
3	Marital separation	65
4	Jail term	63
5	Death of close family member	63
6	Personal injury or illness	53
7	Marriage	50
8	Fired at work	47
9	Marital reconciliation	45
10	Retirement	45
11	Change in health of family member	44
12	Pregnancy	40
13	Sex difficulties	39
14	Gain of new family member	39
15	Business readjustment	39
16	Change in financial state	38
17	Death of close friend	37
18	Change to different line of work	36
19	Change in number of arguments with spouse	35
20	Mortgage over $10,000	31
21	Foreclosure of mortgage or loan	30
22	Change in responsibilities at work	29
23	Son or daughter leaving home	29
24	Trouble with in-laws	29
25	Outstanding personal achievement	28
26	Wife begin or stop work	26
27	Begin or end school	26
28	Change in living conditions	25
29	Revision of personal habits	24
30	Trouble with boss	23
31	Change in work hours or conditions	20
32	Change in residence	20
33	Change in schools	20
34	Change in recreation	19
35	Change in church activities	19
36	Change in social activities	18
37	Mortgage or loan less than $10,000	17
38	Change in sleeping habits	16
39	Change in number of family get-togethers	15
40	Change in eating habits	15
41	Vacation	13
42	Christmas	12
43	Minor violations of the law	11

From Holmes and Rahe, 1967, Table 3, p. 216.

Bridging the Gap Between Stressful Life Events
and Ecological Principles

In the literature reviewed above, the question—under what conditions will the population at risk be largest?—is ignored, giving the impression that stressful events are assumed to occur randomly over time. Included on the list of stressors identified by Holmes and Rahe and modified by other researchers, however, are clusters of life events which can be reasonably expected to occur in predictable patterns. Table 5-3 shows a hypothetical factoring of stressors into life cycle, economic well-being, and random occurrence clusters, and the sums of each cluster's stress values. Conceptualizing stressful events as falling into these clusters suggests that the level of stress experienced by a population over time can be predicted. While the frequency of occurrence of any of the random events may not be predictable, as a cluster they form a "background" or "baseline" stress level which, over time, may remain relatively constant in a population. Added to this baseline stress would be the events best predicted by the age profile of the population, and the prevailing economic conditions. If, for example, a population exhibited an anomalous increase in its birth rate, as did the United States after World War II, that cohort, as it moves through time, would account for increases in the total population's rate of stress-related health and behavior problems, as the predictable life cycle stressors such as finishing school, leaving home, or being married, were experienced. These periods of increased community stress could be predicted from age/sex profiles.

The stress experienced by a given population should also be greatly affected by economic conditions. Some of the events listed in the economic change cluster will occur when the local economy is expanding, others when it is contracting. Given that events perceived as good as well as bad are considered stressful, it can be expected that economic changes considered improvements, as well as setbacks, will produce social costs measured in terms of health and behavioral problems.

Brenner (1973) has measured the relationship between health problems and economic change. He has found a strong inverse relationship, for the period 1915 to 1967, between fetal, infant, and maternal mortality rates and national unemployment rates. The relationship has become particularly strong in recent years and medical advances have reduced the number of deaths attributable to non-stress related factors. Extrapolating from his findings, Brenner hypothesizes that the often cited differences between the United States infant mortality rate and those of several Western European countries is due to variations in national policy on unemployment and economic changes.

Heart disease mortality has also been found to be associated with economic change. Brenner (1971) conducted a correlational study using New York State and national data for economic change and heart disease mortality. As in the mental health and infant mortality studies, Brenner found a consistent inverse relationship between the two variables.

Table 5-3. Hypothetical Factoring of Stressful Life Events

Life Cycle		Economic Wellbeing		Miscellaneous (random)	
Event	Score	Event	Score	Event	Score
Divorce	73	Fired at Work	47	Death of Spouse	100
Separation	73	Business Readjustment	39	Jail Term	63
Marriage	50	Change in Financial State	38	Death of Family Member	63
Reconciliation	45	Change to Different Work	36	Personal Illness or Injury	53
Retirement	45	Mortgage Over $10,000	31	Change in Health of Family Member	44
Pregnancy	40	Foreclosure of Mortgage	30	Sex Difficulties	39
Gain of new Family Member	39	Wife Begins or Stops Work	26	Death of Friend	37
Arguments with Spouse	35	Change in living Condition	25	Trouble with Inlaws	29
Son or Daughter Leave Home	29	Trouble with Boss	23	Personal Achievement	28
Begin or End School	26	Change in Work Hours	20	Change in Sleeping Habits	16
Personal Habits	26	Change in Residence	20	Change in Eating Habits	15
		Change in Schools	20	Vacation	13
		Change in Recreation	19	Christmas	12
		Change in Church Activities	19	Violations of Law	11
		Change in Social Activities	18		
		Mortgage less than $10,000	17		
		Family Get-Togethers	15		
TOTAL LCU	479		472		523

In light of Brenner's work and that of Theorell showing a relationship between stressful life events and premature myocardial infarction, a causal path from economic change to heart disease mortality can be hypothesized. Economic change increases the population at risk by precipitating stressful life events, which, in turn, trigger the output of catecholamines. This increase in catecholamines precipitates the onset of myocardial infarctions.

In an analysis conducted for the United States Congress, Brenner (1976) reported findings suggesting that several indicators of societal well-being (general mortality, mortality for cardiovascular-renal disease and cirrhosis of the liver, suicide, imprisonment, and mental hospital admissions) are related to economic conditions. The national unemployment rate emerged as the most potent economic predictor (inversely related) of fluctuations in the dependent variables. Brenner argued that his findings suggest that the social costs of unemployment have not been sufficiently considered in economic policymaking.

Stress and the Ecological Paradigm

Based on the work of Selye and the others cited above, it would seem that enough evidence exists to offer a testable explanation of how ecological variables affect the rate of spatial arrangement of stress-related health problems in a community. The early ecologists hypothesized a homeostatic relationship between a community's economic base and its demographic characteristics. One could predict the size and age structure of a community by knowing its economic function in the larger system of collection, production, and distribution. The ecologists further predicted that as the size or nature of the economic base shifted, the population experiencing changes in roles, mores, and living space increased. These changes supposedly required readjustment, during which the population at risk would be more likely to exhibit behavioral problems. Given that those who lived nearer the zone in transition were experiencing the most change, the ecologists expected that the problems would be greatest near the CBD and decrease as distance increased.

The above "ecological" understanding of community dynamics can be combined with the stressful life events research to provide an explanation of the incidence and spatial distribution of stress-related health problems. Roughly two-thirds of the life events identified as stressful by Holmes and Rahe fall into the life cycle and economically precipitated clusters. Given that research suggests that the age structure of a metropolitan area can be reasonably predicted from its economic function (Kass, 1972), the proportion of the population likely to be experiencing life cycle stressors can be estimated. Changes in economic base, moreover, should increase the number of persons experiencing those stressors listed in Table 5-3 as economically precipitated.

Catalano and Dooley (1977a) have empircally tested the hypothesis that shifts in regional economies affect the incidence of stressful life events. Using life event survey data collected by the National Institute of Mental Health in

Kansas City, Missouri, over 16 months, the researchers measured the longitudinal relationship between eight economic measures and the incidence of life events. The economic measures included national, metropolitan, and hinterland (Missouri and Kansas less Kansas City metropolitan area) unemployment rates, as well as five measures of change in size and mix of the metropolitan labor force. The latter variables were differentiated into those measuring change *per se* and those capturing the desirability of change. The relationship between the variables was measured both in synchronous (economic change correlated with life event scores of the same month) and lagged (life events scores correlated with economic change of one, two, and three previous months) configurations. Results showed that, as hypothesized, the incidence of life events varied significantly with several measures of economic change. Also as hypothesized, the relationships were more frequently significant in the lagged configuration.

Findings also suggested that measures of absolute change, or change *per se*, were more predictive of variation in life events than were measures which captured the direction or desirability of change. The stress level present in a community could, therefore, be computed from knowing its economic function. The incidence of stress-related disease in that community would, theoretically, vary over time with the index of stress. The spatial distribution of stress-related problems can also be predicted given that there appears to be an inverse relationship between income and experienced stress (Dohrenwend, 1973; Dooley & Catalano, in press). This relationship would result in an ecological gradient similar to that manifested by behavioral problems.

An Ecological Perspective on Non-Biological Toxins

Ill health can be a product of substances in the environment which do not cause infection, but are destructive of tissue and upset bodily functions. While there are naturally occurring non-biological toxins, they are rare, leaving this category represented mostly by man made pollutants. In recent years public health experts have become, as has the entire population, increasingly interested in man made substances which pose threats to human wellbeing. The simple fact that germ theory does not apply to such substances was one of the principal reasons for the current search for a new public health paradigm.

In a given community, pollutants can be either ambient or place-specific. Ambient means they are present throughout the community in some medium such as air or water. Place-specific usually refers to pollutants found in a particular environment such as a factory, home, or shop. The place-specific problems covered in this section will be those associated with the work environment. It will be suggested that the same principles described by Haig and McKenzie to explain the differentiation of human communities can be used to explain the variations in ambient and work related pollutants among communities.

Ambient pollutants usually are broken down into air and water pollution. As shown in Tables 5-4 and 5-5 most air pollution is a product of industrial

Table 5-4. Major Air Pollutants

Pollutant	Characteristics	Principal sources	Principal effects
Total suspended particulates (TSP)	Any solid or liquid particles dispersed in the atmosphere, such as dust, pollen, ash, soot, metals, and various chemicals	Natural events such as forest fires, wind erosion, volcanic eruptions; stationary combustion, especially of solid fuels; construction activities; industrial processes; atmospheric chemical reactions	Directly toxic effects or aggravation of the effects of gaseous pollutants; aggravation of asthma or other respiratory or cardio-respiratory symptoms; increased cough and chest discomfort; increased mortality
Sulfur dioxide (SO$_2$)	A colorless gas with a pungent odor; SO$_2$ can oxidize to form sulfur trioxide (SO$_3$), which forms sulfuric acid with water	Combustion of sulfur-containing fossil fuels, smelting of sulfur-bearing metal ores, industrial processes, natural events such as volcanic eruptions	Aggravation of respiratory diseases, including asthma, chronic bronchitis, and emphysema; reduced lung function; irritation of eyes and respiratory tract; increased mortality
Nitrogen dioxide (NO$_2$)	A brownish-red gas with a pungent odor, often formed from oxidation of nitric oxide (NO)	Motor vehicle exhausts, high-temperature stationary combustion atmospheric reactions	Aggravation of respiratory and cardio-vascular illnesses and chronic nephritis
Hydrocarbons (HC)	Organic compounds in gaseous or particulate form, e.g., methane, ethylene, and acetylene	Incomplete combustion of fuels and other carbon-containing substances, such as in motor vehicle exhausts; processing, distribution, and use of petroleum compounds such as gasoline and organic solvents; natural events such as forest fires and plant metabolism; atmospheric reactions	Suspected contribution to cancer
Carbon monoxide (CO)	A colorless, odorless gas with a strong chemical affinity for hemoglobin in blood	Incomplete combustion of fuels and other carbon-containing substances, such as in motor vehicle exhausts; natural events such as forest fires or decomposition of organic matter	Reduced tolerance for exercise, impairment of mental function, impairment of fetal development, aggravation of cardiovascular diseases

Source: United States Government Publication

Table 5-5. Nationwide Emission Estimates, 1976
(10^6 metric tons/year)

Source category	TSP	SO_x	NO_x	HC	CO
Transportation	1.2	0.8	10.1	10.8	69.7
Highway vehicles	0.8	0.4	7.8	9.3	61.4
Non-highway vehicles	0.4	0.4	2.3	1.5	8.3
Stationary fuel combustion	4.6	21.9	11.8	1.4	1.2
Electric utilities	3.2	17.6	6.6	0.1	0.3
Industrial	1.1	2.6	4.5	1.2	0.5
Residential, commercial & institutional	0.3	1.7	0.7	0.1	0.4
Industrial processes	6.3	4.1	0.7	9.4	7.8
Chemicals	0.3	0.3	0.3	1.6	2.4
Petroleum refining	0.1	0.7	0.3	0.9	2.4
Metals	1.3	2.4	0	0.2	1.9
Mineral products	3.2	0.5	0.1	0	0
Oil & gas production and marketing	0	0.1	0	3.0	0
Industrial organic solvent use	0	0	0	2.9	0
Other processes	1.4	0.1	0	0.8	1.1
Solid waste	0.4	0	0.1	0.8	2.8
Miscellaneous	0.9	0.1	0.3	5.5	5.7
Forest wildfires and managed burning	0.6	0	0.2	0.8	4.8
Agricultural burning	0.1	0	0	0.1	0.5
Coal refuse burning	0.1	0.1	0.1	0.1	0.3
Structural fires	0.1	0	0	0	0.1
Miscellaneous organic solvent use	0	0	0	4.5	0
TOTAL	13.4	26.9	23.0	27.9	87.2

Source: United States Government Publication.

processes and transportation technology. How serious a health problem pollution becomes also depends on the topography of the site a community occupies and its climatological conditions. To understand the air pollution problems of a given community, one must know the types of industrial processes located there, how dependent the population is on the internal combustion engine, and the community's topographical and climatological characteristics. These three factors are closely related to those Haig and the early ecologists saw as necessary to understanding the size, mix, and spatial distribution of the human community.

The type of industry present in a given metropolitan area is clearly a product of its function in the larger system of collection, production, and distribution—its economic base. How dependent a community is on the internal combustion engine is best predicted by the time at which it emerged as an integral part of the larger system. The cost of overcoming friction dropped drastically from 1900 to 1970, making it possible for urban areas to spread over much more area without losing the ease of exchanging goods and information. If a metropolitan area experienced most of its growth after the advent of cheap mobility, as did Los Angeles for example, it can be expected to be more dependent on the internal combustion engine than older communities. The topography and climate of a metropolitan area were considered by the ecologists to be integral components of the abiotic elements of urban ecosystems. These variables are often determining factors in choosing among sites which may be equally well suited in terms of markets and raw materials. Temperate climates, for example, offer lower transport costs than those where cold and snow mean investment in special tires, batteries, etc., and more days lost due to inclement weather.

Assuming the above to be accurate, there should be a measurable relationship between the economic function of a community and the type of ambient air pollution it is plagued with. Several preliminary studies conducted in the past decade have indicated that such a relationship exists (McMullen, 1967; Ozolins, 1966; Welson and Stevens, 1970). As air pollution monitoring technology evolves and more longitudinal data are collected, such studies will become more definitive.

The types of pollutants found in a metropolitan area's water also are affected by its economic base. While "spill-overs" from other communities along the Mississippi certainly account for much of the pollution in, for example, the water reaching New Orleans, that city's own industrial and agricultural activities greatly affect the quality of local ground water. It is, in summary, necessary to understand the abiotic elements, that is, the economic base and natural setting, of any community in order to explain and control its ambient air and water pollution.

A community's work-related health problems caused by non-biological toxins are clearly related to its economic base. The relationship is much more obvious in "primary service communities," as McKenzie referred to those areas whose function was as unifaceted as a coal or asbestos mining community. Coal workers have long been plagued by the dreaded "black lung" disease produced by breathing coal dust. As research documents the carcinogenic affect of asbestos, it becomes clearer why communities based on industries using that substance have higher than expected rates of cancer. In communities with more diverse economic bases, work-related diseases become more numerous. Each distinctive type of industrial process has its health and safety hazards, and to the degree that a community's economic function can be specified, public health officials will be able to predict the types of problems they will have to deal with. It should also be noted that work related health problems are not limited to those caused by biological and non-biological toxins. Stress-related problems, such as heart disease and ulcers, are more likely to appear among those with high pressure jobs. Communities with corporate headquarters and a high concentration of management personnel can expect to have a higher incidence of stress-related health problems. Coughlin (1973), for example, found that metropolitan areas which had enjoyed the most success in attaining economic goals, also had significantly higher rates of death by ulcer.

An Ecological Perspective on Safety Hazards

Safety hazards, the last factor cited as a source of community health problems, can include such diverse phenomena as natural disasters, fires, residential, recreational or work accidents, and automobile crashes. A community's safety hazards can best be predicted by understanding its abiotic elements—economic base and natural setting.

The natural disasters—floods, storms, earthquakes etc.—a community is prone to are, of course, products of its location and natural setting. Populations which perform collective, productive, or distributional functions in flood plains, fault areas, or areas of frequent storms will suffer natural disasters. Those who render public health services to populations at risk are, or should be, specially prepared to help the victims of such disasteers.

A community's susceptibility to fire is a product of complex factors. Among the more important are age and density of structures. The older a building is, the less likely it is to be fire resistant, and the more likely it is to have faulty electrical and heating systems. The denser structures are, the easier it is for fire to spread. Climate is also important. In dry, cold climates, for example, the combination of drier flammable materials and greater need for heating systems tends to increase the likelihood of fire. Given these factors, one would expect that, among communities, the older metropolitan areas in the northeast would be most susceptible to fire. Within any metropolitan area, fires should exhibit an ecological gradient. They should be more common in the older, denser areas surrounding the CBD and decrease as distance from the center increases.

The types of residential accidents a population will experience depends on the type of housing it occupies. Homes closer to the central business district typically have more stairs which are usually older and more likely to be in ill repair. Falls, therefore, could be expected to exhibit an ecological gradient. Accidents associated with yard work, such as lacerations and burns from power lawn mowers, on the other hand, would be expected to manifest a reverse ecological gradient. The distributions of other home-related health problems, such as poisoning from lead based paints, could also be predicted from ecological principles. Lead paint is much more common in old structures, which tend to be closer to the CBD, producing an ecological gradient of lead poisoning.

Recreational accidents are clearly related to climatological factors. Each sport has its typical health problems, and the location and climate of communities will influence the population's athletic pursuits.

The National Safety Council (1976) reported 58,000 deaths resulting from work and auto accidents in 1975. Motor vehicle accidents alone were the leading cause of death among persons aged 1 to 44 years. In addition to loss of life, work and auto accidents injured four million persons seriously enough to cause them to lose at least one day's normal activity, in addition to that lost on the day of the accident. Beyond pain and suffering, work and auto accidents cost an estimated $47.1 billion.

As in the case of health problems caused by work-related pollutants, each industry and type of employment has its characteristic safety hazards. In addition to black lung, coal miners, for example, are threatened by cave-ins. Those who work with heavy machinery are at risk of injury due to carelessness. Agricultural workers, secretaries, retail clerks, and policemen are all exposed to different sets of hazards. Understanding the structure of the local economy is, therefore, central to predicting the types of work-related safety hazards a population faces.

The factors which affect the incidence of auto accidents in a community include such obvious variables as climate, dependence on automobiles, and road design. Driver-related variables are, however, the most immediate causes of accidents. It is, after all, the mistake in driver judgment which precipitates the accident. Increasing societal concern over the costs of accidents has led to a growing body of research concerned with both the environmental (Koch & Reinfurt, 1974; Robertson & Baker, 1976; Satterthwaite, 1976; Viner & Tamanini, 1973) and human (Forbes, 1972) characteristics contributing to increased accident risk. The concept of "accident proneness," for example, has been operationalized and debated (Cameron, 1975; Carlson & Klein, 1970; Crawford, 1971; McGuire, 1970; Schuster & Guilford, 1964), and considerable attention has been given to the influence of alcohol (Ferreira & Silverman, 1976; Zylman, 1974), and drug use (Binder, 1971; Blomberg & Preusser, 1976; Waller, et al., 1974) on driver and worker performance.

Among the individual factors which have been associated with reduced capacity to avoid accidents is the experience of life events which require adaptation behavior (McMurray, 1970; Selzer, 1969; Selzer, et al., 1968; Selzer &

Vinokur, 1974). Selzer and Vinokur (1974) administered a battery of instruments, including mood, life event, aggression, paranoid thinking, and suicidal tendency scales, to 532 male drivers over the age of 20. The group was divided into those with (n = 258) and without (n = 254) a history of alcohol problems. When the instrument scores and demographic characteristics of both groups were compared with auto-accident records during the previous year, life stress proved to be a more powerful predictor of accident records than personality measures, demographic characteristics, or alcohol use.

The importance of Selzer and Vinokur analyses is established by the finding (Catalano & Dooley, 1977a) that the incidence of stressful life events experienced by a metropolitan population varies with economic fluctuations. Stressful life events reported by representative samples of the Kansas City, Missouri, population over a 16-month period were found to be related to several measures of previously occurring (one to three months) change in the size and mix of the metropolitan economy.

The findings described above suggest the general hypothesis that economic expansion will lead to an increased incidence of injury-causing auto and manufacturing accidents by increasing immediate environmental hazards, and by decreasing individual capacity to deal with the hazards.

Individual capacity to cope with environmental risks should be affected by economic expansion. Increased work hours, new job, increased income, change in leisure activities or work responsibilities, and other events associated with economic growth are among the life events found to be stressful. These events are not only fatiguing or distracting, but may also lead to increased use of drugs and alcohol (Brenner, 1975). By increasing the pace of production, hours worked, and the number of new, less experienced employees, economic expansion also adds to the risks in the work environment. Economic growth should also increase the environmental risk of vehicular accidents by increasing the number of, and miles traveled by, commerical vehicles and work commuters. Increased income should also escalate the immediate environmental risk by increasing the number of leisure miles traveled.

This hypothesis has been supported by a recent analysis (Catalano, 1978) of auto and work accident injuries in Syracuse, New York, and Los Angeles, California. Using accident rates of contiguous communities to control for weather, definitional changes, and trends, the analysis found that accident injuries were positively related to economic expansion.

The Elements of the Ecologal Alternative
While an ecological paradigm for public health has not fully emerged, an outline of its elements can be inferred from recent ecological analyses of health problems.

I. *Basic Assumptions.*

An ecological perspective on community health problems would assume:

A. An individual becomes ill when he or she cannot resist or avoid:
   1. Biological organisms and their by-products
   2. Non-biological toxins (pollutants)
   3. Safety hazards
B. Given the homeostatic relationship between abiotic elements (economic function and natural setting) and biotic elements (size, roles, and spatial distribution of the population), health problems exhibited by a community are explainable as follows:
   1. Epidemic diseases are attributable to highly virulent microorganisms entering a community through its interaction with other communities. As the system of collection, production, and distribution becomes more complex, the spread of epidemic diseases becomes more difficult to predict.
   2. Rates of endemic infectious diseases will vary over time with resistance of individuals to ubiquitous microbes. Resistance is lowered by stress which can be expected to be more common when the economic base of a community shifts in size or mix.
   3. The type of health problems attributable to non-biological toxins (pollutants) will depend on the community's economic base and natural setting which control:
      a. The type of ambient pollutants present in the environment.
      b. The type of pollutants present in the work environment.
   4. The types of health problems attributable to safety hazards will be controlled as follows:
      a. Safety hazards posed by natural disasters are best predicted from the location and natural setting of a community.
      b. Residential hazards are best predicted by housing age and type which are functions of ecological processes.
      c. Work related hazards are predictable from a community's economic base.
      d. Injuries due to recreational hazards are best predicted from climate and setting.
      e. The rate of automobile accidents is affected by climate, dependence on autos, and stress levels, all of which are related to a community's abiotic elements.
C. The spatial distribution of health problems within a community can be predicted by ecological factors.

II. *Analogies.*

The analogy which underlies the use of ecological principles to explain health problems is the metropolis as ecosystem model first posed by Park, Burgess, and McKenzie.

III. *Conventions.*

The conventions guiding the public health use of ecological principles would be similar to those common to all ecological research.

A. Empirical Epistemology. Identification and measuring of indexes of a community's health would be essential to ecological analyses of health.
B. Quantitative description
C. Naturalistic Research. Since many crucial factors affecting the health of individuals cannot be replicated or controlled in the laboratory, ecological research is naturalistic. Such research, often referred to as "epidemiological," focuses on measuring the relationship between rates of illnesses and community characteristics.
D. The Community as Unit of Analysis. Based on the assumption that individual resistance and safety risk levels are affected by community characteristics, ecological analyses focus on the community rather than the individual.
IV. *Exemplars.*
While a definitive exemplar has not yet emerged, the rationale for using ecological principles to analyze community health problems can be traced to:
A. Burgess' "The Growth of a City: An Introduction to a Research Project"
B. McKenzie's "The Ecological Approach to the Study of the Human Community"
C. Selye's (1946) "The General Adaptation Syndrome and the Diseases of Adaptation."
D. Brenner's (1971 & 1973) analyses of heart disease and infant mortality.

An Ecological Perspective on Genetic Diseases

There are health problems which occur more frequently among blood relations than in the general population. It appears that the ability to resist certain diseases can be affected by genetic factors. In a population equally stressed and equally exposed to the same toxin or hazard, some persons will, therefore, become ill and not others because of constitutional factors inherited from their parents. As stress levels rise in a given community, those with genetic "predispositions," or lower than average resistive capacity, will become ill before those with average and above average tolerance.

Other genetically controlled health problems do not involve external toxins or safety hazards, but are traceable to natural selective forces which equip a population to survive in one environment but place it at a disadvantage in another. Among the best known of these illnesses is Sickle Cell Anemia which affects blacks almost exclusively. It appears that in several ecosystems in Africa a genetic permutation occurred which increased the resistance of individuals to malaria. Because malaria was endemic in these areas, this permutation, which involved the genes controlling blood cells, became increasingly common in the population. The drawback to this selected characteristic is that if a man and woman both have the trait, the chances are one in four that their child will have sickle cell anemia. This condition is extremely debilitating, for, when the victim becomes tired or stressed, his or her blood cells change shape from the usual round configuration to crescent, or sickle-like, bodies which tend to catch on one another forming clots. These clots block the flow of blood through small capillaries causing extreme pain and degeneration of tissue. Clotting also increases the number of heart attacks and strokes, and often retards growth. Victims rarely live beyond 30 and can not pursue a normal life style which exposes one to stress and exertion.

With the advent of slave trading, many blacks with the permutation were brought to the Western Hemisphere where the threat of malaria was not as great. The result has been that many more individuals without the trait have survived making it less frequent in the population. The chances of two people with the trait meeting, however, are still considerable and, therefore, sickle cell anemia has continued to be a problem among black populations.

The ecologists' interest in a disease such as sickle cell anemia goes beyond its basis in the natural selective adaptation process. The fact that the disease affects mostly black Americans tells the ecologist that the disease will exhibit an ecological gradient reflecting the concentration of minorities in central cities. Since episodes of the disease are apparently triggered by stress, the ecologist also expects rates to be higher at times of economic fluctuation.

The Distribution of Physicians: An Ecological Perspective

Physicians are, obviously, crucial to maintaining an acceptable level of health in a community. In American society, the right of the private physician to serve whom he pleases where he pleases has been highly valued. Physicians are free to locate their practices wherever they feel they can maximize professional opportunity and pursue the life style they please. This mobility, coupled with the fact that, according to several estimates, this nation has only half the physicians it needs (Joroff & Navarro, 1971), has made the distribution of physicians an important issue to many communities.

Mardin (1967) attempted to measure the relationship among several characteristics of metropolitan areas and urban counties and their physician-to-population ratio. As might be expected, he found size to be the most important predictor. The larger a community was the more physicians per population unit it tended to have. While this was less true for general practitioners, the apparent need for specialists to function as groups close to major facilities led to a strong positive relationship between size and physician-to-population ratio. While the variation in physician-to-population ratios among communities in the same size group was smaller than that among different size groups, the differences were significant. Attempting to explain why communities of the same size had different ratios, Marden measured the relationships among educational attainment, age structure, racial characteristics, hospital beds available, and variations of physician-to-population ratio from the expected value given a city's size. He found that in communities of one million or more the two most important variables were race and age. The higher the percentage of black population a community had, the fewer physicians it was likely to have. The more persons aged under 5 and over 65, the more physicians a community was likely to have. In communities of one half to one million, the two most important variables were educational attainment and hospital beds available. The relationship for both was positive, that is, the more of one or both, the greater the ratio of physicians to population. For communities of 100,000 to a half million, age and number of beds available were most important and were positively related with physician-to-population ratio. Age stood out as the most predictive variable for communities of 50,000 to 100,000. The relationship was positive. For urban areas of less than 50,000, beds and race were the most important predictors. The relationship between beds available and physician-to-population ratio was positive, and between race and ratio was negative.

Most of the community characteristics Mardin found important in predicting the ratio of physicians to population are ecologically determined. Population size, age structure, educational attainment, and racial mix are best understood as functions of a community's role in the larger system of collection, production, and distribution. Not only will an ecological perspective help predict the distribution of health problems, it also is helpful in understanding the distribution of health care.

An Important Change Indicated by the Ecological Alternative

If public health is to contend with the illnesses precipitated by stress, non-biological toxins, and safety hazards, it must become more familiar with the economic and social processes which shape the human community. The relationships among demographic and economic characteristics of a community and the health of its population will have to be carefully measured. Such measurement will facilitate both the remedial and preventive functions of public health.

While public health has strived to develop preventive strategies which reduce the number of persons becoming ill, much of its effort is still spent reacting to problems which could not be avoided. The success of these remedial efforts depends on how well a community is prepared to deal with the problem. By measuring the influence of ecological variables on health, public health officials will be able to better predict the onslaught of stress-related and pollution-caused problems. Prediction is prerequisite to effective preparation.

Perhaps the greater value to public health are the preventive strategies which arise from an ecological perspective. After measuring the relationship between ecological variables and health problems, several obvious interventions may emerge. It may be that the most effective way to reduce stress-related illnesses, for example, is to stabilize the local economy, thereby reducing economic stress and normalizing the age structure. Another intervention might involve educational programs designed to increase the ability to cope with life cycle and economic stress. What must be remembered, however, is that the community is a complex ecosystem, and that the wisdom of interventions cannot be assessed without accounting for all the suspected costs, as well as the obvious benefits.

Table 5-6. Disciplinary Matrix of Public Health

Paradigm	Basic Assumptions	Analogies	Conventions	Exemplars
Ancient Ecological	1. Ill health is a manifestation of imbalance among the bodily humors. 2. Environmental factors such as temperature and humidity affect humor balance. 3. Life style factors such as eating, drinking, and sexual habits, as well as work and recreational behavior affect humor balance. 4. The health problems of a community can be predicted from its environmental characteristics and economic function.	The Humor Balance Model	1. Empirical Epistemology 2. Qualitative Description 3. Naturalistic Research 4. Community as unit of analysis	1. The volumes of Hippocratic tradition, especially *Airs, Waters, and Places*
	NO NORMAL SCIENCE—DOMINANCE OF MIASMA THEORY			
Germ	1. Disease symptoms are produced by bacteria which invade the human body, and multiply to the point that they, or their toxic byproducts, interfere with normal functioning. 2. Each disease has a specific causal bacteria. 3. Bacteria is spread through several media, including water, insects, animals, and utensils. 4. Disease can be controlled by isolating bacteria, eliciting immunity, and destroying insect vectors.	Bacterial infection is an attack by microbial agents	1. Empirical Epistemology 2. Quantitative Description 3. Laboratory Research 4. Individual as unit of analysis	1. Henle's *Pathologische untersuchungen* 2. Koch's Anthrax experiment
Modern Ecological Alternative	1. An individual becomes ill when he cannot resist or avoid biological and non-biological toxins and safety hazards. 2. Epidemic diseases are caused by virulent toxins which enter a community through its interaction with other communities. 3. Resistance to ubiquitous biological toxins can be lowered by stress which is more common during periods of economic change. 4. The type of ambient and work-related non-biological toxin present in a community is predictable from its economic function and natural setting. 5. Safety hazards, associated with residential, recreational, and work environments, as well as natural disasters are predictable from economic base and natural setting. 6. The spatial distribution of health problems in a community can be predicted by ecological factors.	Human community is like a natural ecosystem	1. Empirical Epistemology 2. Quantitative Description 3. Naturalistic Research 4. Community as unit of analysis	1. McKenzie's "Ecological Approach to the study of the Human Community" 2. Selye's "The General Adaptation Syndrome and the Diseases of Adaptation" 3. Brenner's analyses of heart disease and infant mortality

Before choosing among courses of action which affect the economic roles or living spaces of the population, the health, behavioral, and economic costs of each alternative must be weighed against its expected benefits. While fraught with measurement problems, and dependent on political processes, for the assignment of values to variables, such a decision strategy would maximize community well-being.

CONCLUSION

If the ecological perspective becomes the paradigm which guides public health's expanding interests, the discipline's paradigm succession (see Table 5-6) will come full circle. The new ecological paradigm will be more exact in its measurement of such community dimensions as economic function and natural environment, but it will assume the same relationships between these dimensions of health as were posited by the ancient Greeks. In the words of Hippocrates:

> When one comes into a city to which he is a stranger, he ought to consider its situation ... the winds ... the rising of the sun ... the waters ... the grounds ... and the mode in which the inhabitants live and what are their pursuits ... for if one knows all these things he cannot miss knowing either the disease peculiar to the place or the particular nature of common diseases.

6 Paradigm Succession in the Study of Abnormal Behavior

Abnormal or deviant behavior has perplexed organized societies from earliest times. Evidence exists, for example, that neolithic man performed craniectomies, or surgical openings of the skull, to release spirits causing behavioral problems (Selling, 1943). The preparadigmatic phase of the study of abnormal behavior includes several enlightened treatises dating to the fourth century B.C. The general lack of political and economic stability characteristic of the "Dark Ages," however, precluded the formation of self-perpetuating communities of scholars to test and expand upon early explanations.

Paradigmatic study of abnormal behavior began late in the nineteenth century. Abnormal psychology's first paradigm, the organic paradigm, was heavily influenced by the germ paradigm of public health. When reading this chapter, the student should keep in mind that the organic paradigm assumed that behavioral problems were symptoms of a physiological disorder. This assumption led to the use of Henle's logic in testing explanations of abnormal behavior.

The organic paradigm, and its preoccupation with physiological causation, was thrown into crisis when Freud demonstrated that psychological processes could elicit physiological symptoms. This reversal of the causal assumption triggered a rush from the biologically oriented organic paradigm to the less empirical anxiety defense paradigm.

This chapter also describes the learned behavior paradigm which has come to dominate abnormal psychology. The student should carefully consider the parallels between the behavioral propositions of the Chicago School and the basic assumptions of the learned behavior paradigm. Also of importance is the alternative perspective offered by social labeling theory. This alternative perspective is congruent with the early ecologists' assumptions concerning the processes by which behavior was judged abnormal.

In addition to the paradigm succession summarized above, several important topics will be discussed here. One of these is the concept of "mental illness" which is commonly used to describe abnormal behavior. The concept was spawned at the turn of the century when the assumptions of the organic paradigm were combined with the desire of reformers to de-spiritualize the layman's understanding of behavioral disorders. The mental illness concept and its implications will be described more fully in this chapter.

Another important topic is the difference between the organic and Freudian assumption that abnormal behavior is symptomatic of a deeper, unseen disorder, and the learning theorists' assertion that behavior is the disorder, not the symptom. This disagreement should be understood because it demonstrates the basic difference between the anxiety defense and learned behavior paradigms. It also explains their differing approach to treatment.

Other concepts which should be noted include: "defense mechanism," "conditioning," "stressful life event," and "deviant careers." All these are important to the chapter's development and continue the theme that adaptation can precipitate health and behavioral problems.

The concepts in this chapter are not only important in the history of abnormal psychology, but are also central in the development of criminology. While the chapter may appear to be a self-contained discussion of abnormal psychology, remember that it also forms the intellectual connection between what has gone before and the discussion of criminal behavior which follows.

THE PREPARADIGMATIC PHASE

Early Enlightenment

Hippocrates' (460-357 B.C.) words, "I do not believe that the human body is ever befouled by a God" (Lewis, 1941, p. 37), reflect his precociously enlightened approach to the study of human health. Even in his contemporary Athens, "madness" was primarily seen as a symptom of demonic possession, to be cured through exorcisms ranging from incantations to drinking ominous potions, to starving and flogging. In contrast to the dominant demonic explanation, Hippocrates attributed abnormal behavior to organic defects, especially of the brain. Based on detailed observation of supposedly possessed persons, he devised general categories of abnormal behavior, and prescribed treatment for each. His prescriptions included some very current therapies (such as changes in diet, environment, or life style), as well as some rather crude suggestions (such as bleedings and imbibing concoctions to alter "humors" or bodily fluids). Unlike his recommendations regarding public health, Hippocrates' prescriptions for, and explanations of, behavioral problems appeared to have little impact on the practices of his day. His theoretical and taxonomic, or classifying, work, moreover, was not furthered by colleagues or students.

Plato and Aristotle, while less empirical than Hippocrates, also posited several explanations of abnormal behavior. Aristotle reiterated Hippocrates' theory of organic causation, while emphasizing the role of bodily fluids. Plato's comments on abnormal behavior are notable for two reasons. First, he argued that those suffering from mental disorder should not be punished as criminals if they commit criminally proscribed acts. Second, Plato asserted that man's behavior could be better understood if viewed as often motivated by natural drives or appetites common to all living things.

Several Roman physicians expanded their interests and studies to include behavioral problems. More than a century before Christ, Asclepiades differentiated chronic and acute behavioral problems, developed classifications for hallucinations, and worked to stop the bleeding and incarceration of persons with behavioral problems. In the first century A.D., Aretaeus observed that mania and melancholy were extensions of common personality types, and not necessarily organically caused. Galen (1916) in the second century A.D., collected and synthesized the existing knowledge of abnormal behavior. He also dichotomized the causes of abnormal behavior into physical and mental precipitants. Among the physical causes, Galen listed injuries to the head, alcoholism, menstrual changes, and changes in the stages of life cycle, especially from childhood to adolescence. Non-physical causes included fear, broken love affairs, and economic reversals. Galen's work could well have precipitated normal science had not the Roman empire begun to crumble and the Dark Ages to engulf the Western World.

The Dark Ages and Demonic Possession

The lack of organized research into behavioral problems characteristic of the fifth to eighteenth centuries cannot be attributed to a lack of abnormal behavior. Evidence shows that there were mass exhibitions of abnormal behavior which included "dance" hysteria, such as tarantism and St. Vitus' dance, as well as mass lycanthropy, or assuming the behavior of wolves and other animals (Stone, 1937). Without strong secular institutions to balance religious organizations badly in need of enlightenment, the belief that such behavior was symptomatic of moral corruption and demonic possession became widespread, and was endorsed by such eminent persons as Martin Luther and Pope Innocent the VIII. Belief that possessed persons could actually inflict calamity on, or corrupt, others led Pope Innocent to issue a decree in 1484 directing the clergy to identify possessed persons, or witches, and put them to death. During the next two centuries, thousands of people throughout Europe, Britain, and America were tortured to elicit confessions of witchery, and were put to death. The general assumption that "madness" was the product of moral corruption or demonic possession remained dominant in Western society through much of the eighteenth century.

Humanitarian Reform

While institutionalization of persons with behavioral problems began to replace witch-hunting and torture late in the eighteenth century, "asylums" were, with few exceptions, miserable dungeons. While the assumption of demonic possession may have become less widespread, the person with behavioral problems was still treated in a sadistic, inhumane manner, and was assumed to be incorrigible.

The most widely recognized break with the tradition of dungeon-like asylums came in Paris in 1792. The leaders of the French Revolution placed Phillippe Pinel (1745-1826) in charge of "La Bicetre," a prison-like asylum. Pinel released the inmates from their chains, cleaned their cells, allowed them to exercise in the fresh air and sunshine, and ended the practice of torture. He insisted that the insane be treated as human beings who, because of traumatic experiences, had lost their ability to cope with reality. This assumption led to a "treatment" of normalizing the social environment of the hospital, discussing the subject's problem and its causes with him, and providing occupational training. This humane approach to rehabilitating those who had been indiscriminately committed to institutions met with immediate success. Former inmates were released as cured and assumed normal lives.

Word of the success of Pinel's humane treatment, often referred to as "moral therapy," spread throughout Europe and America. Reformers such as Tuke in England, and Rush and Dix in America, worked to humanize the treatment of mental patients, and convince the public that behavioral problems were not signs of moral corruption, but were maladies precipitated by life events, and could be cured (Zilboorg & Henry, 1941). In the course of their attempts to educate the public, these reformers often drew analogies between behavioral problems and organic illnesses. While this may have served to enlighten society's understanding of abnormal behavior, the analogy, unfortunately, led to confusion over the causes of behavioral problems. The moral therapy of Pinel and the reformers assumed that many behavioral problems were precipitated by experiences which debilitated the victim's practical or moral reasoning, thereby precluding or interrupting normal functioning. The behavioral problem, therefore, could be lessened through remedial socialization and managed re-entry into society. The analogy to illnesses was meant to emphasize that many victims were basically "normal," and that after recuperation and treatment could resume productive lives. It was not intended to foster the theory that behavioral problems were caused by organic diseases and could be treated medically. For several reasons, to be discussed shortly, the latter hypothesis became increasingly popular and formed the core of abnormal psychology's first modern paradigm.

The work of Pinel and other reformers failed to generate paradigmatically-defined normal science, because their efforts were primarily centered on reforming practice, not conducting scientific inquiry. The theoretical basis for moral therapy was rooted more in humanistic ethics than empirical research. While the modern world was fortunate to have been humanized by reformers such as Pinel, their influence, based primarily on dynamism and charisma, passed with their deaths. Their legacy of humanism could not satisfy the growing scientific curiosity concerning the causes of abnormal behavior.

THE ORGANIC PARADIGM

Historical Development

The late nineteenth century was a period of intense intellectual activity. The scientific method had shed light on such profound mysteries as the origins of the species. Darwin's work dramatized the usefulness of observation, measurement, and classification, as had the break-throughs in identifying the microbial causes of diseases. Even more impressive to those interested in abnormal behavior were the series of discoveries shedding light on the relationship between syphilis and a particular group of behavioral problems referred to as "general paresis." General paresis, which most commonly afflicted the middle aged, typically began with personality changes characterized by increased carelessness and indifference. The early stage degenerated into forgetfulness, sentimentality, and often to promiscuity. Physical symptoms appeared, such as thickening of speech and a peculiar gait. As the disease progressed, the victim became increasingly moody and withdrawn, and eventually reached a stage of nearly complete inactivity. Seizures followed and, before the advent of penicillin, usually led to death. During the mid-nineteenth century, several physicians noted the relationship between syphilis and paresis, and in 1869 the relationship between syphilis infection and degeneration of the nervous system was clearly demonstrated. While conclusive proof of the causal relationship between syphilis and paresis did not come until 1897, the ongoing medical research and resulting enlightenment encouraged many in the last two decades of the nineteenth century to search for organic causes of other behavioral problems.

Kraepelin's Consolidation of the Organic Paradigm

The movement to find the organic causes of abnormal behavior reached its zenith in the work of Emile Kraepelin (1857-1926), whose *Textbook in Psychology* (1896) spawned the organic paradigm. Kraepelin was convinced that behavioral problems, such as fevers or rashes, were symptoms of an organic imbalance or impairment in the body. Borrowing from the history of medical diagnostics, he posited that the primary chore of psychology was to observe and classify behaviors, so that causal agents could be identified. Kraepelin proceeded to collect a great deal of data on the occurrence of behavioral problems, and eventually grouped these into two general classes. The symptoms in each class often appeared concurrently, or in sequence, leading Kraepelin to view the classes as syndromes analogous to the symptom syndromes associated with organic diseases, such as smallpox or measles. The first, or "manic-depressive" syndrome, was characterized by recurring moods of deep depression or extreme excitement, which were unrelated to environmental factors. The second class, or schizophrenic syndrome, was marked by increasingly detached behavior, less and less predicted by environmental variables. Kraepelin carefully devised sub-classes of both categories in the hope that logical ordering would lead to break-throughs, such as the discovery of the syphilis-paresis link. While continuing the immense task of classification, Kraepelin wrote and lectured on the relationship between organic factors and abnormal behavior. He hypothesized that manic-depression was caused by metabolic irregularity and that schizophrenia would be traced to chemical imbalances rooted in glandular malfunction.

While few, if any, of Kraepelin's hypotheses have been proven true, the basic assumption of his work, that behavioral problems were symptoms of organic im-balances, was transmitted to students and colleagues. For the next three decades, the organic paradigm dominated the study of abnormal behavior, and remains an important force today.

The Elements of the Organic Paradigm

Kuhn has suggested that a paradigm be thought of as having four elements: basic assumptions, analogies, conventions, and exemplars. The elements of the organic paradigm are as follows:

I. *Basic Assumptions.*

The most obvious assumption underlying the organic paradigm is that ab-normal behavior is symptomatic of some organic imbalance or impairment. The principle corollaries to this assumption are, first, that the classification of abnormal behaviors into syndromes will allow the eventual identification of the organic causes, and second, that medical treatments for many of the or-ganic causes will be found.

II. *Analogies.*

The explicit analogy used to illuminate the basic assumptions is that drawn between behavioral problems and disease symptoms. Kraepelin, and those who accepted his basic assumptions, constantly cited the physiological re-search and diagnostic procedures of modern medicine as the models for psychologists to emulate in studying abnormal behavior.

III. *Conventions.*

Evolving from their commitment to the organic explanation of abnormal be-havior, the followers of Kraepelin have devised conventions similar to those found in biological and medical research. The organic paradigm, therefore, would be characterized as *empirical*, as opposed to intuitional in its episte-mology. Their description of that data tends to be highly *quantitative*, as opposed to qualitative or impressionistic. The research growing from the organic paradigm tends to be *laboratory* oriented and very similar to that of basic biology. A direct outgrowth of the assumption of organic causation is the paradigm's emphasis on the *individual*, or "patient," as the unit of analysis.

IV. *Exemplars.*

The works of Kraepelin, especially his *Textbook in Psychology* and *Lectures on Clinical Psychiatry*, are most often cited as the classic statements of the organic paradigm. While Kraepelin's work is certainly central to any list of classic works embodying the organic paradigm, it does not meet one of Kuhn's important criteria for exemplary works. That criteria is the applica-tion of the basic assumptions and conventions to devise and substantiate an hypothesis concerning the discipline's subject matter. In fact, Kraepelin's hypotheses concerning the glandular and metabolic causes of abnormal be-havior were never substantiated. The most widely cited demonstration that behavioral problems can have organic causes is the series of research findings establishing the syphilitic basis of general paresis. This research, extending over eight decades, concluded with Noguchi and Moore's identification of the *syphilitic spirochete* as the brain damaging agent in patients dying from general paresis. Any list of exemplars for the organic paradigm should include the general paresis research as well as Kraepelin's work.

The Organic Paradigm and the "Mental Illness" Controversy

The reform movements of Pinel and Dix, and the influence of the organic para-digm did a great deal to humanize the western world's conceptualization of behavioral problems. The reformer's emphasis on treatment and cure, and the organic paradigm's explicit analogy to physical disease, however, led to a popular misconception of behavioral problems. Inevitably, such behavior became known as "mental illness," or that which is symptomatic not only of organic disorder, but also of some sort of "emotional sickness." This popularized form of the organic paradigm assumed people were stricken with some disease, not organic in nature, yet curable by medical or quasi-medical treatment.

The mental illness concept differs from Pinel's "moral therapy" in that the latter assumed the subject's moral and practical reasoning had been disrupted by some traumatic experience, or had never developed because of improper or in-complete socialization. The subject, therefore, had to be morally and practically re-educated, or rehabilitated, to function in the dominant social and economic structure. This assumption underlay the "normalizing" of the "patient's" en-vironment and treatment. The restored subject was one who saw the fallacies in his practical or moral reasoning and the importance of correcting them through his own effort. The "mental illness" concept, on the other hand, portrays the subject as stricken by some disease over which he has no control and from which he can be delivered only by treatments he does not understand. Being "cured" means returned to the state of moral and practical reasoning manifested before being "stricken."

Some psychologists and psychiatrists have expressed the fear that the belief in "mental illness" has become more than just a laymen's misconception, and has actually influenced their colleagues. Thomas Szasz (1960), for example, has argued that the acceptance of the mental illness concept by psychiatrists has led to the untenable situation in which the person with the problem considers himself sick and in need of outside help in the form of expert treatment. The psychiatrist, however, knows no cure for the "illness," and hopes that it runs its course while he goes through treatment procedures mainly for their placebo effect. Price (197?), summarizing Szasz's indictment of the mental illness concept, writes:

> . . . the responsibility both of the patient and of the psychiatrist are obscured when problems in living are seen as products of mental illness. In particular, the patient is relieved of responsibility for his actions when he is able to view his behavior as mental illness—a condition over which he has no control. Similarly, the psychiatrist by implication is absolved of his responsibility to take action on the behavior of the individual who has problems in living, since he views the behavior as mental illness for which there is no known cure.

The Crisis Stage of the Organic Paradigm

The simple fact that no break-throughs followed the solving of the general paresis puzzle made it difficult for many to accept, or continue to support, the organic paradigm. As is often the case in periods of normal science, researchers, who had begun their work assuming the organic paradigm to be sound, uncovered and documented facts that were not explained by it. Hysteria, a syndrome of behaviors which especially perplexed the followers of Kraepelin, deserves note, for experience with treating it led Freud to posit the anxiety defense paradigm.

Hysteria was a condition most often occurring in women who manifested such symptoms as paralysis of an arm, loss of hearing, or the loss of sensitivity to touch in localized areas. These physical symptoms were often accompanied by behavioral problems typified by extreme anxiety. The condition came to the attention of researchers interested in abnormal behavior because physicians could find no organic cause for the symptoms. In a series of investigations conducted at the turn of the century, it was discovered that these symptoms could be replicated in otherwise normal persons through hypnotic suggestion. More importantly, it was also found that persons who had developed the symptoms could be cured through hypnosis. This led some of the most respected researchers of the day to break with the organic school and posit that there were psychological processes which the conscious self could not describe or control. These processes were described as "subconscious" and suspected of influencing behavior and, therefore, of possibly causing abnormal behavior.

The theory that the mind functioned on a subconscious level influenced many investigators, who were either frustrated by the painstakingly slow progress of organic research, or convinced the assumption of organic causation was erroneous. The community of researchers, interested in abnormal behavior, was ripe for the revolution by the end of the first decade of the twentieth century.

THE ANXIETY DEFENSE PARADIGM

Few people have had as great an impact on modern thought as Sigmund Freud (1856-1939), whose work precipitated the normal science phase of the anxiety defense paradigm. Freud began his work as a physician in Vienna, where he studied and lectured on neurology. After losing his university position for making a diagnostic error, Freud went to Paris, where he was influenced by researchers using hypnosis to study hysteria. He became convinced that there were functions of the mind which could not be described by the subject because they were subconscious, and could not be empirically measured by the observer because they were nonorganic. Freud believed that these functions, despite their elusive nature, controlled much of man's behavior, and that understanding them would lead to a parsimonious explanation of abnormal behavior.

Freud's Model of Mental Processes

Freud's early attempts to get at these difficult to define functions involved the use of hypnosis. He found that hysterical patients under hypnosis would often talk of traumatic events, or ongoing problems, which were never mentioned in nonhypnotic discussions. These disclosures under hypnosis often involved emotional outbursts, which seemed to relieve the patient of his symptoms. In addition to often solving the patient's problem, such hypnotic sessions provided Freud with clues about the nature of subconscious processes.

Freud found that by encouraging patients to discuss their fantasies, remembrances, or feelings, he could gather information about the subconscious forces affecting their behavior without hypnosis. This process of doctor-patient interaction, intended to define subconscious precipitators of behavioral problems, became known as "psychoanalysis." After years of dealing with patients through psychoanalysis, Freud, in a series of lectures, papers, and books, offered a description of elusive, subconscious forces. From this description, the Freudians drew the explanation of abnormal behavior upon which the anxiety defense paradigm is based.

Freud's system is based on the assumption that man, aware of his vulnerability to environmental threats, has established an organized society which generates survival-enhancing goods. This organization requires that each of its members behave in a nonthreatening, if not supportive, fashion. Social organization requires trust, respect of rights of weaker members, and obedience to authority exercised in the name of general welfare. Freud claimed that the basic drive to dominate by force and corollary instincts, to gratify immediate sexual urges, and to dissipate anger through violence had to be curbed.

Freud claimed that the conflict between the behavior expectations of organized society and man's instinctual drives was reflected in the mediating function of the conscious self. The conscious self, or "ego," had to control the instinctual drive to behave in a way threatening to the division of labor. The sum of these drives, or "id," formed a subconscious element of the psyche which could not be described by the conscious self, and could only be observed indirectly through fantasies and dreams. While the id demanded asocial behavioral responses, the conscience, or "super ego," demanded altruistic behavior. The super ego was the internalization of the social contract's behavioral expectations transmitted through the socializing efforts of parents, schools, churches, and others.

Abnormalcy as Functional Inadequacy

Freud's model of a conscious ego, balancing the demands of a selfish id and a selfless super ego, formed the basis for his contention that abnormal behavior was an overextension of pain-averting strategies. Freud's explanation of abnormal behavior began with the concept of "anxiety," or psychic pain. Anxiety can arise from three general circumstances involving the ego's relationship with reality, the id, or the super ego. When the ego perceives a threat or problem in reality which requires adaptive measures, it experiences *reality anxiety*. Concern over the ability to control id drives, and fear of subsequent punishment, is referred to as *neurotic anxiety*. *Moral anxiety* is the product of the ego's contemplating, or deciding to do something in conflict with, the conscience or super ego.

Anxiety is very much a part of living. Almost anything the ego does leads to anxiety in one form or another. The ego defends itself from psychic pain by distorting reality enough to relieve the anxiety-causing demands on it. This distortion is not the product of an explicit decision, but is set in motion at the subconscious level. Freud claimed that the most common distortions, or "defense mechanisms," could be separated into five classes. The first class is *repression*, or the dismissing of anxiety-causing fantasies, remembrances, or impulses from the ego. Rejecting sexual fantasies involving blood relations, or dismissing impulses to react strongly to unnerving habits of close friends are examples of normal repression mechanisms. A second group of defense mechanisms identified by Freudians is *reaction formation*, or inversion of feelings to relieve moral anxiety. An often cited reaction formation is dramatic expressions of disgust at the suggestion of sexual intimacy. Such expressions are seen as attempts to avoid the moral anxiety likely to result from the admission that such intimacy is desired. A third type of defense mechanism, *projection*, involves the attributing of one's potential anxiety-causing problems to some other person or thing. The most common example is claiming someone whom we hate or love, hates or loves us, and thereby expects us to react similarly. A fourth distortion of reality used to defend the ego against anxiety is *denial*. This defense strategy, most commonly attributed to children, and used only to describe the relieving of reality, anxiety, refers to one's simple denial that an anxiety-causing problem exists, when in fact it does. The last general class of defense mechanisms involves assuming the behavior of an earlier stage in life development to avoid an anxiety-causing problem. Children extremely afraid of school, for example, may revert to infantile behavior in an attempt to avoid school. Similarly, someone extremely anxious about retirement might begin to behave as he had thirty years earlier. This type of defense mechanism is called *regression*.

Freud claimed that everyone resorts, to varying degrees, to defense mechanisms in coping with anxiety. As long as such behavior helps one function in his day-to-day occupational and social context, it is neither pathological nor abnormal. Defense mechanisms, according to Freud, become abnormal only when they become so extreme as to affect the individual's economic or social functioning. Given the conviction that abnormal behavior is essentially the extension of normal strategies to relieve anxiety, the objective of therapy is clear. The analyst should first attempt to trace through the defense mechanism to the obscure subconscious to identify the neurotic, or moral, source of anxiety. If the problem is identified, it is brought back to the patient's ego in the hope that it can be solved, or that a new, less debilitating, defense can be found. Tracing back into the subconscious is not something one does with scalpel, X-ray, or mathematical coordinates. It is, supposedly, an intuitive skill which is developed through experience and case study, if at all.

The Elements of the Anxiety-Defense Paradigm

Freud's work was immediately embraced by those who felt the organic paradigm could shed little light on abnormal behavior not obviously associated with physical disease. While never questioning the assumption that there were subconscious processes at the root of abnormal behavior, some of Freud's students did posit alternative theories of how these processes produced such behavior. Among the better known of these students were Carl Jung and Alfred Adler. Freud, his orthodox students, as well as Adler and Jung, have enough in common to subsume them in the anxiety-defense paradigm. That paradigm has the following elements:

I. *General Assumptions.*

   The most basic assumption of the anxiety-defense paradigm is that abnormal behavior is the extension of anxiety-relieving defense mechanisms to the point of interference with occupational and social functioning. Other important assumptions include the belief that the psyche performs functions, such as initiating defense mechanisms, not measurable by observers or readily describable by the conscious self. Also central to the paradigm is the assertion that anxiety or "psychic pain" is a product of friction between man's instinctual drives and societal need for predictable, nonthreatening behavior.

The principal assumption regarding treatment is that by bringing the anxiety-causing problem closer to a patient's consciousness, he is given the opportunity to resolve it or to devise a less debilitating defense. Psychoanalysis, or the technique of cutting through defenses to the underlying conflict and bringing it to the patient's awareness, is essentially an interviewing and interpreting process. The analyst must rely on intuitive, qualitative inference from patients' self-reporting.

II. *Analogies.*

For Freud the analogy, or model, used to demonstrate his basic assumptions is the id-ego-super ego construct. Freud claimed that the origin of anxiety and defensive reactions can be understood most easily as a product of conflict among these three elements of psychic processes. Much of the valid criticism of Freud centers on the nature of this trichotomy. Are these separate awarenesses? Are they separate electro-chemical neural systems? Do they exist concurrently, or in sequence? Such questions have never been answered adequately and they underscore the paradigm's greatest weakness—the subconscious processes it assumes cannot be observed. These processes must be inferred from patients' qualitative descriptions of images, feelings, fantasies, remembrances, and dreams. The impediments such obscure data create for normal science are made most obvious by the paradigm's conventions described below.

III. *Conventions.*

By asserting that subconscious processes are not measurable and are extremely difficult to characterize, the Freudians have acknowledged that they must depend on a highly *intuitive epistemology*. Their principal subject is intangible, and its detection not only defies mechanical processes but requires inferential ability, which seems to be more a gift than a teachable skill.

The nature of subconscious processes necessitates that they be described *qualitatively*, as opposed to quantitatively.

Research, or the testing of hypotheses generated from basic assumptions, presents a major problem for Freudians. The hypothesis that anxiety is triggered in most cases by subconscious unobservable processes is impossible to test (Hook, 1959; Nagle, 1959). One may be tempted to assert that because psychoanalysis is based on Freudian assumptions, and because the technique reportedly relieves anxiety, the assumptions must therefore be valid. Among the glaring weaknesses of this argument is the assumption that psychoanalysis is a standardized intervention logically based on Freudian assumptions. The fact is that the technique is highly individualized, and varies not only among analysts but also with an analyst's application to different patients. This variance makes it difficult to show that therapeutic techniques flow from Freudian theory and, in turn, that those theories have anything to do with the techniques' effectiveness.

Assuming the techniques were standardized, logically connected with Freud's assertions, and produced a lessening of anxiety, it would still have to be shown that the lessening was attributable to the intervention and not some other variable, such as passage of time. One researcher, for example, has reported that from a group of persons seeking psychoanalytic help, an equal proportion (two-thirds) of both those who saw the analyst and those on the waiting list reported a relief from anxiety (Eysenck, 1952).

While the Freudians have not pursued hypothesis testing in the traditional scientific sense, they have gathered extensive clinical data based on their work with patients. These data are considered valuable in developing a fuller understanding of subconscious processes, and in teaching therapeutic skills. The information is usually gathered in therapy sessions, and ordered and disseminated in the form of case studies or qualitative descriptions of a patient's problems and his progress under certain therapies. While the case study is not analogous to experimentation, it can be scaled on the laboratory-naturalistic dimension of the convention's element. Freudian case study could be classified as *laboratory* in the sense that data are collected in interviews in analysts' offices. Until very recently, little effort had been made by analysts to gather data on the patient's working or social environment, and such observation remains rare.

The Freudians, clearly, are preoccupied with *individual* abnormal behavior, not its occurrence among groups, or its treatment through environmental change. The unit of analysis is the single patient. The diagnosis centers on his or her psyche, and the therapy is devised to apply to him or her only.

IV. *Exemplars.*

The exemplars of the anxiety-defense paradigm are clearly the major works of Freud, which are replete with case studies demonstrating the application of his principles to the analysis and treatment of abnormal behavior. Among the best known of his works are *The Psychopathology of Everyday Life* (1901), *The Ego and the Id* (1923), and *New Introductory Lectures on Psychoanalysis* delivered at Clark University (1909) and appearing in several collections of his lectures.

The Contributions of the Anxiety-Defense Paradigm

Freud's impact on Western thought has been immense. His principles have been used to reinterpret history, to explain all sorts of social phenomena, and even to analyze the works of Shakespeare. His explanation of abnormal behavior not only replaced the organic paradigm, but became the basis of most organized attempts to deal with such behavior. Two specific impacts of Freud's work are worth emphasizing. The first was its focusing of attention on non-organic causes of abnormal behavior. While many dismiss Freud's concepts of ego, id, super ego, and subconscious as abstractions without referents, most admit that the process of coping with anxiety not attributable to organic causes can be related to behavioral problems.

A second important aspect of Freud's work was the assertion that much abnormal behavior is socially defined. Behavior becomes abnormal when it hinders functioning in work, family, and social settings. An important corollary to this assumption is that abnormal behavior is often the extension of normal behavior and coping strategies into settings in which they hinder, rather than facilitate, functioning.

The Crisis Phase of the Anxiety-Defense Paradigm

Freud's theoretical work, and the anxiety-defense paradigm that it spawned, freed the study of abnormal behavior from the restrictive assumption of organic causation. The paradigm's preoccupation with non-measurable forces and resulting inability to generate testable hypotheses, however, precluded its adherents from adding to psychology's knowledge of subconscious processes. Freud's vague, intuitive descriptions of these forces could not be refined into more specific and predictive laws. The empirical organic paradigm, which could explain only a tiny fraction of abnormal behavior, gave way to the intuitive anxiety-defense paradigm, which claimed to explain a great deal, but could not demonstrate the truth of its explanations. The Freudians' only claim to validity was the alleged success of psychoanalysis. That technique, however, soon proved ineffective in dealing with serious behavioral problems. It seemed, rather, to be most effective at relieving the anxiety of persons well-educated or wealthy enough to be willing to spend considerable time and money in analysis. While the anxiety-defense theory remained the most often cited explanation of abnormal behavior until the learned behavior paradigm fully emerged at mid-century, it would not be inaccurate to characterize abnormal psychology as in a crisis stage from approximately 1930 to 1950. During this period several attempts at explaining abnormal behavior were made by researchers who were not trained as psychologists, psychiatrists, or biologists. These explanations never assumed the status of paradigm for abnormal psychology, but offered insights into behavioral problems which facilitated the emergence of the learned behavior paradigm, and precipitated the social-labeling paradigm. Among these was the ecological explanation emerging from the Chicago School of Human Ecology.

EARLY ECOLOGICAL ANALYSIS OF BEHAVIORAL PROBLEMS

The students of the Chicago School used the basic axioms of the ecological paradigm to generate hypotheses concerning the incidence and spatial distribution of a series of behavioral and health problems. Among the earlier attempts to devise and test hypotheses concerning abnormal behavior was the work of H. Warren Dunham.

Dunham's Analysis of Functional Psychoses in Chicago

The ecologists believed that behavior could be considered abnormal when not predicted by societal laws or mores, functional role, or immediate environment. Borrowing from the ecosystem concept, the ecologists posited that the individuals experiencing change in moral reasoning, functional role, and principal habitat must abandon old, and learn new, behavior patterns. During this transition, the individual was more likely to exhibit incongruous behavior than in periods of stability. Populations in transition, therefore, could be expected to exhibit higher incidence of abnormal behavior than more established populations. The ecologists also posited that communities could expect rates of abnormal behavior to be higher at times of change in economic base, and lower during periods of economic stability.

Chicago, in the four decades spanning 1880 to 1920, had experienced rapid economic change, and its rates of criminal and abnormal behavior were alarmingly high. The Chicago School found itself in the midst of an ideal laboratory in which to test hypotheses emerging from the beliefs listed above. Such research appeared to have as much societal as academic value, for the city was looking for means to reduce the problems it faced. These circumstances led to a series of ecological analyses of crime and abnormal behavior conducted by the students and colleagues of McKenzie and Burgess.

At the 1936 meeting of the American Sociological Association, H. Warren Dunham, from the University of Chicago, presented a paper entitled, "The Ecology of the Functional Psychoses in Chicago." Dunham's paper is important for two reasons, the first of which is its explicit statement that the preoccupation of both the organic and anxiety-defense paradigms with the individual was an impediment to understanding abnormal behavior. In describing the few previous attempts to delineate the impact of social factors on behavior, Dunham (1937, p. 469) wrote:

> Those scattered attempts . . . were the only studies purporting to investigate insanity in relation to the social milieu in which it develops. In the evolving scientific division of labor the study of mental disease and abnormality had come to be the exclusive concern of the medical men both in Europe and America. This resulted in the very definite tendency to study mental disease by the same methods as had been used in studying physical disease, and consequently this tended to hinder and restrict other approaches to this problem.

The second, and most widely cited, aspect of Dunham's paper was its presentation of research findings supporting several hypotheses evolving from the ecologists' assumptions concerning abnormal behavior. The ecologists' hypothesis that populations experiencing changes in moral reasoning, functional role, and habitat would have higher rates of abnormal behavior could be empirically tested. Dunham collected information from Chicago's public and private psychiatric institutions on the patients they had treated between 1922 and 1934 for the two main diagnostic categories of serious behavior problems: manic-depression and schizophrenia. These categories were the same as those devised by Kraepelin. Manic-depression was still used to describe either deep melancholy or extreme excitement unrelated to environmental factors, and schizophrenia to describe behavior patterns which became increasingly unrelated to environmental factors or life events. It should be noted that the latter problem was considered more serious in that treatment at that time was seldom effective.

Dunham found that the hospitals kept so little information on the recent life histories of patients that he could not ascertain how many patients had experienced changes, and, therefore, could not compare their change rate to that of the "normal" population. He was, however, able to get the patients' addresses, and attempted to draw conclusions based on available data describing their neighborhoods. Dunham assumed that residents of areas of high migration from rural or foreign areas would have been exposed to new or conflicting moral codes and assumptions about compliance. Such areas also were characterized by high rates of job insecurity due to the marginality of unskilled-labor markets. A highly mobile population also meant that new arrivals were adjusting to a new environment, and existing residents had to constantly adjust to new neighbors replacing old. Dunham concluded that ecological assumptions would be supported if psychiatric patients came disproportionately from these areas.

Extrapolating from Burgess' work, which reflected the findings of economists such as Haig, Dunham also expected to find an ecological gradient of rates of abnormal behavior. That is, he expected the rates to be highest in the zone in transition, where low rents made it possible for migrant, economically marginal populations to survive. Dunham proceeded to plot the addresses of 10,575 patients diagnosed as schizophrenic, and 2,311 as manic-depressive, on a map of Chicago divided into 120 "sub-communities." Rates for each sub-community were computed by dividing the sum of cases by the number of persons aged 15-64 residing in that area in 1930. Each subcommunity was then shaded to show into which of six intervals of rates it fell (Fig. 6-1 and 6-2).

Dunham's expectations were confirmed in the case of schizophrenia. The rates varied from 14 to 150 per 100,000, with the highest found around the CBD and the lowest at the periphery. As he had expected, statistical analysis showed an inverse relationship between schizophrenia and rent; that is, the higher an area's rent, the lower its schizophrenia rate tended to be. There also was an inverse relationship with education; that is, areas with higher median school years completed tended to have lower rates of schizophrenia.

The findings describing manic-depression, however, showed no apparent

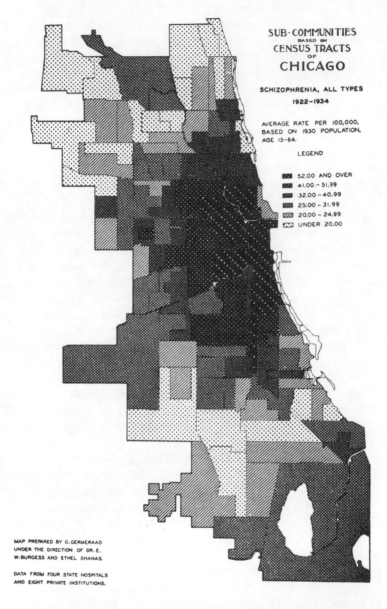

Fig. 6-1. Spatial Distribution of Schizophrenia from Dunham Analyses of Chicago
(Dunham, 1937. Reprinted by permission.)

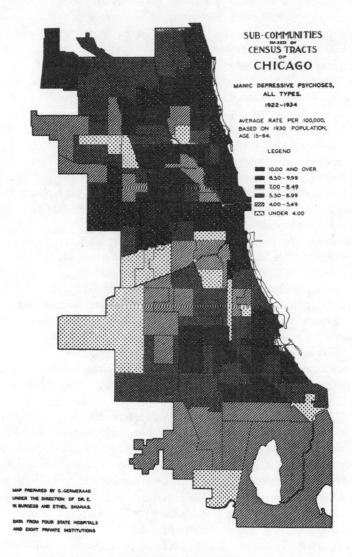

Fig. 6-2. Spatial Distribution of Manic-depressive Psychoses from Dunham Analyses of Chicago (Dunham, 1937. Reprinted by permission.)

relationship with distance from the zone in transition. The rates ranged from 1.5 to 19.3, with high and low rates apparently randomly dispersed throughout the city. In contrast to the schizophrenia rates, manic-depression seemed positively related to rent and education; that is, among those communities with manic-depression cases, the higher the level of education and rent, the higher the rate of manic-depression tended to be.

Dunham was careful in drawing conclusions from his findings. He suggested that, in the case of schizophrenia, the findings could be interpreted as supportive of the ecologists' belief that populations experiencing social and environmental change tend to exhibit more abnormal behavior. Also supportive of the ecological paradigm was the finding that schizophrenia was distributed along an "ecological gradient."

The findings regarding manic-depression led Dunham to suggest that social and environmental factors were not important factors in precipitating manic-depressive behavior. This, he claimed, lent support to those who had posited an hereditary or constitutional causation.

Dunham also made several observations, based on his work, that are rarely cited, but which include comments as historically important as his findings. One observation involved the validity of the diagnostic processes by which someone was labeled manic-depressive as opposed to schizophrenic. Dunham noted that very few of the schizophrenic patients, but over half of the manic-depressive cases, were diagnosed at private hospitals which tended to service the middle and upper classes. As a possible explanation of this phenomenon, Dunham mentioned that psychiatrists had told him that at private hospitals the label "schizophrenic" was often avoided, because it usually meant an incurable condition requiring institutionalization. Wealthier families, of course, would rather avoid such stigmatizing diagnoses and have the patient returned home "cured" as soon as possible. This was made more likely by a manic-depressive diagnosis. At public hospitals, however, the patient or his family, if he or she had one, knew little of diagnostic processes, and usually was overwhelmed by the bureaucracy, and confused by the language, leading to strange behavior regardless of actual condition. Moreover, the family may not have been able to afford to keep the patient at home, and actually desired the schizophrenic diagnosis to make committal to a public institution possible. The result is the more frequent diagnosis of schizophrenia for persons living in lower rent areas than in neighborhoods of higher socioeconomic class. This observation raised the possibility that what Dunham had actually found was evidence pointing to the subjectivity of professional diagnosis, and the tendency to label marginal, or culturally-different, persons more severely than the dominant class.

A second observation Dunham made regarding the implications of his findings dealt with the "drift effect." He noted that one explanation of the concentration of schizophrenics in the zone in transition could be that their behavioral disorder reduced their economic competitiveness, thereby reducing income and requiring them to seek out low-rent areas.

Replication, Misunderstanding, and Abandonment

Dunham's work triggered a series of replications of mapping studies both in America and other nations. Within a decade of the first appearance of Dunham's work (1936), nine similar studies had been conducted, all of which supported his original spatial findings (see, for example, Green, 1939; Queen, 1940; Schroeder, 1942). All found an ecological gradient of schizophrenia rates, while manic-depression tended to be less concentrated around the zone in transition.

An observation commonly made in these studies was that racial and ethnic groups which were in the minority in a given sub-community had higher rates than similar groups in sub-communities where they formed the majority. This fact led some, including Dunham, to posit the isolation theory of schizophrenia. Essentially, the theory stated that individuals and families needed regular inter-action with others in order to develop and maintain a sense of expected be-haviors. If linguistic and cultural barriers precluded such interaction, the minority group could lose the sense of participation in dominant society and exhibit abnormal behavior. This "isolation" explanation eventually gave way to the assertion that when a culturally different group is dominant in an area, it can mark out its own "turf," and behave in a fashion expected by others of the group. When the group is small, however, it must interact more fully with the dominant society, making its behavioral differences highly visible and more likely to be labeled deviant. Aware of this phenomenon, minority groups will form enclaves where critical mass allows behavior patterns to change more slowly, with less interference from the dominant society. This latter explanation becomes an important element in the social-labeling paradigm of abnormal psychology.

Another observation made by the early ecologists was similar to those later associated with the learned behavior paradigm of abnormal psychology. Frederick Thrasher, whose work primarily focused on juvenile delinquency and will be described more fully in the next chapter, noted that criminal behavior among gangs in Chicago became a learned behavior. He believed that the boys in areas of low involvement by the dominant society devised their own trophic organization supplied by illegal, as well as legal, sources of scarce goods. This behavior was passed on from generation to generation of gang members, as long as it provided the desired material or social resources not available from the greater division of labor or social structure. This "learning explanation" of at least one form of abnormal behavior did not influence the work of Thrasher's fellow ecologists concerned solely with functional psychoses. It did, however, later serve to connect ecological theory to the work of learning theorists such as B. F. Skinner.

It is unfortunate that most of the research spawned by Dunham's work focused on the spatial distribution of functional psychoses. In the drive to map more data describing cases of severe disorder, the successors of Dunham ne-glected to develop a theoretical connection between their work and the basic ecological assumptions concerning abnormal behavior. In essence, those assumptions saw "abnormalcy" as incongruous or non-predicted behavior, not just the extreme withdrawal from reality requiring institutionalization. Moreover, the etiology, or causal factor, of such behavior was thought to be the adjustment to economically precipitated changes, which increased the chances of acting in an unpredictable way. No assumption was made of "illness" or "loss of touch with reality," but simply that the transition from old behavior patterns to new ones created a population at risk which could be expected to exhibit behavior appropriate in old settings but not in new, or behavior reflective of an, as yet, incomplete understanding of new moral systems, role expectations, and physical surroundings. The early ecologists believed, further, that an understanding of economics and economic geography could help identify the populations at risk. Rather than operationalizing and testing these early propositions and beliefs, Dunham and his successors became mappers of addresses of institutionalized psychiatric patients. Their work became increasingly atheoretical as it moved further from its roots in human ecology. By positing such weak theories as the isolation effect, the replicators of Dunham led others not familiar with the work of Thomas and Znaniecki, Simmel, or McKenzie, to conclude that ecological analysis was merely an exercise in cartography.

Perhaps the most unfortunate result of the diversion into spatial analysis was the erroneous impression, given to many, that human ecologists believed the causal factor was the physical environment of the zone in transition. None of the seminal works in human ecology suggest that bad housing, density, pollution, or physical decay cause insanity or criminal behavior.

Criticism of the overemphasis on spatial distributions became increasingly common through the 1940s, and a more serious logical problem was pointed out by W. S. Robinson (1950), when he demonstrated the error inherent in the use of correlation analysis to infer association between place specific rates and the behavior of individuals. This criticism and the emergence of the learning paradigm reduced interest in the ecological paradigm's explanation of abnormal behavior. Some researchers did continue to study the incidence of behavioral problems among different socioeconomic groups. The most often cited of these efforts is Hollingshead and Redlich's (1958) study of social class and abnormal behavior in New Haven, Connecticut. They found, as the ecologists would predict, that the economically marginal population accounts for a disproportionately large number of the cases of severe behavioral problems (Liem & Liem, 1978). The Hollingshead and Redlich study has been replicated several times in this country (Myers & Bean, 1968; Srole, Langner, Michael, Opler, & Rennie, 1962) and cross culturally (Kohn, 1968), and its findings have been supported.

While a great deal of intellectual effort went into describing the spatial and socioeconomic distributions of severe behavioral problems, very little was invested in testing the most easily operationalized of the ecological theories; that is, that fluctuations in economic base will precipitate increases in abnormal behavior. By mid-century, few psychologists remained interested in ecological analysis. The attention of the discipline had been drawn to the controversial work of learning theorists such as B. F. Skinner. Except for the work of isolated researchers, progress in reformulating and testing ecological hypotheses was suspended for over a decade. As will be described shortly, however, growing interest in community mental health during the middle and late 1960s led to a reconsideration of the impact of ecological variables on behavior. Research, not directly motivated by familiarity with the work of the early human ecologists, began to substantiate their basic assumptions.

THE LEARNED-BEHAVIOR PARADIGM

During the period dominated by the Freudians and the anxiety defense paradigm, a number of psychologists reacted strongly to the intuitive quality of the work describing subconscious processes. Qualitative case studies, and the techniques used to generate them, were considered unscientific. Among the more outspoken of these critics was John B. Watson (1879-1958) who argued that the role of psychology was to predict behavior as parsimoniously as possible without resorting to obscure abstractions. He also suggested that this task could be most efficiently pursued by looking at behavior as "learned." The concept of learned behavior had become a subject of considerable interest to natural scientists at the time of Watson's most widely disseminated criticism (1914). This interest had been occasioned by the work of the Russian scientist Ivan Pavlov.

The Precursors of the Learning Paradigm

At the turn of the century, Pavlov was conducting research on the digestive processes of dogs, when he discovered a peculiar phenomenon. He found that a stimulus occurring simultaneously with one which instinctively elicits a particular response can eventually elicit the instinctive response. Pavlov's classic example of substituting a stimulus through association involved the ringing of a bell each time a dog was fed. Eventually the dog could be made to salivate at the sound of the bell, even when food was not present. Pavlov further observed that the salivating at the sound of the bell alone eventually stopped if the ringing were not occasionally accompanied by food. This led him to speculate that the dog learned to associate the bell with food, and the association led to salivation as long as it was occasionally reinforced. The response elicited through association and reinforcement became known as a "conditioned reflex."

Respondent Conditioning

Pavlov's work was expanded upon and applied to humans by several psychologists, the best known of whom was the team of Watson and Raynor. Their classic demonstration (1920) that conditioned reflexes could be elicited from humans involved an 11 month old boy who was given the opportunity to play with white

rabbits. At the outset, the boy showed no fear of the animals and enjoyed playing with them. The experimenters then began to pound a steel bar behind the
boy each time he reached for the rabbits. The noise was distractingly loud, and
frightened the child at each repetition. Soon the child was reluctant to touch the
rabbits out of fear of the noise. Eventually, he became afraid of the rabbits
themselves, and carried the association over to stuffed white animals. Watson
and Raynor concluded that fright, which instinctively and normally followed
hearing the loud unexpected noise, could be elicited by neutral stimuli, such as
stuffed animals, through conditioning.

Work such as Watson and Raynor's indicated that behavior could be "controlled" to the degree that an "abnormal" response to a stimuli could be
produced by associating that stimuli with one which normally elicits the desired
response. The process of producing non-instinctual responses through association
and substitution of stimuli became known as "respondent" or "classical conditioning."

The concept of conditioned behavior contributed to abnormal psychology by
explaining certain types of behavioral problems, and in obviating their treatment. The type of problem most obviously associated with respondent conditioning is phobia, or fear of phenomena not normally considered harmful.
Citing Watson's experiment with the young boy, some psychologists posited that
stimuli attendant to, but not causal of, traumatic experiences may elicit the
anxiety of the trauma when experienced later in life. This type of conditioning
can be reversed, supposedly, by associating the stimuli with one the subject finds
pleasant until its anxiety-causing effect is neutralized (Jones, 1924).

Early in the development of respondent conditioning (1913), an American
psychologist, E. L. Thorndike, posited the "law of effect" based on work such as
Pavlov's and Watson's. Essentially, the law states that responses to stimuli which
bring rewarding consequences are reinforced and repeated, while those which
bring unpleasant consequences are weakened and eventually avoided. The observation that the organism perceives the effect of his behavior, and learns from it,
was to lead some researchers, such as B. F. Skinner, to go beyond the
respondent-conditioning model and claim that behavior is learned through
conditioning processes involving positive and negative reinforcements.

The Emergence of the Learning Paradigm

In 1953, B. F. Skinner's *Science and Human Behavior* argued that the concept of
conditioning had a much wider application than that posited by Watson, and
others interested in respondent conditioning. Skinner argued there was an
"operant conditioning" which took place constantly in the course of life, and
determined how man behaves in response to stimuli. Everyone, according, to
Skinner, has basic needs and drives which they seek to fulfill through varying
behaviors. Behaviors which bring them closer to their goals are reinforced and
repeated, while those which do not help, or which hinder, are weakened and

avoided. The classic example of operant conditioning is the hungry rat placed in a cage where there is a lever which will deliver food when pressed. At first the rat scurries around the cage looking for food. Each time he touches the lever a piece of food is dropped in the enclosure. Eventually, he associates, or "learns" to touch the lever to get food. At this point, food is no longer given for merely touching the lever, but only when it is depressed. Soon the rat learns to press the lever when he is hungry. The rat will continue, for a period, to press the lever when hungry, even though no food is given. Without occasional reward, however, the response will eventually stop.

Negative reinforcements can also be used to elicit a desired response. For example, a rat which is delivered an electric shock after a light goes on in his cage, unless a lever is depressed, will continue to depress the lever after he learns it precludes the shock. This behavior will continue each time the light goes on, even though no more shocks are received.

Extrapolating from such experiments, Skinner posited that human behavior can be seen as "shaped" by the successes and failures experienced while attempting to fulfill basic needs. Reinforcers are established societally, as well as naturally, and therefore can be used to intentionally shape man's behavior. Indeed, Skinner (1971), in his more recent works, has argued for the use of operant conditioning to create more perfect societies.

Operant Conditioning and Abnormal Behavior

Since Skinner's first presentation of operant conditioning, other psychologists have replicated his work and expanded on his theories. Among the better known of these works are Eysenck and Rachman's *The Causes and Cures of Neurosis* (1965), Ullman and Krasner's *A Psychological Approach to Abnormal Behavior* (1969), and Wolpe's *Psychotherapy by Reciprocal Inhibition* (1958). There is agreement among these researchers on several points concerning abnormal behavior. The most basic agreement is that there is no inherently normal or abnormal behavior. "Normal" and "abnormal" are labels given a person's behavior by others, depending on how predictable or congruent it is with social and environmental variables. Most persons "learn" to behave in a predictable way through a societal operant-conditioning program which reinforces predictable behavior, both positively and negatively, and punishes non-predictable behavior. The conditioners include parents, school systems, employers, voluntary organizations, and the state.

Based on this understanding of behavior, the learning theorists differentiate two classes of abnormal behavior. The first is the phobic behavior mentioned earlier, or responding to a stimulus not in predictable fashion but in a way conditioned by its association with some traumatic stimulus. The small boy conditioned by Watson to be frightened by stuffed animals is an example of phobic abnormal behavior.

The second class of abnormal behavior results from the failure of social conditioning to reinforce acceptable behavior or punish non-acceptable behavior. The failure of social conditioning can result from ineffective reinforcement or punishment by parents or other conditioners, or from functioning in a subgroup whose reinforcements are more immediate than the larger society's, but whose behavior expectations are different. The inability of the individual to associate reinforcements with his actions also can preclude effective conditioning.

Treatment Strategies Flowing From the Learning Paradigm

One of the most attractive qualities of the learning paradigm is its clear indication of treatment strategies. Since the maladaptive behavior itself is seen as the problem and not the symptom of some deeper imbalance, the obvious treatment is to use conditioning or other learning techniques to deter or elicit behavior. This strategy, or "behavior modification," assumes varying forms, depending on whether the behavior is of the first, or phobic, class, or a product of incomplete socialization.

To treat phobic reactions, behavior modifiers attempt to reverse the process Watson and Raynor used to produce a phobic reaction in the boy conditioned to be frightened by stuffed animals. In a classic example, Jones (1924) removed a child's phobic fear of rabbits by bringing rabbit-like toys to the child's attention while he was responding normally to enjoyable stimuli such as eating. The toys were replaced by real rabbits, and brought increasingly closer to him during meals. Eventually, the boy was conditioned to associate the rabbit with the pleasant stimulus of food, and his frightened behavior gave way to more normal responses.

In the cases of incomplete or ineffective societal conditioning, the behavior-modification process takes on the characteristics of operant, rather than respondent, conditioning. Perhaps the most widely known form of such treatment is "aversion therapy," or the attempt to condition the patient to associate unpleasant outcomes with certain behaviors, thereby decreasing the behavior's occurrence. Alcoholics, for example, can be treated by administering drugs which cause extreme nausea when alcohol is consumed. The patient may come to associate the nausea with alcohol and, therefore, reduce his drinking. While such extreme forms of aversion therapy are prescribed, and have been effective, as elements of larger programs of therapy, they are not representative of behavior modification therapy in general. More typical of such therapy is the process described by Bandura (1969). The elements of the process are:

1. providing the subject with a "model" or person whose behavior demonstrates the normal response in a range of environments,
2. reinforcing the subject with rewards when he or she emulates the behavior of the model,
3. transferring the rewarding process to the subject so he or she evaluates his own behavior and extends the reinforcing program to his unmonitored periods, and

4. replacing material or explicit rewards with more abstract self-administered feelings of satisfaction and disatisfaction analogous to conscience.

Elements of the Learning Paradigm

While the learning paradigm is new and still emerging, it has manifested all of Kuhn's elements.

I. *The Basic Assumptions.*

The basic assumptions of the learning paradigm include:

A. Abnormal behavior is either phobic response to environmental stimuli or behavior incongruent with societally-sanctioned means to ends.

B. Phobic responses to environmental stimuli are learned through respondent conditioning.

C. Behavior incongruous with societally-sanctioned means to ends is a product of ineffective or subcultural operant conditioning in the form of socialization.

D. Phobic and incongruous behavior are themselves the problem, not the symptoms of deeper imbalance.

E. Behavior can be modified through reinforcement and punishment.

II. *Analogies.*

The learning theorists emphasize that the process by which one comes to exhibit abnormal behavior should be considered analogous to that by which we come to exhibit any behavior—by learning it. They consider all behavior to be the outgrowth of experience and conditioning.

III. *Conventions.*

Because the learning theorists believe that abnormal behavior is not symptomatic of anything deeper, they claim it is best studied the way any observable phenomenon is studied; that is, through careful measurement, classification, hypothesizing and experimentation. Their epistemology, in other words, is *empirical.* Given their emphasis on measurement, moreover, the learning theorists tend to be *quantitative* in describing their subject matter.

Reflecting their roots in the work of Pavlov, Watson, and others who considered themselves scientists, the learning theorists have maintained a tradition for *laboratory research.* The strategies for treatment which flow from the learning paradigm, however, are more naturalistic than either the organic or the anxiety-defense paradigms. The difference is that the learning theorists see the individual's social and organizational environment as the conditioner of his behavior. Without an understanding of the reinforcements and punishments the individual is subject to in his everyday life, a therapist could not devise a schedule of effective behavior-modifying interventions.

While sensitive to the fact that individual behavior can be studied as a product of, and often predicted by, social forces, the adherents to the learning paradigm maintain the traditional bias of psychology, and emphasize the *individual* as the unit of analysis.

IV. *Exemplars.*

The best known adherent to the learning paradigm is B. F. Skinner. All his works have proselytized for conditioning, and his *Science and Human Behavior* (1953) is widely recognized as influential in precipitating the learning school. As at least one observer (Price, 1972) of the old field has noted, however, abnormal psychology was most influenced by learning theory through Wolpe's *Psychotherapy by Reciprocal Inhibition* (1958).

While both these works have played central roles in exposing students to the paradigm, no list of examplars would be complete without Watson and Raynor's experiments demonstrating the principles of respondent conditioning.

Similarities Between the Ecological and Learning Paradigms

The ecological and learning paradigms have several striking parallels in their assumptions concerning behavior. Both emphasize that "abnormal" is a label attributed by society to behavior which is not predicted by environmental context or societal mores and laws. The ecologists and learning theorists also agree that behavior can be viewed as an adaptation strategy intended to further one's chances of survival at a given standard of living. This strategy, moreover, is seen by both as regulated by rules established societally to insure order in the division of labor. Conditioning, in the form of positive and negative reinforcement as well as punishment, plays an important role in both the ecological and learning paradigms, for, through conditioning, individuals learn to behave in the most predictable fashion. Another interesting similarity between the two schools is their explanation of why individuals behave abnormally. Both talk of ineffective socialization or the lack of models, reinforcers, and punishment as preconditions of abnormal behavior.

The major difference between the schools centers in their basic unit of analysis. The learning paradigm focuses on the individual and his or her behavior as the objective reality to be measured and studied. The reasons for ineffective conditioning, or phobic association, are searched out in each individual case, in the hope that generalizing from such cases will provide classes of causes, such as lack of parental conditioning, inability to associate reinforcers or punishments with a specific behavior, or conditioning to behavior patterns in conflict with the dominant expectation. This emphasis on the individual case is perpetuated by the tradition of the discipline and the obvious need to devise treatment for particular individuals rather than groups of individuals.

The ecologists were more interested in the fact that the societal conditioning process seemed to be more effective among some groups than others and at different times. They wanted to determine which conditions led to the weakening of learned behaviors, or precluded the learning of sanctioned behaviors. Also of interest was the phenomenon of conditioning to subgroup norms and expectations which were in conflict to the dominant mores. These subjects all were more parsimoniously studied, the ecologists believed, by observing and measuring group behavior.

While both the learning and ecological paradigms posited that the labeling of behavior as "abnormal" was a subjective process in that norms, mores, and values change, neither was preoccupied with the sociology of norm formulation. Some ecologists, including Dunham, realized that the subjectivity of labeling could lead to persons being institutionalized because they belonged to subgroups with behavior expectations at variance with the majority. The potential abuses of this "norm clash" were not fully illuminated, however, until the emergence of the social labeling paradigm.

THE SOCIAL LABELING PARADIGM

The subjectivity of the normal-abnormal differentiation was assumed by both the ecologist and learning theorists, but the implications of that subjectivity were most dramatically demonstrated by a group of social psychologists and sociologists. Their work has been very controversial, and has forced abnormal psychology to recognize the importance of social forces in the diagnosis and treatment of abnormal behavior. While it may be premature to refer to this body of literature as "paradigmatic," the issues it raises have become so central to abnormal psychology that its consideration is essential to any overview of the field.

Residual Rule Breaking and Mental Illness

The social labeling paradigm considers abnormal behavior to be that which violates the expectations of the dominant society. These expectations take the form of explicit and implicit rules. When the rules are explicit, such as laws or religious mores, the violator's behavior is labeled criminal or immoral, and he is subjected to the corresponding legal or social sanctions. In addition to explicit rules, there are, according to the social paradigm, some rules of behavior which are unstated, and govern actions for which there appears to be no rational purpose except to demonstrate a lack of awareness of social context. Goffman cites "away" behavior as typical of that proscribed by implicit rules. One should not act as if he is away from people when there are others present who are directing their attention to him. He should not talk to himself, act obviously preoccupied, stimulate his genital organs, etc. There are no explicit rules applying to "away" behaviors, but everyone knows not to manifest them. Breaking such implicit rules is called "residual rule breaking," to refer to that group of abnormal behaviors which are "residual," or left over when explicitly prohibited behaviors are subtracted from the total class of proscribed behaviors. The cause of residual rule breaking, claim the social theorists, has in the past been attributed to witchcraft and possession, and now to "mental illness."

The controversial aspect of the social labeling paradigm is its description of the process by which residual rule breaking becomes labeled mental illness, and the tendency of the labeling itself to elicit classical symptoms of psychological disorder. It is important to note that the social theorists believe most everyone indulges in residual rule breaking, but few are labeled because those present did not detect it, were more tolerant than the majority, were not aware of the majority opinion of the behavior, were reluctant to label it mental illness, or were in an inferior power position and could not label it mental illness. The "audience," therefore, becomes, for the social theorists, an important element in understanding abnormal behavior. The family, for example, often performs the initial labeling, and variations in its values can mean the same behavior exhibited by different persons can lead to one person's institutionalization and another's being considered eccentric.

While the social labeling theorists acknowledge that residual rule breaking can be caused by organic problems, or improper conditioning, they claim most is an outgrowth of attempts to cope with anxiety. Such attempts usually involve changes in one's values or beliefs, or engaging in behaviors which have a relaxing effect. These changes may or may not relieve the anxiety, but they are highly visible to those in the social environment. If these "significant others" see the behavior as unusual but resulting in better adjustment, nothing further might happen. If, however, the significant others view the behavior as residual rule breaking, the exhibitor may begin what the social theorists call the "deviant career."

The Deviant Career

Once someone's behavior has been labeled as residual rule breaking or abnormal, the social theorists claim he is increasingly conditioned to behave in a way typical of the "mentally ill." This conditioning process has three stages, during each of which the "patient" is rewarded for acting "ill" and punished for acting "normal" (Sarbin, 1969).

The first of these stages is the *pre-patient* phase, during which others first regard the individual's behavior as "sick." These others in his environment begin, out of sincere concern, to insulate him from "stressful" situations, and may begin to react differently to his moods to avoid "upsetting" him. The subject may either object to such treatment, which tends to reinforce the others' perception of him as "out-of-sorts" and irrational, or he can acquiesce, which confirms their diagnosis. In either case, he will develop real anxiety over his situation, and this will lead to even more unpredictable behavior. At some point, a doctor is called and, noting that the patient has no physical problem that would cause his anxiety and abnormal behavior, might suggest psychiatric observation. Once a medical expert concurs that the problems are probably "emotional," the patient begins to accept that perhaps he is "ill."

The second stage of the process, or *unsettled patient* phase, begins with voluntary or forced institutionalization for "observation." Once in the institution, the patient is forced into the hospital routine, and any reaction, resistance, or acquiescence is seen as indicative of the patient's disturbed condition. The only behavior which elicits judgments that one is improving is that expected by the therapist, who assumes the patient is emotionally disordered. To act normally in the therapeutic context, therefore, is to act in a way the larger community judges abnormal.

After the patient reaches the passive stage he might be released as "rehabilitated" or he may remain institutionalized. If the passive patient is not released, he enters the *stabilized-patient* role, which can mean extended institutionalization and concurrent loss of social skills. Once the patient loses his social skills, he becomes dependent on the institution for all his needs, making his ability to function in the community problematical even if released. Eventually, the individual becomes "converted," or accepts the diagnosis of mental illness, since functioning in the external world seems a frightening impossibility.

The Treatment Strategies

Few of the authors identified with the social school have addressed themselves to the problem of treating those whose behavior has been labeled "abnormal." Given their belief, however, that it is the diagnostic and treatment process which actually leads to the severe forms of abnormal behavior (i.e., the stabilized patient), they have little faith in existing programs to rehabilitate individuals. Since the social school believes residual rule breaking to be primarily the product of anxiety over problems in living, it posits that part of the problem's solution is to reduce the societal precipitators of anxiety. It is not clear that there is agreement on which are the societal precipitators and how they are to be changed, but most prescriptions call for the reform of institutions which rigidify behavior expectations.

The prescription which flows more obviously from the social perspective is the suggestion that residual rules be made explicit so their worth to society can be evaluated. Those that are frivolous could be discarded, and those that are based on societally-held moral values could be incorporated into the legal system. Such reassignment of rules would at least make the status and the rights of the rule breaker more clear (Szasz, 1960). Given the social school's preoccupation with the labeling process rather than with behavior, its adherents would have to conclude that tolerance of unusual non-criminal behavior, not caused by organic problems, is the ultimate "solution."

The Elements of the Social Paradigm

Unlike the others considered in this chapter, the social paradigm has not completely emerged. Its elements, therefore, are not as well defined, and their listing requires some extrapolation. The following list is based on as little extrapolating as possible.

I. *General Assumptions.*

Among the more important of the social paradigm's basic assumptions are:

A. Abnormal behavior is the breaking of residual rules, detected by others with little tolerance for such rule breaking, and with the power to bring such behavior to the attention of professional diagnosticians.

B. Residual rule breaking is usually part of a strategy to relieve anxiety over problems in living.

C. The system of professional treatment for those who break residual rules actually conditions them to behave abnormally and maladaptively.

D. Solutions to the problem of abnormal behavior must involve societal reform and increased tolerance.

II. *Analogies.*

The social paradigm has not devised a distinct analog for the process described in the basic assumptions. Several authors, however, have suggested analogies for various elements of the process. The first step of the process, or labeling of residual rule breaking, has been likened to *audience reaction* to demonstrate the subjective nature of the "abnormal" label (Price, 1972, p. 78). The result of conditioning patients to act in an ill or abnormal fashion has often been referred to as the "deviant career" (Scheff, 1966).

III. *Conventions.*

At this early stage in its development, the social paradigm has not produced a great deal of research, yet indications as to its conventions seem clear. Its epistemology, given that the subject of its study is an observable labeling process, is *empirical*. Its description of that process, at this point, is *qualitative* as opposed to quantitative. Critics have charged that those adhering to the social school have ideological commitments to radical social change, which reduce objectivity in observation and description (Price, 1972). While this may be so, it is difficult to determine whether such commitment preceded the analysis of the effects of therapy on individuals, or if the findings of the analysis precipitated the commitment. If the latter were the case, the commitment may well be a logical outgrowth of objective assessments, and should be considered as legitimate a prescription as psychoanalysis or behavior modification.

The research of the social school has been *naturalistic*, and will probably continue to be so, simply because the labeling process cannot be replicated in a laboratory, nor would such replication provide any added validity to findings. An example of recent naturalistic research suggested by the social paradigm involved placing eight normal volunteers in mental institutions (Rosenhan, 1973). They gained admittance by reporting hearing noises and voices, but once in the institution they acted normally in response to directives, and never again mentioned noises. None of the eight normal volunteers was detected by the professional staffs of any of the institutions. Their behavior was seen as abnormal because it was so labeled at the time of commital. All the pseudopatients were eventually discharged, but not because they were recognized as normal. Each was released with a diagnosis of schizophrenia "in remission."

The emphasis on labeling and "audience reaction" as the keys to understanding abnormal behavior clearly differentiates the social paradigm from those previously considered. The latter's preoccupation with the individual is replaced by the social school's study of the group. The social paradigm's level of analysis, therefore, is the *community*.

IV. *Exemplars.*

The exemplars of the social paradigm include the work of Irving Goffman, whose *Asylums* (1961) was particularly influential in shaping the paradigm. Scheff (1966) provided the best synthesis of the work generally considered as typical of the social school in his *Being Mentally Ill: A Sociological Theory*. Sarbin's (1969) "Schizophrenic Thinking: A role theoretical analysis" includes an often cited description of the "deviant career" concept central to the social school.

Similarities Between the Social and Ecological Paradigms

The social paradigm has one striking similarity to the ecological paradigm and its behavioral axioms. Both recognize the crucial role played by audiences in the labeling of abnormal behavior. This realization leads both to assume that the incidence of such behavior is most parsimoniously explained by studying society's rule-making process and the forces affecting compliance to rules.

The most glaring difference between the social and ecological paradigms is their explanation of why some people are more likely to be labeled abnormal than others. The ecologists claim the populations at risk are those experiencing adaptation to new roles, moral perspectives, and physical environments made necessary by dynamic industrial economies. The social theorists have no well formulated hypotheses to explain the variations among groups, except to point out that the poor's higher rates are probably due to the more anxiety-generating life events which supposedly accompany economic marginality.

SOME RECENT RESEARCH SUBSTANTIATING ECOLOGICAL ASSUMPTIONS

While Dunham and those preoccupied with spatial distributions of abnormal behavior became identified as the "ecological school," their work never tested the basic assumptions of human ecology concerning abnormal behavior. In recent years, however, psychologists and sociologists have conducted research which tends to substantiate the behavioral axioms listed in Chapter 4. This work, while not explicitly motivated by the desire to test ecological hypotheses, is, nonetheless, of great value to ecologists, and justifies a reconsideration of the ecological paradigm as a useful alternative for abnormal psychology.

Role Change as Precipitator of Behavioral Problems

Among the changes cited by the ecologists as increasing the individual's chances of exhibiting non-predicted or abnormal behavior was change in functional role or job. Several studies have focused on job change to determine its association with behavioral problems. Among the better known of those is Clausen and Kohn's (1959) study of Hagerstown, Pennsylvania, in which they found persons who changed jobs to higher or lower paying positions had more behavioral problems than those who did not. One criticism of such research is that it cannot be established whether the job change contributed to the onset of the behavioral problem, or the behavioral problem led to the job change. This is not as great a problem for the ecologists as one might believe, as long as the labeling or institutionalization occurred after the job changes. The ecological model does *not* claim that the change causes psychological trauma manifested by behavioral problems, but that it increases the likelihood of the individual exhibiting behavior likely to be labeled abnormal in the new context. If the individual is a quick learner in the behavioral sense, and thereby minimizes his response mistakes and transition time, he may change jobs any number of times without exhibiting enough incongruous behavior to be labeled abnormal. His chances of being so labeled, however, are greater than the chances of as quick a learner who does not change jobs. Job changing for slow learners is more precarious, for their chances of exhibiting incongruous behavior and of being labeled abnormal are greater than the quick learner given the same number of job changes. In a period of rapid economic change, therefore, the ecologist expects more behavior labeled as abnormal even though the psyche of the changers has not been traumatized.

Another study, which tends to support the ecological hypothesis that economic fluctuations can increase rates of abnormal behavior, indicates that the families of job changers may be affected by such shifts. Kantor (1965) monitored over 800 families in a school district for two years to try to determine if job changes of the parents affected the children's behavior at school or at home. Families who left the district were dropped from the sample because any changes in the child's behavior could then be attributed to school changes. Of the remaining families it was found that those children whose parents had experienced an upward, lateral, or downward job change had significantly more behavior problems either at school or at home, or both, than the group whose parents had not changed jobs. The impact of the parents' job changes appeared significant whether the change involved moving to a new residence in the district or not.

Life Events as Precipitators of Behavioral Problems

For at least the past 25 years, researchers have noted that the behavioral problems among psychiatric patients were often preceded by some aversive life event (Arieti, 1959; Leff, et al, 1970; Meyer, 1948; Paykel, et al., 1969). The relationship is not simple. It is affected by such characteristics as social support (Gore,

1978) and individual assessment of stress severity. Findings continue to suggest, however, that those who develop behavioral problems experience (prior to their symptoms) more life events requiring adjustment than the normal population (Eaton, 1978; Dohrenwend, et al., 1978; Paykel, 1969).

The relevance of such work for the ecological paradigm lies in the types of events identified as precipitative of behavioral problems. Holmes and Rahe (1967) devised a ranking of such events by asking people to consider a list of 43 potential life changing events, and to rank each as to its strength of impact (see Table 5-2 in Chapter 5). The ranking was done by arbitrarily assigning marriage 500 points and asking that the other events be given the appropriate number of points *vis-a-vis* marriage. The list of stressful life events can be separated into life-cycle, economic well-being, and random clusters (see Table 5-3 in Chapter 5). The events listed in the economic cluster can all be expected to occur more frequently during periods of increasing, decreasing, or shifting economic base.

Migration and Behavioral Problems

Related to the life events research is the extensive body of findings describing the effects of physical and social mobility on the incidence of abnormal behavior. A long line of research has established that migrant populations more often exhibit behavior labeled as abnormal than the stable population from which they originated. This relationship holds true after controlling for age and sex differences. These findings led some to conclude that mobility itself caused people to become less stable. Closer investigation, however, clarified that the move itself was not as predictive as the setting into which the migrant moved. For example, Faris and Dunham (1960) compared the rates of abnormal behavior among migrants who had moved into areas where their ethnic group was a small minority, and into areas where there were large concentrations of people of the same ethnic background. He found the former situation produced significantly higher rates than the latter. Astrup and Odegaard (1960) studied Norwegians who migrated from town to town, and from small towns to the metropolis of Oslo. They found that the rates among those moving from small town to small town did not vary, while those migrating from such towns as Oslo were significantly higher. The ecological explanation of such findings is that the greater the difference between the origin and destination of the migrant, the more new behavior he must learn, and the greater his chances are of exhibiting behavior considered abnormal by the dominant population.

Economic Change and Abnormal Behavior

Thus far in this section, research findings have been cited which indirectly support the ecological assumptions concerning abnormal behavior. Other recent work comes much closer to testing the ecological assumptions concerning economic change and behavioral problems. The two best examples of such research are "ecological psychology" and the recent discovery of meaningful relationships between economic trends and committals to mental institutions.

Without apparent familiarity with the work of McKenzie, Burgess, and the other early human ecologists, Roger Barker, a psychologist, began a rather unique line of research in the early 1950s called "ecological psychology." Barker was trained by Kurt Lewin (1951) who argued that if psychology was to understand behavior, the discipline would have to abandon its complete preoccupation with controlled laboratory experiments. The social and physical context in which behavior took place and derived its meaning was, for Lewin and his students, at least as important as data gathered by observing and measuring individuals in controlled settings.

Inspired by Lewin's perspective, Barker assumed the task of identifying and classifying "behavior settings," or places in which socially purposeful functions took place, and which tended to predict the behavior of the individuals who used them. Some obvious examples of such settings are churches, schools, and stores where those present can be accurately predicted to be exhibiting behaviors characterized as worshipping, studying, or shopping.

After extended observation of two small towns, one in Kansas and the other in Britain, Barker (1961) noted that the American town had 20 percent more behavior settings than the British town, despite having half the population. This meant, according to Barker, that the population of the Kansas town had to participate in more behavior settings to keep them manned. Under such conditions, Barker hypothesized, the participants would be required to take on more responsibilities than in the British town, where there were more persons and fewer settings. He further suggested that such increased participation and responsibility meant that the community was dependent on all its members, with few people being discouraged from participation. This situation supposedly led to stronger community identity, more social cohesion, and a greater feeling of importance for the individual. Undermanned situations also mean that children are prepared to take meaningful roles in a community at a younger age.

Barker and Gump (1964) attempted to test some of these hypotheses by observing the behavior and participation rates in a high school with a high ratio of behavior settings to students and in a larger school with a lower ratio. They found that more students in the smaller school, in fact, participated directly in more activities and identified more strongly with the institution.

Based on these findings, Barker theorized that in systems where there are enough, or more than enough, individuals to perform the needed functions in all behavior settings, deviant behavior can more easily lead to being labeled abnormal since the individual can be easily replaced. In situations where there are slightly fewer persons than functions, on the other hand, there is more tolerance of deviant behavior because the individual would be difficult to replace. Severe undermanning, however, can lead to strain and increased intolerance.

Barker's hypotheses have been operationalized and tested in other institutions with findings generally supportive of his hypotheses (Wicker, 1968; Willems, 1967, 1972). Barker has also replicated and extended his earlier comparison of the undermanned American town and the optimally or overmanned British town (Barker & Shoggen, 1973), and found the differences supportive of his hypotheses.

The overmanned-undermanned dichotomy and its behavioral correlates add weight to McKenzie's assertion that the relationship between a community's economic base and population size is predictive of its rate of behavioral problems. In fact, McKenzie and the early ecologists believed the optimal situation was growth of the economic base at a rate that would provide just enough roles for the natural increase of births over deaths. This equilibrium state is analogous to the slightly undermanned condition described by the ecological psychologists as maximizing both the tolerance toward unusual behavior and the population's feeling of participation and responsibility.

The growing awareness that many behavioral problems are parsimoniously explained as products of societally unacceptable adaptation strategies has led to the emergence of a "community" psychology (Heller & Monahan, 1977). At the core of this movement is the belief that the incidence of behavioral problems can be most effectively managed by "treating" the environment as well as the individual. This tenet has inevitably led to the use of the ecological paradigm as a guide to intervention.

The work of Kelly (1966) is generally considered seminal in establishing the ecological perspective on community mental health services. This perspective has yielded prescriptive recommendations such as the expansion of functional roles in the community so that the probabilities of an individual finding an acceptable niche are maximized (Mills & Kelly, 1972). Kelly's more profound contribution, however, has been the infusion of an awareness of ecological interdependence into community psychology. This awareness had led to an appreciation (Trickett, Kelly & Todd, 1972) of the need for ecological modeling of communities so that the outcomes, both intended and unintended, of potential interventions can be anticipated.

While the work of Barker and Kelly offers theoretical support to the general assumptions of the human ecologists, its contribution to empirical testing of these assumptions has been surpassed by research demonstrating a strong relationship between committals to mental institutions and economic change. Using data collected in New York State between 1914 and 1960, Brenner (1973) found that the manufacturing employment index was inversely associated with institutionalization rates for most of the population, but that the association was proportional for the poor, the elderly and for women with more than high school education.

While Brenner's findings support the ecologists' contention that shifts in the economic base of a community will precipitate increases in abnormal behavior, they did not identify the intervening variables between economic change and institutionalization (Dooley & Catalano, 1977). Brenner's findings can be explained by at least two rival hypotheses:

1. Economic change increases the incidence of stressful life events and thereby the population at risk of acting abnormally (Catalano, 1975).
2. The rate of abnormal behavior remains relatively constant, but institutions
   are used as shelters for the dependent and infirm when the economy precludes care at home.

In the most definitive test of the ecological hypothesis, Catalano and Dooley
(1977a) analyzed data describing the experience of stressful life events and the
mood of a monthly sample of the Kansas City metropolitan area population.
These survey measures were correlated with unemployment and measures of
change in the employment structure. If the ecologists, and hypothesis one above,
are correct, one would expect that mood and life events would be related to the
economic measures. The analyses showed that the survey measures were strongly
related to the economic indices. Mood was best predicted by unemployment
rates, while the incidence of stressful life events was more strongly correlated
with change in employment structure. Further analysis (Catalano & Dooley,
1977b) of the Kansas City data showed that change in the basic industries was
more highly associated with stressful life events than was change in services in
industries. Disaggregating the population into demographic and socioeconomic
subgroups (Dooley & Catalano, in press) showed that low income families were
more adversely affected by economic change than were middle or high income
families. These findings are supportive of McKenzie's hypothesis that the incidence of adaptation demands among metropolitan populations would be greatest
when the economic base shifts in size or mix. Burgess' contention that the
impact of economic change would be most pronounced in those areas where low
income populations were predominant is also reinforced by the Kansas City
analyses.

A DISCIPLINARY MATRIX OF ABNORMAL PSYCHOLOGY

Kuhn suggests that the paradigms a given discipline has adhered to during its
development can be compared by using a "disciplinary matrix," as described in
the first chapter. Following the discussions of the paradigms dealt with in this
chapter, the elements of each were described. Those elements have been abbrevi-
ated and arrayed in the disciplinary matrix shown in Table 6-1. An "ecological
alternative" has been added to the matrix to emphasize the fact that, although
they were preoccupied with spatial distributions, the early ecologists had addressed themselves to behavioral problems. The ecological alternative is separated by double lines from the others to indicate that it was never adopted by
abnormal psychology as a paradigm.

EMERGENCE OF AN
ECOLOGICAL-LEARNING-SOCIAL SYNTHESIS?

There are several key commonalities among the ecological, learning, and social labeling paradigms which could lead to a synthesis and the emergence of a new, more holistic, paradigm. Such a synthesis would include at least the following general assumptions:

1. Man is capable of a wide range of behaviors, not all of which are societally acceptable.
2. The dominant society rewards some behaviors and punishes others, creating a conditioning system which shapes behavior into predictable patterns.
3. One of the negative reinforcers is the "abnormal behavior" label which can lead to remedial conditioning and behavior modification.
4. Application of the abnormal label will not be universally objective. The same behavior will be labeled differently depending on, among other variables, the tolerance of the audience, the manning of the setting, and the power of the person exhibiting the behavior.
5. The high risk periods, during which one is more likely to exhibit behavior labeled as abnormal, occur when moving from old role routines, moral systems, and behavior settings to new ones. How likely one is to make the transition without being labeled depends on his learning skills. "Learning skills" in this sense is not necessarily the same as "intelligence" as popularly understood.
6. The population at risk is likely to be largest when the economic system is in flux—that is, when the mix and/or size of the metropolitan area's division of labor is changing through increases or decreases in cash flows from basic industries.

A paradigm based on assumptions similar to those above would be greater than the sum of the learning, ecological, and social paradigms. It would necessitate abnormal psychology's assimilation of skills and concepts from economics and sociology. Such broadening is not easy, but the potential reward of more parsimonious explanations of abnormal behavior is inspiring many to make the effort.

Table 6-1. Disciplinary Matrix of the Study of Abnormal Behavior

Paradigms	Basic Assumptions	Analogies	Conventions	Exemplars
Organic	1. Abnormal behavior is symptomatic of some organic imbalance or impairment. 2. The classification of abnormal behaviors into syndromes will allow identification of organic causes. 3. Medical treatments for many of the organic cases will be found.	Behavior problems are like physical illness	1. Empirical epistemology 2. Quantitative description 3. Laboratory research 4. Individual is the unit of analysis	1. Kraepelin's *Clinical Psychology* 2. General Paresis research
Anxiety Defense	1. Abnormal behavior is the extension of defense mechanisms to the point of functional interference. 2. The psyche performs non-observable, subconscious functions to defend against anxiety. 3. Anxiety is psychic pain caused by the friction between instinctual drives and the social contract. 4. Treatment involves bringing the anxiety-causing problem to the conscious level for resolution or less debilitating defense.	Ego-Id-Superego construct	1. Intuitive epistemology 2. Qualitative description 3. Case study 4. Individual is unit of analysis.	Freud's *The Ego and the Id, Psychopathology and Everyday Life, Introductory Lectures on Psychoanalysis*
Ecological Alternative	1. Abnormal behavior is behavior perceived as incongruous with role, laws or mores, or place. 2. The chances of one's behavior being perceived as abnormal increase when role changes, moral reasoning changes, or norms clash, or place changes. 3. The population experiencing changes is largest when economic base is changing in size or character.	The metropolis or human community is like the natural biome	1. Empirical epistemology 2. Quantitative description 3. Naturalistic research 4. Community is unit of analysis.	1. McKenzie's "Ecological Approach to the Study of Human Community", 2. Dunham's "The Ecology of Functional Psychoses in Chicago"

Learning Paradigm	1. Abnormal behavior is either maladaptive response to stimuli, or behavior not societally sanctioned as a means to an end. 2. Maladaptive responses to stimuli are learned through respondent conditioning. 3. Behavior not societally sanctioned as a means to an end is a product of incomplete or ineffective operant conditioning. 4. Maladaptive or non-sanctioned behavior are themselves problems, not symptoms of a deeper disorder. 5. Abnormal behavior can be extinguished through respondent and operant conditioning.	The process leading to one's behaving abnormally is like his learning to do anything	1. Empirical epistemology 2. Quantitative description 3. Laboratory research 4. Individual is unit of analysis	1. Watson and Raynor's conditioning experiment 2. Skinner's *Science and Human Behavior*
Social Paradigm	1. Abnormal behavior is the breaking of residual rules detected by those with low tolerance and power to label. 2. Residual rule breaking is usually part of a strategy to relieve anxiety over problems in living. 3. The system of professional treatment for those who break residual rules actually conditions them to act abnormally. 4. Decreasing abnormal behavior means societal reform and increased tolerance.	1. The process leading to one's being labeled abnormal is like audience reaction 2. Once labeled, the treatment process leads to a life situation like a deviant career	1. Empirical epistemology 2. Qualitative description 3. Naturalistic research 4. Community is level of analysis	1. Goffman's *Asylums* 2. Scheff's *Being Mentally Ill: A Sociological Theory* 3. Sarbin's "Schizophrenic thinking: A role theoretic analysis"

7 Paradigm Succession in the Study of Criminal Behavior

Criminal behavior is often considered a subset of abnormal behavior and has been studied through a paradigm succession similar to that described in the previous chapter. Criminology's first paradigm, the moral atavism paradigm, clearly reflects the nineteenth century preoccupation with physiological causation. Unlike abnormal psychology's organic paradigm, however, the assumptions of the moral atavism paradigm were based more on popular interpretations of natural selection than on the logic of bacteriological research. In fact, the research which ended the moral atavism paradigm's dominance of criminology was based on experimental logic typical of bacteriology.

Criminology's second paradigm is essentially the Freudian based anxiety defense paradigm described in the previous chapter. The student, however, should give special attention to the reasoning by which Freud's work was extended to criminal behavior. This reasoning is still much with us in the form of the frustrated aspiration paradigm.

Of the three disciplines dealt with in this volume—public health, abnormal psychology, and criminology—the last has been the most influenced by the Chicago School. The human ecologists saw crime as precipitated by three circumstances: *norm clash*, or the branding of newly arrived migrants as criminal because their moral codes were different than the majority's; *anomie*, or the condition of normlessness experienced by migrants who either had not internalized the social contract or who were confused by the apparent relativity of the many moral codes exhibited in diverse urban populations; and *weakened dedication to the social contract* caused by unrewarded compliance and increased moral dilemmas common in unstable economies.

These three circumstances might have explained an increase in crime in communities experiencing rapid growth or decline in economic base, but the early ecologists had no way to explain the consistently high crime rates in well-defined areas of cities in times of relative economic stability. Their students, however, especially Thrasher, offered theories to explain the transmission of crime. These included explanations eventually expanded upon by Sutherland to become the influential theory of "differential association."

Students should note that the Chicago School did *not* attribute the high rates of crime in the zone in transition to physical conditions such as poor housing or high density. Much of the reason for criminology's rejection of ecological analysis was based on the incorrect assumption that the Chicago School claimed physical conditions "disorganized" people, leaving them without moral reasoning. This misunderstanding was reinforced, as will be discussed, by the work of Shaw and McKay who were associated with the Chicago School.

Another aspect of this chapter which should be noted is the suggested synthesis of the "learning" and the ecological perspectives on crime. The suggestion that this synthesis may predict fluctuations in the crime rate over time is especially important. The fact that the ecological perspective ties criminal behavior to economic change should also be noted. This connection is vital to one of the central themes of this book—that much health and behavioral disorder can be viewed as the external cost of ill-informed decisions.

Before describing the preparadigmatic phase of criminology, the concept of criminal behavior must be clarified. All organized societies are based on an implicit understanding of the social contract. In exchange for the increased security made possible by participation in the division of labor, each participant is expected to behave in a way nonthreatening to, if not supportive of, the trophic organization. Some behaviors (e.g., paying taxes or debts) are seen as so necessary to the orderly functioning of the system of collection, production, and distribution that failure to perform them is punished by decreased security, while others (e.g., theft or murder) are seen as so threatening that they are proscribed under threat of decreased security. The enforcement of the contract requires an institution, the state, with the power to monitor behavior and to punish those who do not comply. The actions of this institution are legitimate when taken in behalf of the general welfare and when the list of expected and proscribed behaviors is agreed upon by a majority of the participants in the community. This "list" usually takes the form of statutes and codes which include a description of the punishment likely to be incurred by violation.

In the broadest sense, criminal behavior refers to avoiding the expected, or exhibiting the proscribed, behaviors. As will become obvious as the chapter progresses, however, the subject matter studied by classical and contemporary criminologists is usually more narrowly defined. Criminology is concerned with behavior proscribed by a subset of public statutes referred to as "criminal" as opposed to "civil" law. While the distinction between criminal and civil wrongs is often obtuse, it is usually based on the seriousness of the threat to the division of labor. In general, civil law deals with settling disputes between two individuals, one of whom has sought the intervention of the state. Civil trials bear such titles as "Smith v. Jones" and their outcomes usually involve decisions on the payment of damages. Criminal law deals with offenses threatening enough to the division of labor that society is seen as offended as much as the victim. In criminal trials the state represents the general welfare and titles such as "The People v. Jones" are used. The outcomes of criminal trials involve deciding if the accused avoided or committed an expected or proscribed act, and, if so, setting the punishment to be administered by the state. Some acts or their avoidance are both criminally proscribed and entitle the victim to seek damages under civil law. Beating someone, for example, can lead to criminal punishment for assault and to being sued in civil court for the damage inflicted on the victim.

One other point deserves mention before proceeding to the historical development of criminology. While the difficult task of collecting reliable data describing the phenomenon being studied is prerequisite to all science, the controversial nature of criminology's subject matter has led to its findings being carefully scrutinized to detect measurement errors. While this chapter will minimize the discussion of methodological issues, their importance should not be underestimated. Very little, for example, can be concluded concerning the actual amount of criminal behavior exhibited by a community, since most studies use *reported* crime. Such data include police and citizen reports based on observations and discretionary judgments never tested in court. Acts not reported to authorities by witnesses, if any, or victims are excluded. It should also be noted that only a minority of the crimes committed are "solved" in the sense that the guilty individuals are apprehended and convicted. This means that great care must be taken in characterizing the criminal population based on its subset in jail. There is good reason to suspect that the jailed sample is not representative of those who violate criminal law.

CRIMINOLOGY'S PREPARADIGMATIC PHASE

Because crime has been a problem for all organized societies, it has been the subject of considerable discourse. Much of the recorded comment on the causes of crime parallels that on abnormal behavior in general. The Greeks and Romans viewed some criminal behavior as predictable from physical characteristics as well as from social conditions. This early enlightenment apparently did not influence the intellectuals of the Dark Ages, when criminal behavior was attributed to moral inferiority or demonic possession.

Beginning in the sixteenth century, attempts to scientifically explain crime became more common. These attempts fell into two traditions, the biological and social. The more important works of each tradition will be described briefly for they presaged two of the more influential of criminology's modern paradigms, the moral atavism and the ecological paradigms.

The Biological Tradition

Physiognomy, the early belief that anatomical characteristics of an individual were predictive of his personality, is best represented by the work of J. Baptiste de la Porte (1535-1615). Porte studied the cadavers of convicts in the expectation that they would measurably differ from those of noncriminals. He believed the differences would define a population which contributed more than its proportional share to the incidence of criminal behavior. This population at risk could not be cognitively dissuaded from criminal behavior for its inclination to such acts was physically innate. Based on his observations, Porte (1586) claimed the criminally inclined population was characterized by small ears and nose, thickened open lips, bushy eyebrows, shifty eyes, and long thin fingers.

Physiognomy continued to be popular among those interested in the scientific explanation of personality. Lavater (1741-1801) published his *Physiognomical Fragments* in 1775, and added considerable impetus to the search for anatomical predictors. He focused attention on facial characteristics: beard, chin shape, eyes, and nose. He anticipated the advent of phrenology, the study of cranial characteristics to predict personality.

The first phrenologist was Franz Gall (1758-1828), an anatomist who spent considerable time measuring and categorizing the crania of prison and asylum inmates. While principally interested in the functions of the brain, Gall insisted that personality characteristics could be predicted from bumps and irregularities of the skull. His works, especially *On the Functions of the Brain* (1825), were widely disseminated and attracted several disciples, the most influential of whom was Johann Spurzheim (1770-1853), who lectured extensively in Europe and America. Through Spurzheim's efforts phrenology gained a wide following on both continents. In Europe Carus (1840) and Lauvergne (1841) advocated the use of phrenological analysis to predict criminality, while Caldwell (1824) published a popular phrenology text in America.

While phrenology presaged modern criminology's first paradigm, the most immediate precipitator was Benoit Morel's (1809-1873) theory of "degeneracy" which first appeared in 1857. Morel posited that man's physical characteristics, intelligence, and moral sensitivity were normally distributed. These distributions, supposedly, resulted primarily from genetic diversity; but deviations from the norm, in the case of intelligence and moral sensitivity, could be increased through environmental factors such as the presence or lack of education and moral training. The negative extremes of the distributions of intelligence and moral sensitivity were, according to Morel, populated by genetically inferior individuals unredeemed or made more deviant by environmental factors. Morel referred to this population as "degenerate" based on their position at the extreme of the distribution where the measured characteristics decrease rapidly or "degenerate." Morel further claimed that while moral degeneracy was primarily genetic, it was highly associated with physical degeneracy. This belief led him to posit that the population of physically degenerate individuals would produce more than its proportional share of criminals.

Morel's tenets influenced Cesare Lombroso who was to cast criminology's first paradigm by synthesizing the degeneracy theory with popular versions of Darwin's theory of natural selection. Before turning to the Lombrosian, or "moral atavism" paradigm, another important preparadigmatic tradition was the precursor of the Chicago School's application of ecological analyses to criminal behavior.

The Social Tradition

During the first half of the nineteenth century several researchers were attempting to identify the causes of criminal behavior using techniques very different from those associated with the physiognomists and phrenologists. These men had access to data describing the incidence of crime and other characteristics of nation states and communities. Using these data they attempted to test several popular beliefs about the causes of crime.

The first of these researchers was a French bureaucrat, A.M. Guerry, who in 1829 became the official collector of judicial statistics for the City of Paris. In this capacity, Guerry was constantly reviewing government data describing many aspects of French life measured by government statistics. He noticed that the data he reviewed did not appear to substantiate three of the more commonly cited causes of crime: poverty, illiteracy, and high density. To determine if there was a measurable relationship among these variables, Guerry divided France into five areas which were aggregates of departments (roughly the equivalent to American counties). Data describing the five areas' crime rates, demographic characteristics, climate, education levels, wealth, and degree of urbanism were collected; and for each characteristic a map of France was prepared comparing the area's rates by degrees of shading. By comparing these maps, Guerry was able to graphically test the hypothesized relationship between, for example, education and crime. Guerry reported that there did not appear to be a consistent relationship between poverty, illiteracy, or high density and crime. Some of the poorest districts, for example, had the lowest crime rates, leading Guerry to note that there must be something worth stealing before thieves will risk being caught. Those areas with a juxtaposition of rich and poor would, he hypothesized, have more crime than either those with only the wealthy or the poor. Based on his data, he also concluded that a more educated population did not mean an area would have low crime rates. The areas with more educated populations had, in fact, higher crime rates. Density, moreover, did not appear to be strongly related to crime. While the department with the largest cities did have the highest crime rates, many with large cities had rates lower than those with predominantly rural populations.

While Guerry's analyses were methodologically crude by modern standards, they were seminal for several reasons. The most important of these was his use of data describing communities rather than individuals. By using the group as the unit of analysis, Guerry implied that the causes of crime were environmental, or social, as well as inherent in the psycho-biological makeup of individuals. He was attempting to identify the conditions under which a population could be expected to exhibit relatively greater or lesser rates of criminal behavior. The fact that he used maps to facilitate his correlation of measured variables reinforces the categorizing of Guerry's work as antecedent to the Chicago School.

Another of the nineteenth century researchers attempting to identify the environmental determinants of criminal behavior was Englishman Henry Mayhew, whose work was precocious both in its methods and its conclusions. Mayhew (1812-1887) was a man of letters whose diverse endeavors included playwriting, reporting, and editing of the influential journal of satire, *Punch*. While a journalist, Mayhew became interested in the plight of London's poor, and over the period 1851 to 1865 published a series of articles and volumes describing the life of the marginal classes. Included in these were two volumes, *The Criminal Prisons of London* (1862) and *London labour and The London Poor* (1864), which, among other topics, were concerned with crime in England. While Mayhew based these works on several sources, including his countless interviews with prisoners and criminals, it was his correlation of several characteristics of geographic areas which makes his conclusions compelling.

As had Guerry, Mayhew grew increasingly skeptical of the popularly accepted assertions that poverty, illiteracy, density, or moral degeneracy caused crime. To test these relationships, he collected the following data for the years 1841-1850 for each of the counties of England and Wales:

1. population density,
2. overall crime rate,
3. illiteracy rate,
4. size and age of the female population,
5. number of marriages below age of legal independence,
6. number of illegitimate children,
7. committals for rape,
8. committals for "carnally abusing girls,"
9. committals for operating brothels,
10. concealments of birth,
11. attempts at abortion,

12. assaults,
13. committals for bigamy,
14. committals for kidnapping,
15. committals for prostitution.

Using these data, Mayhew computed as many rates as possible, and depicted the variations among counties on maps by shading each county according to the interval of rates into which it fell. A map was prepared for each rated variable allowing the rough correlations of rates across counties. Based on this carto-graphic technique, and on a ranking of the counties for each variable, Mayhew concluded that on the county level, one could not predict the criminality of the population knowing its density, rate of illiteracy, or wealth.

Mayhew did notice, however, that the counties with the largest cities had the highest rates of many types of crime. Attempting to explain this phenomenon, he collected the same data listed above for each of the police districts of London. Using the mapping and ranking techniques, Mayhew replicated his correlations and found the following:

1. Crime was not evenly distributed throughout the city.
2. While high crime areas were usually dense, few dense areas were high crime areas.
3. While high crime areas were usually poor, not all poor areas were high crime areas.
4. While high crime areas had high illiteracy rates, not all areas with high il-literacy rates were high crime areas.
5. Not all areas characterized by high density, poverty, and illiteracy had high crime rates.
6. Areas of high crime rates tended to have had a history of high crime rates, even though the population there may have changed.

Based on these findings, on visits to the high crime areas, and on interviews with inmates and criminals, Mayhew concluded that poverty, density, illiteracy, and degeneracy did not cause crime. Crime, he claimed, was a business—a means to survival emerging from need and opportunity. The criminal learned his trade the same way a craftsman learned his, by being born into a family of thieves, or by being exposed to the "trade" early in life. Through association with crimi-nals, the child learned criminal skills and pursued the behavior as a means of survival. Mayhew (1862, p. 413) wrote:

Crime, we repeat, is an effect with which the shape of the head and the form of the features appear to have no connection whatever . . . the great mass of crime in this country is committed by those who have been bred and born to the business, and who make a regular trade of it, living as systematically by robbery or cheating as others do by commerce or the exercise of intellectual or manual labour.

Mayhew observed that the children of the poor and illiterate will, because of the economic forces described in Chapter 3, live in dense areas and will need to find some role in the division of labor. In those poor, dense areas with criminal traditions, the child will come to view criminal behavior as a viable trophic role, while another poor child in an equally dense area without such traditions will not have as immediate an opportunity to learn the "trade." The result, Mayhew claimed, is that some areas characterized by poverty, illiteracy, and density will have high juvenile offender rates, while others will not. These juvenile offenders mature into professional criminals as they devote time and practice to developing their skill. Those areas with high juvenile offender rates are, therefore, the areas with high adult crime rates.

Mayhew's view that crime is essentially learned behavior likely to occur more frequently among a population exposed to a criminal tradition was to be reformulated and expanded in the twentieth century. Before criminology returned to the social tradition's emphasis on environmental variables, however, it progressed through two paradigms which riveted the discipline's attention on the individual as unit of analysis. These were the moral atavism and anxiety defense paradigms.

THE MORAL ATAVISM PARADIGM

The last quarter of the nineteenth century was marked by the pervasiveness of Darwinism. While Darwin's impact on modern Western thought was immense and complex, two concepts often attributed to him can be cited as seminal to criminology's first modern paradigm. The first of these is the theory of "evolution," or the popular understanding of the process of natural selection. Natural selection, described in more detail in Chapter 2, is the process by which the mean physical characteristics of a geographically defined population change, as environmental factors affect the gene pool. The genetically controlled characteristics best suited to a particular environment will become the mean for the population it supports. The popularized version of natural selection held that a species slowly perfects its physical qualities as the weaker, inferior individuals die out, and their representation in the gene pool is reduced. The assumptions that evolution means progress, and that civilization grows more perfect as man evolves, underlie the theories referred to as "social Darwinism." Figure 7-1 depicts the social Darwinists' understanding of evolution. At time two, the mean perfection has increased as has that of the advanced and the retarded extremes.

A corollary to the theory of evolution was that individuals would be born whose qualities would be more typical of a much earlier time period. These would fall in the extreme end of the retarded side of the distribution. This condition, referred to as "atavism," supposedly accounted for persons born with webbing between toes or fingers or with scaly skin. Physical atavism became a popular explanation for many birth defects and physical anomalies considered repugnant or undesirable. Darwin himself has been quoted as saying (1882, p. 137):

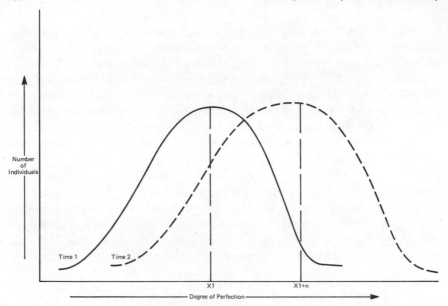

Fig. 7-1. Social Darwinist understanding of "evolution."

With mankind some of the worst dispositions which occasionally without any assignable cause make their appearances in families, may perhaps be reversions to a savage state, from which we are not removed by very many generations.

In the context of this popularized theory of evolution, Morel's theory of moral degeneracy, predictable from physical characteristics, assumed a more credible scientific stature. The most influential of those who synthesized the theories of atavism and degeneracy was the Italian physician, Cesare Lombroso, often referred to as the father of modern criminology.

The Emergence of Criminology's First Paradigm

Cesare Lombroso began his medical training in 1852 at age 18, and soon distinguished himself as an outstanding scholar as well as surgeon. It was, in fact, his dissertation research on cretinism, published in 1859, which led to Lombroso's lifelong preoccupation with the biological basis of human behavior. This interest was whetted by his experience as an army physician (1859-1862), during which Lombroso devised an anatomical measurement and classification system. He used this system in an attempt to correlate the physical characteristics of 3,000 soldiers with their home region in Italy. Lombroso lost interest in the relationship between physique and place of origin as he detected what he considered a significant relationship between anatomical characteristics and behavior. This apparent correlation led to his work in a mental institution, where he became convinced that organic defects and imbalances produced abnormal behavior.

During the decade 1863-73, Lombroso continued his research in insane asylums compiling data on the organic bases for behavioral problems such as cretinism and pellagra. In the last half of this decade of research, Lombroso turned his attention to the criminally insane. One investigation involved an autopsy on a well-known outlaw Lombroso had observed prior to death. He found the criminal's brain marked by depressions and anomalies more characteristic of lower forms of animals than of man. Describing the moment of his discovery, Lombroso (Ferrero, 1911, p. xxii) wrote:

> At the sight of that skull, I seemed to see all of a sudden, lighted up as on a vast plain under a flaming sky, the problem of the nature of the criminal—an atavistic being who reproduces in his person the ferocious instincts of primitive humanity and the inferior animals. Thus were explained anatomically the enormous jaws, high cheekbones, prominent superciliary arches, solitary lines in the palms, extreme size of the orbits, handle-shaped or sessile ears found in criminals, savages and apes, insensibility to pain, extremely acute sight, tatooing, excessive idleness, love of orgies, and the desire not only to extinguish life in the victim, but to mutilate the corpse, tear its flesh and drink its blood.

Lombroso believed that society's behavioral expectations became increasingly sophisticated as man's intellectual capacity evolved and society became more complex. The ability to internalize these expectations and to utilize them in moral reasoning required cognitive apparatus evolved to a level approaching the norm of the dominant society. Atavism of the cognitive apparatus, therefore, increased its victim's chances of exhibiting proscribed behavior. Most importantly, Lombroso believed that cognitive atavism and collateral moral insensitivity were highly associated with physical atavism.

The Normal Science Phase of the Moral Atavism Paradigm

The work which most compellingly presented Lombroso's tenets was *The Criminal Man*, which appeared in 1876. *Criminal Man* explained Lombroso's version of moral atavism and its indication by physical stigmata. These indicators included (Ferrero, 1911, p. 10):

> ... deviation in head size and shape from the type common to the race and region from which the criminal came; asymmetry of the face, excessive dimensions of the jaw and cheekbones, eye defects and peculiarities, ears of unusual size or occasionally very small, or standing out from the head as do those of the chimpanzee; nose twisted, upturned, or flattened in thieves, or aquiline or beaklike in murders, or with a tip rising like a beak from swollen nostrils; lips fleshy, swollen, and protruding; pouches in the cheek like those of some animals; peculiarities of the palate, such as large central ridge, a series of cavities and protuberances such as are found in some reptiles, and cleft palate; abnormal dentition; chin receding, or excessively long or

short and flat, as in apes; abundance, variety, and precocity of wrinkles, anomalies of the hair, marked by characteristics of hair of the opposite sex; defects of the thorax, such as too many or too few ribs, or supernumerary nipples; inversion of sex characteristics in the pelvic organs; excessive length of arms; supernumerary fingers and toes; imbalance of the hemispheres of the brain (asymmetry of cranium).

Lombroso knew that his conclusions would be controversial and require extensive substantiation in the form of empirical data. While the first edition of *Criminal Man* cited the findings of his measurement and observation of numerous criminals, each of the succeeding four editions included additional measurements made by Lombroso and his disciples. The result was that the fifth and last edition (1897) was nearly nine times larger than the first (250 pages).

Lombroso attracted several followers from Europe and America who helped make his moral atavism paradigm dominant at the turn of the century. Americans who accepted Lombroso's tenets, or variants of them, included criminologists Auguste Drahms (1900), Arthur McDonald (1893), William Noyes (1888), James Weir (1894), and Hamilton Wey (1890). While the most ardent of Lombroso's disciples included a German (Kurella, 1910) and several Dutch criminologists, the great majority were Italians. The Italian, or Positive, School of Criminology, which continues to be preoccupied with morphological correlates of behavior, included such early Lombrosians as Morselli (1908), Ottolenghi (1932), Pende (1928), Vidoni (1923), and others who began their careers by collecting measurements of criminals to support their mentor's assertions.

The normal science stage of the moral atavism paradigm lasted from approximately 1890 to 1913. While several criticisms of Lombroso's conclusions were published during this period, the crisis stage was not precipitated until the appearance of Goring's (1913) *The English Convict*, which will be described shortly.

The Elements of the Moral Atavism Paradigm

It is no coincidence that criminology's moral atavism paradigm and the organic paradigm of abnormal psychology emerged simultaneously. The last half of the nineteenth century was marked by the conviction among intellectuals that the scientific method and Darwinian perspective would answer the profound questions concerning man's nature and behavior. Careful measurement, recording, and organization of empirical facts were seen as the basis of scientific progress. Intuition and normative preconceptions were rejected as sophistry and as incompatible with science. This often naive faith in the power of man's intellect and his ability to be objective in his measurement was the common bond among the social and natural sciences as pursued at the turn of the century. This faith, or Positivism, as it is usually referred to, accounts for the similarities among the elements of the late nineteenth century paradigms described in this and preceding chapters. The elements of the moral atavism paradigm are as follows:

I. *Basic Assumptions.*

The assumptions underlying the moral atavism paradigm arise from the social Darwinist belief that man is evolving to a more perfect physical and moral state. The two principal assumptions the paradigm draws from Darwinism are:

A. Criminal behavior is a product of moral insensitivity caused by atavistic cognitive apparatus.

B. Atavism is detectable from measurable physical characteristics.

II. *Analogies.*

Drawing from social Darwinism, and from Morel in particular, the moral atavism paradigm explicitly analogizes:

A. The assumed evolutionary progress of the physical organism to the development of moral sensitivity. Man's progress as a moral organism is analogous to the process of physical evolution.

B. The phenomenon of physical atavism to the moral condition of the criminal.

III. *Conventions.*

The conventions of the moral atavism paradigm reflect the positivist commitment to empiricism. These conventions are:

A. Empirical Epistemology. Lombroso and his followers were convinced that measurable facts were the only data appropriate to science.

B. Quantitative Description. While not trained as statisticians, Lombroso and his early disciples amassed, and cited massive amounts of, quantitative data describing the physical appearance of criminals. It is ironic that Lombroso's work was eventually discredited due to its crude measurement techniques and invalid inferences drawn from the collected data.

C. Laboratory Research. The search for measurable anatomical correlates to criminal behavior led Lombroso to utilize a series of data-collection techniques ranging from autopsy to production-line-like measurement of prisoners. All assumed that the crucial data was not affected by removing the subject from his or her environmental setting, and that the closer the measurements came to being laboratory controlled, the more reliable the data would be.

D. The Individual as Unit of Analysis. While Lombroso was far too intelligent to assert that social factors played no role in precipitating criminal behavior, he was convinced that biological factors were more causal. The result was the inevitable emphasis on the individual subject as the unit of analysis.

IV. *Exemplar.*

Lombroso's *The Criminal Man* (1876) is clearly the exemplar of the moral atavism paradigm. The work's metamorphosis from a 250 page first edition to a nearly 2,000 page fifth edition, and its translation in several languages reflect its impact on criminology in particular and behavioral science in general.

The Crisis Stage of the Moral Atavism Paradigm

Lombroso and his early disciples claimed that they had proven the association between physical characteristics and criminal behavior through their collection of massive amounts of data describing the physical attributes of criminals. The value of Lombroso's data as proof depends on four conditions. First, the convict population whose characteristics were measured must have been a representative sample of the criminal population. If, for example, only lame criminals were caught because the police could easily catch them, it would be absurd to conclude all criminals were lame. Societal attitudes toward the poor and physically stigmatized, as well as the effectiveness of the police, can make the convict population less than representative of the criminal population.

Assuming the convict population was representative of the criminal population, a second prerequisite would be that the measurement of the convict's physical characteristics was reliable. What one of Lombroso's assistants considered an asymmetrical face or thickened lip must have been considered asymmetrical or thickened by all those whose findings were used as supporting data.

If the data describing the convict population was representative and reliable, a third condition would be that the same measurements be made of a noncriminal population to determine that any characteristics found common to the convicts were not common to the general population. If 99 percent of Italian convicts were found to have brown eyes, very little could be concluded if 99 percent of all Italians had brown eyes.

A fourth prerequisite necessary to accepting Lombroso's data as proof would be the determination that differences between the convict population and the noncriminal population were statistically significant.

While Lombroso's findings were criticized for being insufficient on all four prerequisites, the lack of reliable measurements and adequate control groups were considered the greatest weaknesses. Much of the data Lombroso cited was collected by students and disciples whose techniques were highly subjective and never checked for reliability. While Lombroso understood the need for control groups to validate his findings, none was ever formally established and measured.

Both his critics and disciples urged Lombroso's work be replicated with reliable measures and control groups to determine once and for all whether convicts had stigma which differentiated them from the noncriminal population. Charles Goring, an English doctor and psychiatrist, aided by the influential statistician Karl Pearson, undertook the challenge to test Lombroso's atavism hypothesis. In a study begun at the turn of the century, Goring devised standardized measures for 37 physical traits, and applied the measures to 3,000 convicts and an equivalent control group of noncriminals. The results of his study were published in 1913 under the title *The English Convict*. Goring concluded that Lombroso's hypothesis was not supported by the data describing the convicts and control group. While not rejecting the influence of genetic factors on behavior, Goring demonstrated that the measurements cited by Lombroso as predictive of criminality did not discriminate between the convict and non-criminal population.

The appearance of *The English Convict* precipitated the crisis phase of the moral atavism paradigm. The validity of Lombroso's massive data had been discredited and the atavism hypothesis, by virtue of its inherent dependence on empirical verification, could not stand.

The assumption of an individual defect which precluded normal moral development, however, found its way into criminology's second paradigm. In its new form, the defect assumption was much more difficult to test, for it was attributed to the unmeasurable unconscious.

APPLYING THE ANXIETY-DEFENSE PARADIGM TO CRIMINAL BEHAVIOR

As Goring's work began to erode the influence of the moral atavism paradigm, the Freudian explanation of human behavior became increasingly popular among the intellectuals of the Western world. Criminology's first crisis phase was, as a result, short lived. The ego-id-superego model quickly filled the vacuum left by the discrediting of Lombroso's tenets.

The Freudian-Based Models of Criminal Behavior

The anxiety-defense paradigm assumed that psychic functions include unconscious processes which significantly affect behavior. These processes involve the conscious self's, or ego's, attempt to balance the instinctual selfish demands of the id against the super ego, or internalized behavior expectations of organized society. The ego's concern over adapting to real external demands, checking the drives of the id, and living up to the expectations of the superego, takes the form of anxiety which Freud described as "psychic pain." The ego attempts to protect itself against this pain through defense mechanisms initiated in the unconscious. These mechanisms—including repression, reaction formation, projection, denial, and regression—are used by everyone to minimize anxiety, but can be exaggerated to the point of interference with the individual's social and occupational functioning. When defense mechanisms become dysfunctional or maladaptive, they are considered abnormal behavior. A subset of abnormal behavior would, of course, be that which renders the exhibitor liable to criminal prosecution.

Freud's explanation of abnormal behavior appealed to criminologists, who had just been disillusioned by the empirical discrediting of Lombroso's work, principally because the anxiety defense paradigm maintained the discipline's focus on defects in the individual as the cause of criminality. The concept of an atavistic defect in organic cognitive apparatus, which precluded moral reasoning, was replaced by the claim of imbalance among unconscious, immeasurable, psychic forces which led to criminal behavior through both over- and under-development of moral reasoning.

The anxiety-defense explanation of crime emerged between 1910 and 1930, or nearly simultaneously with similar explanations of abnormal behavior in general. While the anxiety-defense paradigm subsumes crime under abnormal behavior, further refinement by criminologists has led to several psychodynamic explanations of criminal behavior (Feldman, 1964).

The earliest variant of the anxiety defense paradigm devised specifically for criminal behavior claimed that neurotic anxiety, or guilt, drove certain individuals to commit acts which would bring them punishment (Alexander & Staub, 1931). More specifically, this early explanation claimed that persons with overdeveloped superegos felt extreme anxiety in the form of guilt over their natural Oedipal and Electra desires to have intercourse with their parents. In order to relieve this guilt, such individuals seek punishment by engaging in anti-social behavior which may include criminally proscribed acts.

Another of the earlier uses of Freudian theory to explain crime as a subset of abnormal behavior utilized the defense mechanism of reaction formation. Reaction formation involves overcompensating for a weakness one unconsciously recognizes in his ability to cope with real, neurotic, or moral anxiety. In the example cited earlier, a woman relieved moral anxiety over her promiscuous desires by expressing extreme disgust at any suggestion of sexual activity, or by becoming a nun. The reaction formation explanation of crime assumes that everyone desires to achieve the material success and individual recognition valued by industrial societies. Not everyone, however, has the skills to achieve this success because industrial societies inherently become increasingly competitive. The less capable and aggressive individuals intuit their inability to achieve success, and experience reality anxiety, which is relieved by rejecting societal norms and expectations, and behaving in a fashion non-supportive of, or threatening to, the division of labor. When this anti-social, reaction-formation based behavior takes the form of criminally proscribed acts, the individual becomes criminal as well as abnormal (Alexander & Healy, 1935).

A third neo-Freudian explanation of criminal behavior focused on the influence of family interaction on ego development. Healy and Bronner (1936) studied the family life of 105 delinquent children and their nondelinquent siblings to determine if parent-related variables were correlated with delinquency. They concluded that the delinquent children had not received sufficient parental attention in the form of recognition of individuality, encouragement of self-assertion, or reinforcement of a sense of adequacy. The child, supposedly, experiences anxiety over his lack of identity and functional status, and alleviates this by participation in juvenile gangs, which call upon each member to establish some role identity, and which reward performance with status. When the activities of such gangs involve illegal pursuits, the participants are likely to be labeled criminal.

Another Freudian based explanation of criminal behavior assumes that some individuals never develop superegos because of defective socialization (Friedlander, 1947). Without an internalized dedication to the behavioral expectations of society, individuals are, supposedly, unable to control their selfish id impulses. They seek immediate gratification and cannot discipline their pursuit of pleasure or their avoidance of responsibility. Given such personality characteristics they inevitably exhibit anti-social behavior which may include crime. The defective socialization can be attributed to lack of parental interest in the child's moral learning or to the parents' lack of moral reasoning.

Each of the above criminological variants of the basic Freudian model is open to criticism by empiricists for being untestable. If one cannot describe or measure the unconscious processes underlying the hypothesis, it cannot be proven true or false. Before dealing with the criticism of criminology's use of the anxiety defense paradigm, and the crisis stage such criticism precipitated, the paradigm's elements will be described below.

The Elements of the Criminal Behavior Variant
of the Anxiety-Defense Paradigm

I. *Basic Assumptions.*

Given their common bases in Freudian thought, the elements of the criminological and psychological versions of the anxiety-defense paradigm are very similar. The difference is criminology's refinement of Freud's basic assumptions to deal specifically with criminal behavior. The assumptions are as follows:

A. Criminal behavior is the use of legally proscribed acts as defense mechanisms against anxiety. The four psychic conditions most commonly cited as leading to criminal defense mechanisms are:

1. Neurotic anxiety resulting from incestuous desires relieved by punishment incurred by committing criminal acts.

2. Reality anxiety resulting from parental neglect relieved by participation in juvenile gangs.

3. Reality anxiety resulting from competitive inadequacy relieved by anti-social reaction formation.

4. Weak superego resulting from ineffective socialization leading to indulgence of criminal id drives.

B. The processes by which anxiety is generated and defense mechanisms initiated are unconscious, making quantitative description and measurement impossible.

II. *Analogies.*

As in the anxiety defense paradigm the principal pedagogical model is the ego-id-superego construct. Criminologists espousing the psychodynamic paradigm accept the Freudian tenet that the ego, id, and superego cannot be observed, and must be inferred from the subject's descriptions of images, feelings, fantasies, remembrances, and dreams.

III. *Conventions.*

Criminologists accepting the anxiety-defense paradigm subscribe to the same conventions adhered to by psychologists utilizing Freudian theory to explain abnormal behavior. These are:

A. Intuitive Epistemology. All Freudian models assume that important cognitive functions are unconscious and unobservable. Gathering information describing these unconscious functions requires an inferential skill which eschews empirical measurement.

B. Qualitative Description. Given their dependence on intuitive epistemology, the Freudian-based criminologists must resort to qualitative description of cognitive processes. It should be noted that in attempting to demonstrate significant differences between groups whose psyches have been characterized intuitively and qualitatively, several Freudian researchers have used quantitative statistical tests. The Healy and Bronner study cited earlier, for example, used control groups and significance tests to support its findings. Such quantitative tests have been discounted by empiricists, since the data being tested were collected in a subjective, often irreplicable, manner.

C. Laboratory Research. The case study constructed from information collected in therapy sessions or from testing based on indirect measures of assumed unconscious processes is the Freudian's principal research technique. While more recent variations on the Freudian model have come to attribute more importance to environmental factors, naturalistic observation of the individual is not considered essential to reliable basic research.

D. The Individual as the Unit of Analysis. All Freudians assume that the most parsimonious explanations of why some individuals are criminals and others are not will be based on data describing individuals, not groups.

IV. *Exemplars.*

Freud's works, especially *The Psychopathology of Everyday Life* (1901) and *The Ego and the Id* (1923), are the primary exemplars of the anxiety-defense paradigm as applied to criminal behavior. The works which relate Freudian principles explicitly to crime are those cited in the discussion of the four Freudian based explanations of crime. These include Alexander and Staub, *The Criminal, The Judge, and the Public* (1931); Alexander and Healy, *The Roots of Crime* (1935); Healy and Bronner, *New Light on Delinquency* (1936); and Friedlander, *The Psychoanalytical Approach to Juvenile Delinquency* (1947).

The Crisis Stage of the Anxiety-Defense Paradigm

While the intuitive, qualitative nature of the anxiety-defense paradigm was a welcomed contrast to the naive positivism of its predecessor, the Freudian-based assumption that behavior reflects the interaction of immeasurable forces eventually led to the paradigm's rejection by many criminologists. Intuitive epistemology reduces the reliability of data to a level which precludes the logical testing necessary to establish the validity of explanations. Without careful posing and testing of successive explanations, knowledge in the scientific sense does not grow. Acutely aware of this fact, criminologists who considered their discipline a science more than an association of therapists criticized the Freudian-based models described above. These criticisms are based on the inability of Freudian theorists to demonstrate any measurable psychic difference between the criminal and noncriminal populations (Bromberg & Thompson, 1937; Schuessler & Cressey, 1950).

CRIMINOLOGY'S USE OF THE ECOLOGICAL PARADIGM

During the period of the anxiety-defense paradigm's greatest influence, students of the Chicago School began their ecological analyses of crime. Their efforts began with great promise, but as with the ecological analyses of behavioral problems in general, ended in disappointment due to preoccupation with spatial distributions.

Antecedents to Criminology's Use of the Ecological Paradigm
While the work of Guerry and Mayhew described earlier anticipated the Chicago School's use of ecological concepts to analyze criminal behavior, the most immediate precipitator was Thomas and Znaniecki's *The Polish Peasant in Europe and America* (1920). This two-volume work was primarily concerned with the effects of increasing economic organization on the forms of human interaction. In the course of their exhaustive study, the authors collected considerable data describing the behavioral effects of migration and assimilation on newcomers to American cities. Thomas and Znaniecki noted that the change in life styles left the migrant "disorganized" and more likely to be labeled by the receptor community. The authors cited crime as an example of behavioral problems arising from changes in life circumstances. Based on extensive interviews, court records, and analyses of personal life histories, Thomas and Znaniecki hypothesized that the migrant population exhibited higher rates of criminal behavior due to the demand upon it to abandon modes of moral reasoning appropriate to small towns, and to internalize the more abstract modes typical of urban societies. They theorized that behavior in small towns was shaped by primary and peer group pressure operationalized through immediate reward and punishment in the form of respect or ostracism. Urban living, however, required that the individual internalize the social contract concept and behave as expected out of the realization that the division of labor can function only when its participants are supportive. The transition from old to new modes leaves the migrant without strong behavior guidance at a time when he is faced with an exponential increase in moral dilemmas stemming from physical need and the opportunities for crime presented by the urban milieu.

An Ecological Perspective on Crime

McKenzie and the other early ecologists synthesized the work of Thomas and Znaniecki, Adna Weber (1899), and Simmel (1893), and made the synthesis dynamic by adding the economic theories summarized by Haig. The most fundamental hypothesis arising from this synthesis was that the predictability of the size, mix, spatial distribution, and behavior of a human community varies with the stability of its economic base. Observing a community longitudinally (over time), the ecologist would expect rates of abnormal behavior to be higher during periods of change in economic base than during periods of stability. This relationship is expected because normal behavior is that which is congruent with the exhibitor's trophic role, living space, and prevailing societal laws and mores. Increases or decreases in economic base increase the size of the population experiencing changes in its trophic role, living space, and moral reasoning. During the transition from one set to another, the population at risk is more likely to exhibit behavior considered incongruent with either old or new behavior determiners, and to be labeled abnormal. When the behavior determiner violated is the law, the label is "criminal."

Behavior incongruent with laws and mores will increase during times of increasing economic base because communities will experience an influx of migrants who feel relieved from peer and primary group pressure to conform, and who have not yet internalized the social contract. Due either to the desire to indulge previously repressed promiscuous drives, or to the physical need of unaffordable goods, the migrant will experience moral dilemmas at a time when he is cognitively least equipped to cope with them. It should also be noted that the ecologists recognized that "norm clash" would lead to increased labeling of migrants as criminals.

The expected effect of decreasing economic base on criminal behavior was rationalized by the ecologists as a product of increasingly difficult moral dilemmas experienced by a population whose dedication to the social contract was weakened by lack of reward. The population whose previous compliance to the social contract did not preclude the economic deprivation experienced when the community's base decreased, is more likely to commit crime when his or his family's need becomes pressing.

While McKenzie and Burgess did not dwell on crime as a subset of abnormal behavior, they did cite it as one of the behavioral outcomes of economic change. The challenge they posed to their students was to collect longitudinal data describing changes in the economic bases of communities and the incidence of behavioral problems such as crime. The object of ecological analyses was to be the development of predictive models, which would allow more informed economic decision making and more preventive and remedial action by social service and police agencies. For reasons described below, however, the students of the Chicago School did not pursue this research strategy.

Reckless and Thrasher: The Emergence of the Spatial Tangent

The students and colleagues of Park, Burgess, and McKenzie wasted little time in using ecological principles to analyze the incidence and location of criminal behavior in the city of Chicago which had become their "laboratory." Research based on the early theories of Park and Burgess was pursued by students even before *The City* appeared in 1926. Two examples of this early research are important for their exemplar effect on the criminological use of ecological analysis.

Walter Reckless, who was to become a renowned criminologist, was influenced by the work of Burgess while studying sociology at the University of Chicago in the mid-1920s. Reckless became involved in an investigation of prostitution in Chicago, and chose to use Burgess' concentric zone model as a device to organize his data. Reckless collected data from law enforcement agencies describing the number of police actions, including raids and arrests, involving prostitutes during 1922 in the Chicago area. These data included the addresses of the raids and of the persons arrested, as well as descriptions of the manner in which brothels and prostitutes operated. Reckless plotted his data on a base map of Chicago which had been divided into Burgess' zones. Arrayed in this format, Reckless' data showed that while prostitution was found throughout the city, the types of vice operation differed from zone to zone reflecting the ecological pattern of land uses. Prostitution in the CBD was pursued discretely in 1928. There were no obvious brothels, and the prostitutes appeared to be individual entrepreneurs who plied their trade by engaging in what Reckless (1926, p. 169) described as "the social whirl centering about the restaurants, the cafes, the theaters." Reckless attributed the discrete form of prostitution in the CBD to the fact that the downtown areas of major cities were regularly visited by middle class families which would be offended by blatant vice. Businessmen knew this and pressured politicians and police to keep prostitution to an unobtrusive level. He also noted that retailing and office uses drove the cost of rents to the point at which brothels could not compete.

In contrast to the discrete variant found in the CBD, prostitution in the zone of transition was open and operated from highly visible brothels. Reckless claimed that blatant vice concentrated in the zone in transition because much of the population there was not particularly concerned about the presence of vice, and because those that were offended were not politically strong enough to have police resources redirected to vice control. The concerned population, moreover, was usually upwardly mobile and intended to move to the zone of workingmen's homes to escape phenomena such as prostitution.

Reckless noted that vice in the residential zones assumed a third variant. He claimed middle class and workingmen's neighborhoods would be hostile to any form of prostitution, but that working and middle class men still sought out prostitutes. These prostitutes, according to Reckless, operated from high rent apartments which lined the boulevards leading from the center of the city to the

outlying areas. These were not ramshackle areas, nor were the brothels anything
like their counterparts in the zone in transition. Reckless wrote (1962, p. 170),

> The immoral flats (apartments) are really only accessible by taxicab or automobile,
> since they hug the boulevards rather than the streetcar lines. They attract, therefore,
> a high class patronage, a sporting element that does not subscribe to the cheaper
> entertainment provided by the brothel.

Based on the distribution of vice shown by his mapped data, Reckless suggested several characteristics of urban neighborhoods which would lead one to
expect to find prostitution nearby. These included such phenomena as burlesque
shows, rescue missions, other criminal activities such as gambling, large numbers
of single men, succession of residential to commercial land uses, a combination
of high land values and low rents, and a high concentration of immigrants and
racial minorities.

Reckless' work set the precedent for spatial analyses of criminal behavior,
rather than longitudinal testing of the central ecological assumption that economic conditions affect the incidence of crime. His list of neighborhood correlates of vice, moreover, obviously describes only the zone in transition, despite
his findings that vice was found throughout the city. This distortion fueled the
misconception that ecologists assumed poor environmental conditions were the
principal prerequisites of abnormal behavior.

The precedent of spatial analyses of crime was partially reinforced by the
work of another early ecologist. Frederick Thrasher, a student of Park and
Burgess at Chicago, became interested in juvenile delinquency as a behavioral
problem influenced by ecological factors. As his doctoral research, he undertook
a study of juvenile gangs in Chicago during the mid-twenties. Under Park's and
Burgess' supervision he spent considerable time living in Chicago's gang-plagued
neighborhoods observing the behavior patterns and social organization of the
gangs, and interviewing individual gang members. Thrasher published his findings
in a fascinating volume entitled *The Gang: A Study of 1,313 Gangs in Chicago*,
which appeared in 1927. Given the ecologists' roots in the work of Thomas and
Znaniecki, the most likely ecological explanation of juvenile delinquency was
that children whose parents experienced changes in role, moral reasoning, and
living space would also be disorganized. That is, they would have no sense of
role-generated behavior expectations, or of moral criteria, and would be over- or
under-reactive in their interaction with environmental threats and opportunities.
This condition of disorganization would be expected to fluctuate with the
stability of the economy.

Thrasher's experience with the gangs of Chicago, however, led him to reject
the "disorganization" based explanations and to devise an alternate set of
theories based on more elementary ecological principals. The fact that led
Thrasher to abandon the disorganized-parent equals disorganized-child formula
was the obvious organized quality of the gang member's life. The gang provided

members with social and functional roles and had explicit and implicit moral codes which members were expected to honor under the threat of physical punishment or social ostracism. In addition, each gang had a "turf" or physical area which it knew extremely well and patrolled against encroachment by other gangs. In other words, the gang member had all the immediate behavior guidance of the most "organized" member of society. The crucial difference was that the gang often rewarded behavior proscribed, and punished behavior expected, by the dominant society.

Thrasher explained the emergence of urban gangs as a process analogous to that which produced the dominant adult society. The parents of many gang members were indeed "disorganized." They had experienced the shifts in behavior determiners which required learning new roles, moral reasoning, and living spaces. Given their own state of uncertainty the parents' ability to shape the behavior of their children to the expectations of the dominant society was greatly reduced. The other behavior shapers, schools, churches, and similar institutions which reflected dominant value systems—also were ineffectual in dealing with the children of disorganized parents. Without parental conviction that schooling was good, or insistence that children attend school, the child was not likely to take the school experience seriously. Schools in the transitionary area, moreover, were run by administrators and teachers representing other racial or ethnic groups, with little understanding of the culture, or even the language, of the new students. The result was a drastic reduction in the school system's ability to condition behavior.

In addition to the lack of direct conditioning agents, children in the zone in transition were not, according to Thrasher, aware of the interdependence of the social system. This was a result of their parents' ignorance and, more importantly Thrasher felt, of the disinterest of the larger community in assimilating the population not upwardly mobile enough to find its own way into the economic system. This meant that the child did not develop an understanding of the social contract and its implications for behavior.

Thrasher posited that, under those conditions, normal children would develop their own division of labor complete with desired goods, roles, laws and mores, and place. Since the dominant society plays so small a part in determining what those goods would be and what laws and mores would be established, it could be expected that behavior exhibited by members of these microcosmic, trophic organizations would often be considered criminal by the dominant society.

Based on the above understanding of the etiology of delinquent behavior among gang members, Thrasher predicted that the distribution of delinquent gangs throughout a metropolitan area would follow an ecological gradient. That is, as distance from the zone in transition increases, delinquent ganging decreases. Thrasher claimed this was true because:

1. disorganized adults with reduced socializing capability concentrated in the zone in transition;

2. schools and other socializing institutions were weakest in the zone in transition; and
3. the established community was not interested in the population of the transitionary areas.

Thrasher also noted that high delinquency areas are likely to exhibit high rates over time because each child entering or growing up in these areas will face oscracism or violence if he does not participate in the gang. Parents whose ability to shape their child's behavior has been reduced by their own uncertainty about expected behavior, or whose behavioral expectations reflect their own conditioning as former gang members, will not be able to deter their children's participation as effectively as parents dedicated to the behavioral prescriptions of the dominant society.

Based on his findings, Thrasher recommended several remedial actions the community could pursue to reduce the delinquent behavior of gangs. Many of the public and private programs formulated since 1930 to reduce ganging have explicitly cited Thrasher's work as the basis of their intervention strategies. Many "war on poverty" programs, in fact, trace their theoretical underpinnings to Thrasher's work (Moynihan, 1969). Thrasher recommended that the dominant society become involved in the socialization of children in transitionary areas. Thrasher recognized that children would organize into groups, despite all efforts to isolate individuals, and that the primary purpose of community involvement should be to ensure that the gang members see the objectives of their association as consonant with those of the dominant division of labor. The object of interventions should, therefore, be to provide models and situations which demonstrate that compliance with the social contract brings the reward of increased security and respect. The specific types of programs he suggested included: organizing the children's play into team sports, such as Little League, to demonstrate the importance of cooperation, discipline, rules, and impartial judges; the use of "big brothers," or successful male-role models for children with weak families; and the involvement of organizations such as the Boy Scouts to demonstrate the importance of individual moral character to the functioning of society. Thrasher also urged that school curricula and teacher assignments be changed to make school more interesting to children and, therefore, increase its socializing effectiveness. Church congregations should, Thrasher claimed, make attempts to involve themselves in transitionary areas to demonstrate the moral commitment to the success of society.

While Thrasher's work contributed much to the early ecological movement by offering an example of how the behavioral problems caused by economic change could be perpetuated through the normal learning processes of children, his findings became known for their spatial, rather than behavioral, analyses. This preoccupation with the spatial manifestation of criminal behavior growing from the early work of Reckless and Thrasher reached its zenith in the exemplars of the application of ecological principles to the analysis of crime. These were the collected works of Clifford Shaw and Henry McKay.

Spatial Analyses

McKay and Shaw had begun in the early 1920s to collect the addresses of criminal offenders in Chicago. Upon hearing of the work of their colleague, Ernest Burgess, who had begun to map such social phenomena, the two researchers became interested in ecological theory to explain the heavy concentration of crime in several areas of the city. Shaw and McKay proceeded to map all the data they had collected, including the home addresses of 5,158 male school truants, 43,298 alleged juvenile offenders, and 7,541 alleged adult criminals. Their findings, appearing in a volume entitled *Delinquency Areas* (Shaw, Zorbaugh, McKay & Cottrell, 1929), included:

1. The rates of truancy, delinquency, and adult crime exhibited an ecological gradient. The rates decreased as the distance from the central business district increased.
2. There was a high correlation among the truancy, delinquency, and adult crime rates. Those neighborhoods with high truancy rates tended to have high delinquency and high adult crime rates.
3. The high rate areas tended to remain high rate areas over time, even though the population changed.
4. Recidivism rates, the rate of persons apprehended more than once, exhibited an ecological gradient. The further from the CBD a truant lived when first detected, the less likely he was to be later apprehended for delinquency or adult crime.

In a second study, conducted for a special federal commission investigating crime and delinquency in America, Shaw and McKay replicated their analysis in Philadelphia, Richmond, Cleveland, Birmingham, Denver, and Seattle. The results reaffirmed their findings in Chicago.

Perhaps the best known and most influential work of Shaw and McKay was *Juvenile Delinquency in Urban Areas* (1942). Shaw and McKay began their exhaustive study by collecting the addresses of all male alleged delinquents apprehended in Chicago during the following time periods: 1900-06, 1917-23, and 1927-33. These three six-year periods were chosen because the researchers, as will be discussed, wanted to compute delinquency rates for areas of Chicago. To compute a rate, the number of delinquents must be divided by the base population of the given area. By using the three years before and after the decennial censuses, Shaw and McKay felt they could use the census-reported population as a reliable base figure. The 1900-06 period was chosen because juvenile court did not exist in Chicago prior to 1900.

After collecting the addresses for the offenders detected during the three six-year periods, the researchers prepared base maps depicting the city of Chicago in 1900, 1920, and 1930. These maps were divided into the equivalent of mile-square blocks covering the physical extension of Chicago. The physical growth of the city was demonstrated by the fact that the 1900 map yielded 106 square-mile blocks, the 1920 map produced 113 blocks, and the 1930 map required 140 squares to cover the city.

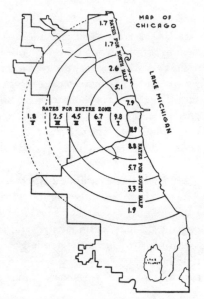

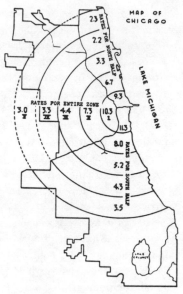

A. Zone rates of male juvenile delinquents, 1927–33 series

B. Zone rates of male juvenile delinquents, 1917–23 series

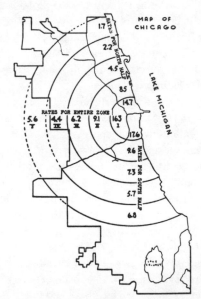

C. Zone rates of male juvenile delinquents, 1900–1906 series

Fig. 7-2. Shaw and McKay's mapping of delinquency rates. (From Shaw and McKay,
1942. Reprinted by permission.)

The census for 1900, 1920, and 1930 was then used to determine how many males aged 10-16 years lived in each block. A delinquency rate was then computed for each block by dividing the number of delinquents detected for each of the three periods by the population of 10-16 year old males.

Once each block on all three maps had been rated, Shaw and McKay overlaid a pattern of concentric zones on each map. This was done by drawing circles at two-mile intervals from the area of highest land value (center of CBD). The mean rate for all the blocks falling in each concentric zone was then computer. Figure 7-2 is a duplicate of the mapped data produced by Shaw and McKay. The data for the three six-year periods confirmed the findings of the authors' 1929 study.

Juvenile Delinquency and Urban Areas also included analyses of delinquency in Philadelphia, Boston, Cincinnati, Richmond, and Cleveland. Each of those studies reinforced the findings of the original Chicago analysis.

In a revised edition of *Juvenile Delinquency and Urban Areas*, appearing in 1969, additional data were added to the original compilation, and the analysis of Chicago was expanded to include its suburbs. The pattern first described in the 1929 study was again reinforced.

Shaw and McKay: Facts Without Explanations

The pattern of delinquency and adult crime so methodically described by Shaw and McKay is a fact that must be explained by any hypothesis intended to explain criminal behavior. By themselves, however, these facts do not explain crime. By far the weakest aspect of the work of Shaw and McKay was their lack of explanation of their findings. Without explicitly establishing a theoretical nexus between their findings and the work of Thomas and Znaniecki and of McKenzie and Burgess, Shaw and McKay added weight to the criticism that ecological analysis was essentially atheoretical mapping.

In the first edition of *Juvenile Delinquency and Urban Areas* (1942), Shaw and McKay suggested an etiology based on Edwin Sutherland's theory of differential association which will be described in succeeding pages. Sutherland's work, however, came to prominence in the early 1930s, a decade after Shaw and McKay had begun their work. In the 1969 edition of *Juvenile Delinquency and Urban Areas*, the authors allude to the frustrated-aspirations model developed by Robert Merton, also described later, in their explanation of the ecological gradient of crime. Merton's work, however, did not appear until 1938. The impression left by their work is that Shaw and McKay were primarily interested in generating facts about the distribution of crime, not in explaining criminal behavior. Because of their lack of clear explanations, several interpretations of Shaw and McKay's findings became popular and were identified incorrectly with the Chicago School. The most glaringly inaccurate of these was that the physical characteristics of the zone in transition caused crime. The assertion that physical surroundings are criminogenic was subsequently criticized for being empircally indefensible. Robinson (1950), for example, criticized the use of correlation analysis to measure the relationship between the characteristics of geographically defined populations and the behavior of individuals. Because so many criminologists accepted the mistaken assumption that the Chicago School believed places to be criminogenic, Robinson's criticisms were seen as refutations of ecological principles, rather than of uninformed interpretations.

A second interpretation offered to fill the explanatory vacuum, left by Shaw and McKay's reluctance to interpret their findings, was that the social characteristics of the zone in transition "disorganized" its inhabitants. The term disorganization was originally used by Thomas and Znaniecki and Park and Burgess to describe the condition experienced by individuals when they changed roles, modes of moral reasoning, and living spaces. While disorganized persons congregated in the zone in transition, the zone in transition did not disorganize people. As Thrasher noted in 1927, delinquents were not disorganized, but, rather, improperly socialized due to the disorganization of their parents and the lack of societal commitment to involving the children of the zone in transition in the division of labor. The reified interpretation of "disorganization" often attributed to Shaw and McKay assumes disorganization is a quality of a spatial area which causes children to become "anomic," or normless, and confused about their roles in society. This corruption of the disorganization concept was appropriately criticized for two reasons. First, it cannot be shown that delinquents or criminals are normless or confused (Jonassen, 1949). Second, the assertion that a disorganized area causes its inhabitants to become anomic and criminal is useless as explanation, due to its circularity. In essence, the "disorganized place" concept states that an area is disorganized when its population exhibits high rates of crime and behavioral problems, and that an area's population is likely to exhibit high rates of crime and behavioral problems when the area is disorganized (Lander, 1954). Because the physical causation and disorganization theories were incorrectly attributed to the Chicago School, their discrediting led to reduced interest in ecological analysis.

The Elements of the Ecological Paradigm as Adopted by Criminology

The elements of the ecological paradigm's criminological variant differ slightly from the ecological paradigm of abnormal behavior. The variation is accounted for by the addition of Thrasher's explanations of "organized" delinquent behavior. The elements are as follows:

I. *Basic Assumptions.*

The criminological variant of the ecological paradigm assumes:

A. Criminal behavior is that which is perceived as incongruous with societal laws and mores.

B. The chances of an individual's behavior being perceived as incongruous with societal laws and mores increase when moral dilemmas are accompanied by changes in modes of moral reasoning or by reduced dedication to the social contract resulting from non-rewarded compliance.

C. The population experiencing changes in moral reasoning increases with growth in economic base; the population with reduced dedication to the social contract increases with a shrinking economic base.

D. Adult populations experiencing changes in moral reasoning or reduced dedication to the social contract are not effective conditioners of children's behavior.

E. Children whose behavior is not conditioned by parents are more likely to form delinquent gangs than other children.

F. The spatial distribution of adults experiencing changes in moral reasoning and reduced dedication to the social contract forms an ecological gradient.

G. The spatial distribution of delinquent gangs forms an ecological gradient.

II. *Analogies.*

The analogy used to demonstrate the criminological variant of the ecological paradigm is the metropolis as ecosystem model first posited by McKenzie and Burgess.

III. *Conventions.*

The conventions of the researchers applying ecological analysis to criminal behavior are the same as the founders of the Chicago School.

A. The data considered necessary for hypothesis testing must be *empirically* derived.

B. The data collected must be *quantitatively* measured.

C. The subjects being studied must be observed in *naturalistic* settings.

D. Behavior is most parsimoniously explained when viewed as a product of *group* interaction.

IV. *Exemplars.*

All spatial analyses traceable to the Chicago School use Burgess' concentric zone model as their basic exemplar. The criminological variant of the ecological paradigm adds the following as exemplars:

A. Frederick Thrasher's *The Gang: A Study of 1,313 Gangs in Chicago* (1927).

B. Shaw and McKay's *Juvenile Delinquency and Urban Areas* (1942, 1946).

Neo-Ecological Studies

While the ecological paradigm lost much of its following after the appearance of Robinson's criticisms (1950), researchers continued to pursue the spatial analysis of criminal behavior (Voss & Petersen, 1971). The principal difference between those more recent analyses and those of Shaw and McKay is the former's use of sophisticated statistical techniques.

Several of these neo-ecological studies deserve mention because of their affirmation of early ecological assumptions. Among the more important of these is Bernard Lander's *Towards an Understanding of Juvenile Delinquency* (1954). Lander's purpose in conducting his study of delinquency in Baltimore was to use sophisticated statistical techniques to test several popular beliefs concerning crime. Among the tenets he was interested in testing was that poor physical surroundings, including bad housing and high density, cause crime. Lander incorrectly attributed this belief to the Chicago School, and assumed his analyses were tests of early ecological theory. His findings, however, actually affirm the assumptions of the early ecologists, while discrediting the inaccurate interpretations of their work. After having characterized Baltimore's 1940 census tracts by a series of variables including density, housing conditions, home ownership, median family income, and racial composition, Lander used partial correlation techniques to determine which characteristics were consistently associated with high delinquency rates. He found that neither housing conditions nor density were consistently related to delinquency. Lander found that the two best statistical predictors of delinquency rates were the number of rental units and the racial characteristics of a census tract. The association was positive; that is, the more rental units or blacks a tract had, the higher its delinquency rate was likely to be. Lander explained this by claiming that many rental units mean a census tract houses a population experiencing considerable life change, which apparently reduces the effectiveness of behavior conditioning. The positive correlation between percent of black population and delinquency reflected, Lander claimed, the fact that blacks were the most recent population experiencing change in economic role and movement to the cities. In a paragraph highly supportive of the ecological assumptions, Lander (1954, p. 173) wrote:

> Unstable community conditions and the consequent weakening of social controls that are congruent with the dominant culture provide fertile ground for the emergence of variant norms and group standards. Sherif's 'Psychology of Social Norms', and the studies of Clifford Shaw and Frederic Thrasher indicate the existence of norms and standards in these areas. The controls and mores of a gang are highly regulatory of the behavior of its members. However, these norms may not be congruent with those of the larger society.

Lander's work has been criticized on several occasions for methodological errors (Borgatta, 1968; Chilton, 1964; Gordon, 1967). None of these criticisms, however, have discredited his basic finding that measures of population change, such as number of rental units and proportion of population accounted for by minority groups, are more predictive of delinquency rates than are measures of physical characteristics, such as density or housing conditions.

Despite the increasing sophistication of the post-Shaw and McKay spatial analysis, many criminologists felt little new insight into the nature of criminal behavior was being gained (Polk, 1969; Rosen & Turner, 1967). The contribution of continued spatial analyses appeared to be the reification of the finding that significant positive correlation existed between the delinquency rates of areal units and indices of physical mobility among lower socioeconomic groups. As mid-century neared, criminology obviously needed a testable explanation of the correlation, not further evidence that the relationship existed. While ecological analysis was credited with helping demonstrate the pervasiveness of the relationship, the ecological paradigm was not seen as a fertile source of parsimonious explanations of the processes that produced the correlation. This was true because many criminologists accepted the misleading assertion that the Chicago School explained crime as a product of the disorganizing effect of places, not of social processes.

Sutherland's Theory of Differential Association

After Shaw and McKay's *Delinquency Areas* appeared in 1929, several sociologists attempted to explain the fact that some areas retained high crime rates over time, while others, with the same socioeconomic and physical characteristics as the high crime areas, exhibited low rates. One of these sociologists, Edwin Sutherland (1939) devised an explanation which was similar to that offered by Mayhew 75 years earlier. Essentially, Sutherland noted that the attitude one holds toward the social contract is learned. If the individual is taught by those with little understanding of the social contract and the necessity for compliance to law, he would be more likely to exhibit criminal behavior when confronted with a moral dilemma, than would another taught by those with a fuller understanding of the social contract. One's propensity to react criminally to moral dilemmas is predictable from whom he associated with during the learning period. Sutherland referred to this observation as the theory of "differential association." It should be noted that Sutherland asserted that *attitudes* toward the social contract were learned, not criminal responses to stimuli. After the advent of the learning paradigm, several psychologists were to posit that criminal responses were learned.

Sutherland's observations can be viewed as an elaboration on Thrasher's allusion to the fact that once gangs form subcultures, new members are assimilated through the same learning processes that perpetuate dominant society. Sutherland's work was important for ecologists because it amplified Thrasher's tenet that gangs were not disorganized, but were, in fact, microcosms of the dominant society which formed in the moral vacuum left by a disorganized adult population. Differential association, in the context of the Chicago School, was an elaboration of step five in the following causal chain:

1. Changes in economic base create a population in transition from one set of roles, living places, and moral systems to another.
2. During the transition period, the population at risk either has not internalized the social contract concept or is cynical about the rewards of compliance.
3. Children of the population at risk are not taught to accept the social contract as a behavioral guide.
4. Delinquent gangs emerge with strong non-majoritarian role assignments, moral expectations, and place identity.
5. The gang as a social organization perpetuates itself by transmitting its values to those who must rely on it for safety, scarce goods, identity, etc.

6. Once an area becomes dominated by a delinquent gang, it can be expected to manifest high rates of delinquency over extended periods of time.

In the context of ecological theory, Sutherland's work appears to be an attempt to make the transmission assumption more empirical. If the number and importance of a child's associations could be measured and categorized as majoritarian or delinquent subcultural, the differential association theory claims that his attitude toward the social contract could be predicted. The tenuous assumption underlying Sutherland's preoccupation with attitudes is that they predict responses to moral dilemmas.

Sutherland's work was not associated with the Chicago School by many criminologists because the concept of differential association was unrelated to the popular understanding of human ecology as strictly spatial analysis. As a result, many commentators on the development of criminology have treated Sutherland's *Principles of Criminology* as the seminal work of a separate paradigm often referred to as the "symbolic interactionist" school (Nettler, 1974). By itself, however, differential association offers no explanation of criminal behavior, only an observation on the transmission of attitudes. Without Thrasher's assumption of disorganized adults, differential association begs the question of why the transmitting group has an indifferent, or hostile, attitude toward the social contract. Attitudes, moreover, have never been shown to predict behavior, and often are attributed to persons after behaviors have been exhibited. It becomes circular reasoning to assert that an attitude produced a delinquent behavior, when the attitude is attributed to the individual because he has exhibited delinquent behavior.

While Sutherland's work was laudable for attempting to explain why high crime areas tend to remain so over time, differential association added little to Thrasher's work, and by itself seemed trivial at best. Explanations of the process by which delinquent behavior was transmitted from one group to another remained at the level of sophistication of Thrasher's work until the advent of the learning paradigm in psychology.

By mid-century, most criminologists had lost interest in sterile spatial analyses and in the trivial observations of differential association. The resulting void was filled by the work of Robert Merton (1938; 1957) which inspired criminology's next paradigm.

THE FRUSTRATED-ASPIRATION PARADIGM

Merton's theory of crime as a product of frustrated aspiration is based on assumptions similar to those the ecologists borrowed from Thomas and Znaniecki and the French sociologist, Emil Durkheim (1897). Essentially, these earlier sociologists saw behavior as shaped by systems of rewards and punishments which included the provision or denial of material security, as well as the allocating of non-material goods such as prestige and respect. The ecologists assumed, perhaps naively, that the desire for more goods and respect were innate and not likely to be satiated. Merton, looking back from mid-century, claims that in order to perpetuate its industrial capitalist economy, the Western world, and the United States in particular, has had to motivate its population to consume far beyond what it needs for survival. This, supposedly, has led to the emergence of advertising and other societal conditioners which instill in the population the desire to acquire more goods and status.

Merton claimed that the drive to achieve is pervasive and becoming stronger as society increasingly describes the ideal existence as one of affluence. The problem with this system is that universal aspiration creates keen competition for scarce resources, and the legitimate means to those resources. Any handicap proves devastating given the limited number of legitimate pursuits which reward people at the level to which they aspire. Intelligence, cleverness, ethnic background, race, physical appearance, and other characteristics which the individual cannot change can become crucial determiners of success or failure.

According to Merton, those who are frustrated by characteristics they cannot control intuit that compliance to the social contract will not be rewarded at the level to which they aspire. This realization creates a cynicism, if not hostility, toward traditional moral codes. When faced with moral dilemmas, these frustrated individuals are more likely to behave criminally than those who feel their aspirations are being met.

The Cloward and Ohlin Explanation of Delinquency

Merton's theory assumed its most influential form in the work of Cloward and Ohlin (1960). In a volume entitled *Delinquency and Opportunity*, Cloward and Ohlin used the frustrated-aspiration theory to explain criminality among lower socio-economic youths, especially racial minorities (see Tittle, Villemez & Smith, 1978 for a recent discussion of the class-criminality relationship). The authors posited that these youths aspire to the same life goals as middle and upper class adolescents. These goals include material affluence and peer respect. Due to societal racism and poor education, however, lower socio-economic minority group adolescents are severely handicapped in the competition for legitimate roles which reward at a level equal to their aspirations. When the youths realize they cannot legitimately achieve their goals, they explore non-sanctioned routes to material success including those dominant society considers criminal.

The basic aspiration-frustration model posited by Merton, and applied to delinquency by Cloward and Ohlin, has several variations differing in the explanation of why frustration leads to crime.

The most frequently cited variant of the frustrated-aspiration model draws from Freudian theory to connect the experience of frustration to criminal behavior. Described earlier under the Anxiety-Defense Paradigm, the "reactive hypotheses," as the Freudian variant is referred to, assumes that the delinquent develops a reaction-formation defense mechanism to cope with the anxiety caused by feelings of competitive inadequacy. The defense mechanism manifests itself in the development of a personality marked by aggression and the rejection of traditional values. This personality supposedly increases the youth's chances of exhibiting criminal behavior when faced with moral dilemmas (Kobrin, 1951).

A second explanation of the relationship between frustrated aspiration and crime assumes that criminal behavior is a product of a rational decision balancing the expected gain against the likelihood of punishment. Recognizing aspiration cannot be fulfilled legitimately, the offender, supposedly, seeks out the illegitimate means which offers the best gain/risk ratio (Rogers, 1973).

The Elements of the Frustrated-Aspiration Paradigm

Based on Merton's description of the criminogenic impact of the disparity between aspiration and means to achievement, the frustrated-aspiration paradigm can be described as including the following elements:

I. *Basic Assumptions.*
   A. Modern industrial societies condition their populations to aspire to increased material acquisition and status.
   B. Lower socio-economic youths aspire to achievement as strongly as middle and upper class youths.
   C. Lower socio-economic youths are less able to compete for legitimate means to success, due to racism and poor education.
   D. The realization of competitive inadequacy leads to frustration and anxiety.
      1. Frustrated aspiration leads to loss of dedication to the social contract or "anomie."
      2. Anxiety leads to reaction formation in the form of aggressive anti-social behavior.
      3. The desire to acquire material symbols of achievement leads to a rational selection of illegitimate means to success.

II. *Analogies.*

   The analogs used to demonstrate the paradigm's assumptions vary with the versions of the paradigm listed under I-D above.
   A. Merton's classic presentation of the frustrated-aspiration paradigm analogizes the process by which frustration leads to crime to Durkheim's concept of "anomie." Anomie is the loss of behavior guidance experienced when primary and peer group pressure is lifted, or when the social contract is rejected or not understood.
   B. The Freudian-based version of the frustrated-aspiration paradigm used the ego-id-superego construct as the explanatory analog.
   C. The rational choice variant analogizes the decision to pursue illegitimate means to success to any decision involving the maximizing of benefits and reduction of costs.

III. *Conventions.*
   The fact that the frustrated-aspiration paradigm has developed the three

variations described above makes generalizing about research conventions tenuous at best. The following characterizations, therefore, may be less precise than those offered for the previously cited paradigms.

A. Epistemology. Given the fact that most of the researchers adhering to the paradigm consider themselves social scientists rather than psychoanalysts, its epistemological preference can be characterized as empirical.

B. Descriptive mode. While most criminologists espousing the frustrated-aspiration paradigm consider themselves to be empiricists, much of their measurement utilizes qualitative description. This is due primarily to the difficult task of measuring such variables as "aspiration" or "frustration." The ambiguity of these terms, in fact, contributed to the current crisis stage of criminology.

C. Research setting. Given the paradigm's emphasis on the impact of economic opportunities and on societal shaping of aspiration, the study of criminal behavior is assumed to be most parsimoniously pursued in naturalistic settings.

D. Level of analysis. For the same reasons cited in C above, the frustrated-aspiration paradigm is preoccupied with the group or social system as unit of analysis.

IV. *Exemplars.*

The most commonly cited sources of the frustrated-aspiration paradigm are Merton's (1957) *Social Theory and Social Structure* and Cloward and Ohlin's (1960) *Delinquency and Opportunity: A Theory of Delinquent Gangs.*

The Crisis Stage of the Frustrated-Aspiration Paradigm

The frustrated-aspiration paradigm reached its peak influence during early and mid-1960s. Even during this period, however, several weaknesses of its basic assumptions were described by commentators. The most telling of these criticisms focused on the assumption that delinquent youths have similar aspirations and values as nondelinquent youths. This contention is simply unsubstantiated. As Nettler (1974, p. 159) notes:

Like many other explanations of human behavior, the opportunity-structure theory starts with what people want. The engine of action is desire. It is assumed that the desires called "aspirations" have been quite similar for all North Americans, if not for all Westerners, at some time in their careers. However, opportunity-structure theory is silent about the life histories of delinquents and hence takes for granted what needs to be known—the extent to which lawful careers and all they entail are preferred or derided.

In fact, substantial research conducted over the last three decades has found considerable differences between delinquent and nondelinquent youths (Beilen, 1956; Burt, 1925; Crockett, 1962; Douvan, 1956; Douvan & Edelson, 1958; Haan, 1964; Srole, et al., 1962; Stacey, 1965; Thompson, 1971). This research indicates that delinquent gangs are subcultures with their own values and symbols of achievement which are substantially different from those of the dominant society.

While the questionable soundness of the assumption of similar values and aspirations reduced the influence of the frustrated-aspiration paradigm, the crisis phase in which criminology now finds itself was principally precipitated by the failure of governmental delinquency control programs based on the Cloward and Ohlin model. The "War on Poverty," as the efforts of the Office of Economic Opportunity are often referred to, included a program intended to reduce ganging by increasing the opportunities for economic achievement among lower socioeconomic groups. This strategy, based on the Cloward and Ohlin explanation of delinquency (Moynihan, 1969), has been widely judged a failure (Hackler, 1966; Hackler & Hagen, 1972; Weissman, 1969).

While the failure of OEO programs to control delinquency is not a direct refutation of the frustrated-aspiration paradigm, criminologists and social scientists were discouraged with the events of the late 1960s. Many felt that Mertonian-based explanations were naive and ignored the unpleasant facts that delinquent subcultures were fundamentally different from the remainder of society, and that the difference could not be reduced with paternalism or cash (Banfield, 1968). General disillusionment with the frustrated-aspiration paradigm has created a Kuhnian crisis condition in contemporary criminology. The resulting search for parsimonious explanations of crime has led to a renewed interest among criminologists in learning theory.

THE LEARNING ALTERNATIVE

Two British psychologists, who have contributed to the learning paradigm described in the previous chapter, have applied their assumptions to criminal behavior to produce a learning explanation of crime. H. J. Eysenck (1964) and G. Trasler (1962) have posited that criminal and delinquent behavior results primarily from the fact that some children are not conditioned to respond to moral dilemmas in societally acceptable fashion. Effective conditioning requires: 1) that there are concerned conditioners in the child's environment, 2) that the conditioners understand the behavioral expectations of society and intend to elicit such behavior, and 3) that the impact of the rewards and punishments administered by the conditioners representing majoritarian expectations is greater than that of any conditioners representing subcultural expectations. When these prerequisites are not met, the individual's response to moral dilemmas is more likely to be societally unacceptable. This conceptualization of the process by which responses to moral dilemmas become more or less likely to be societally acceptable leads to the following hypotheses concerning crime:

   1. Children who do not have parents or surrogates who closely monitor indi-

vidual behavior are more likely to respond unacceptably to moral dilemmas.

2. Children whose parents or surrogates are ambivalent about majoritarian behavior expectations will be more likely to respond unacceptably to moral dilemmas.

3. Children whose environments include delinquent subcultural conditioners which compete with parental conditioning are more likely to react unacceptably to moral dilemmas.

A considerable amount of research attempting to identify the childhood conditions which are associated with later criminal behavior indicate that the above hypotheses are valid. Research dating to 1924 (Theis) has found that children raised in institutions are more likely to exhibit behavioral problems, including criminal behavior (Bowlby, 1952; Freud & Dann, 1951; Goldfarb, 1943, 1944, 1945; Spitz, 1946). Children from "broken homes" have also been shown to be more likely to exhibit criminal behavior later in life (Chilton & Markle, 1972; Gleuck & Gleuck, 1950; Hodgkiss, 1933; Maller, 1932; Monahan, 1957). The concept of broken homes, of course, is crude in that many uni-parent situations are apparently more healthy than the traditional two parent arrangement (Burchinal, 1964; Goode, 1966; Nye, 1957). The evidence appears overwhelming that disruption of the parental monitoring and conditioning process increases the child's later chances of reacting criminally to moral dilemmas.

Parental ambivalence toward majoritarian behavioral expectations and the consistency and mode of eliciting them also have been shown to influence the likelihood of children becoming delinquent (Barker, 1940; Burt, 1925; Gleuck & Gleuck, 1950; Hathaway & Monachesi, 1957; Healy & Bronner, 1936). The hypothesis that competition from delinquent subcultural conditioners will reduce the effectiveness of parental conditioning appears to be amply substantiated by the consistent finding that high delinquency areas tend to remain so over long periods of time.

While the three hypotheses listed above have been separated to demonstrate their connection to learning theory, it should be noted that disrupted parental conditioning, parental ambivalence about societally proscribed behavior, and competition from delinquent subcultural conditioners are conditions which are more likely to exist simultaneously among lower socioeconomic than middle and upper class families. The emerging learning paradigm, therefore, can account for the higher incidence of delinquency and crime among the lower socioeconomic classes as parsimoniously as the frustrated-aspiration paradigm.

A Suggested Synthesis of the Criminological Versions of the Ecological and Learning Paradigms

The explanation of crime offered by the learning theorists is essentially the same as that posited by McKenzie, Burgess, and Thrasher. While the latter may have stated their hypotheses in less formal fashion than the learning theorists, the ecologists' explanation is more holistic given their understanding of economic dynamism and norm clash.

It is unfortunate for criminology that the ecological paradigm has been so strongly associated with the spatial analysis of criminal behavior. This has delayed the realization of the obvious parallels between learning theory and the behavioral hypotheses of the early ecologists. A synthesis of these two intellectual traditions would produce a more holistic hypothesis of greater specificity than either could generate alone. Testing such hypotheses would undoubtedly lead to explanations of criminal behavior, at least as parsimonious as those offered by the frustrated-aspiration paradigm.

The following preliminary synthesis of the basic assumptions of the ecological and learning paradigms is intended to stimulate more sophisticated efforts.

I. Man is capable of a wide range of behaviors, including those which violate criminal laws established to protect the division of labor.

II. The likelihood of criminal responses to moral dilemmas is reduced through conditioning administered by parents and the state.

   A. Parental conditioning involves the monitoring of child behavior and the use of rewards and punishments to shape it into societally accepted patterns.

   B. The state conditions people to avoid criminal responses by threatening to label violators as "criminals" and subjecting them to punishment administered in the name of the general welfare.

III. The incidence of crime and delinquency can be expected to be higher among those for whom:

   A. The effectiveness of parental conditioning is reduced by:

      1. Lack of consistent monitoring by parents or surrogates.

      2. Ambivalence of parents or surrogates toward the behavioral expectations of the dominant society.

      3. Competition to parental conditioning by other environmental conditioners representing subcultural values.

   B. Compliance to law is not likely to preclude hardship.

   C. Crime is a career. This group includes the former juvenile delinquents produced by ineffective early conditioning.

IV. The population at risk, or that portion of the community described by III A, B, and C, is largest when the economic base changes.

   A. When economic base increases in migration and leads to:

      1. Parents who are learning new roles, places and moral codes and who are more likely to:

         a. neglect their monitoring of child behavior.

         b. be ambivalent or unsure about behavioral expectations.

         c. have competition from subcultural conditioners in transitionary areas.

2. Reduced likelihood of compliance among those who do not improve their socioeconomic status despite the prosperity of the surrounding community.
3. Increased opportunity for crime among those for whom noncompliance means increased status.

B. When economic base decreases:
   1. Parents experiencing increased financial hardship are more likely to:
      a. be preoccupied with economic problems and neglectful of monitoring their children.
      b. be cynical about majoritarian behavior expectations.
      c. find increasing competition in conditioning children as delinquent subcultures increase.
   2. Adult compliance is tested more severely and cynicism toward continued compliance increases.
   3. The number of career criminals eventually increases given the increase in delinquents.

C. When communities experience changes in the mix of their economic base, the effects of both increasing and decreasing base are manifested.

D. When the economy is stable, that is, increasing just quickly enough to provide roles for indigenous population increases, criminal behavior remains constant and is accounted for by delinquent gangs which perpetuate themselves in traditional high crime areas, and by those who "graduate" from the gangs to career crime. Each episode of economic change, however, is likely to produce a "bulge" of delinquents which will move over time through the age distribution.

TESTING THE LEARNING-ECOLOGICAL SYNTHESIS

The hypothesis suggested in the outline above can be tested to determine their validity and to facilitate the development of more parsimonious explanations. Such research would have to be naturalistic and longitudinal. This means a metropolitan area would be monitored over time to determine its crime rate and its rate of economic change. These two indices would then be compared to determine if there is a measurable relationship between them. The research design would resemble that devised by Brenner (1973) and described in the previous chapter. Unlike Brenner's retrospective analysis, however, research on crime would have to be prospective simply because most crime data is unreliable. Only in recent years have victimization studies (National Criminal Justice Information Service, 1975) been conducted to compare the actual crime rate with the reported crime rates compiled by the F.B.I.

Table 7-1. Disciplinary Matrix of Criminology

Paradigm	Basic Assumptions	Analogies	Conventions	Exemplars
Moral Atavism	1. Criminal behavior is a product of moral insensitivity caused by atavistic cognitive apparatus. 2. Atavism is detectable from measurable physical characteristics.	1. Man's moral sensitivities evolve as do his physical characteristics.	1. Empirical Epistemology 2. Quantitative Description 3. Laboratory Research 4. Individual is Unit of Analysis	1. Lombroso's *The Criminal Man* (1876)
Anxiety Defense	1. Criminal behavior is the use of legally proscribed acts as defense mechanisms against anxiety. 2. The psychic processes by which anxiety is generated and defense mechanisms initiated are unconscious, making quantitative description and measurement impossible.	1. The ego-id-superego model.	1. Intuitive Epistemology 2. Qualitative Description 3. Laboratory Research 4. Individual is Unit of Analysis	1. Freud's *The Psychopathology of Everyday Life* (1901) 2. Freud's *The Ego and the Id* (1923) 3. Alexander and Staub, *The Criminal, The Judge, and the Public* (1931) 4. Alexander & Healy, *The Roots of Crime* (1935) 5. Healy & Bronner, *New Light on Delinquency* (1936) 6. Freidlander, *The Psycho-analytic Approach to Juvenile Delinquency*

Ecological	1. Criminal behavior is that which is incongruous with societal laws and mores. 2. The population most likely to exhibit criminal behavior is that which experiencing changes in moral reasoning, or that with a reduced dedication to the social contract. 3. The population at risk is highest when the economic base of a community changes. 4. The population at risk is less likely to effectively condition its children. 5. Children ineffectively conditioned will form subcultural gangs. 6. Subcultural gangs perpetuate themselves by conditioning new members.	1. The metropolis as ecosystem model.	1. Empirical Epistemology 2. Quantitative Description 3. Naturalistic Research 4. Community is Unit of Analysis	1. Burgess, "The Growth of the City" (1926) 2. Thrasher, *The Gang* (1927) 3. Shaw and McKay, *Juvenile Delinquency and Urban Areas* (1942)

Frustrated Aspiration	1. Lower socioeconomic youths aspire to the same goals as all youths.
	2. There are fewer legitimate roles to success than aspirants.
	3. Those handicapped by racial discrimination or poor education will be frustrated in their attempts to achieve goals.
	4. The frustrated youth will turn to illegitimate means to material success because of:
	  a. anomie
	  b. reaction formation
	  c. the rational conclusion that "crime pays."
		1. Durkheim's model of counterveiling social pressures.
		2. Freud's ego-id-superego model.
		3. Rational cost/benefit analysis.
			1. Empirical Epistemology
			2. Qualitative Description
			3. Naturalistic Research
			4. Community is Unit of Analysis
				1. Merton, *Social Theory and Social Structure* (1957)[
				2. Cloward and Ohlin, *Delinquency and Opportunity: A Theory of Delinquent Gangs* (1960)

8 The Suburbanization and Segregation of Metropolitan Populations

The concluding chapters of this book are very different from the three in the preceding cluster. The previous three chapters suggest an intellectual convergence of public health, abnormal psychology, and criminology. This intellectual convergence may emerge because of its potential to parsimoniously solve research issues. The fact is, however, that the intellectual separation of crime, ill-health, and abnormal behavior has never reflected the real community where these problems converge in a way clearly predicted by ecological principles. The following chapters attempt to describe the costs of economically driven change and the role of social cost accounting in efforts to reduce those costs.

The American community in the last quarter of the century appears to be very different from the compact, center-city-oriented system described by Haig, McKenzie, and Burgess. The sprawling metropolitan areas of contemporary America can, however, be understood by changing only two factors in Haig's model: increase the disposable income available to the family unit and decrease the cost of friction.

An increasingly diverse and productive economy allowed Americans to greatly increase the amount of income they could spend to achieve their desired life style. This increase, however, required considerable urbanization, especially during and immediately following the massive industrial growth of World War II. Cities were not ready for the in-migration. The war effort precluded investing resources in essential new housing or transportation, water and sewer systems, let alone in traditional urban amenities such as educational, cultural, and health service facilities. The post-war population was, therefore, disillusioned with the urban experience. This disillusion was accompanied by increased purchasing power accumulated during the war when everyone worked, but had fewer consumer products to buy.

The construction of the interstate highway system provided the opportunity for Americans to act on their anti-urban bias and utilize their new purchasing power to leave the city. The American community exploded. Burgess' zones spread over the rural landscape, moving the middle class well beyond the political boundaries of the original central city. This spread was accompanied by a continuation of in-migration. The new migrants, however, were racially different.

This chapter introduces several concepts which the student will find central not only to mastering this book, but to understanding current events. "Standard Metropolitan Statistical Area" (SMSA) refers to that social and economic whole which has been called the "city" through the first seven chapters of this book.* An SMSA includes the "central city," or the political jurisdiction in which Burgess' zones usually were focused, and the "outside central city," or the suburban jurisdictions which now represent Burgess' commuter zone. "Fiscal disparity" is the term used to describe the fact that central cities bear most of the costs of coping with the health and behavioral costs of economic change, but cannot tap the tax bases of suburban jurisdictions which garner most of the benefits. "Socioeconomic status" refers to a measure of an individual's educational background and income. As will be discussed, Coleman found the socioeconomic status of a child's parents to be among the most predictive variables of the child's success in school.

Decisions made over the past 50 years to improve our communities have often generated social costs which may exceed gains. More importantly, the student should note that knowledge of social costs may not have precluded the decisions because those who bear the costs are not always those who accrue the benefits. If those who benefit are powerful, the decision can be made regardless of costs.

This chapter also sets the stage for the difficult questions raised in the closing chapter. These questions deal with the role of the government in balancing the interests of those who pay for, and who benefit from, change.

---

*See table 8-14, p. 246.

INCOME INCREASES AND COST OF FRICTION DECREASES

Haig and Burgess described the urban system of the 1920s as expanding through the supersession of land uses. This process was fueled by increasing economic bases which generated new competitors for central locations. As bidding by new users drove the rents of central locations beyond the ability of existing users to pay, firms had to decentralize functions or move completely to sites further from the CBD. Savings in rent offset the increased cost of friction incurred by such moves. This system remained compact as long as the cost of friction was relatively stable. In the five decades since Haig wrote, however, reductions in the cost of friction and increases in the amount of money available to overcome it, have, with the exception of two important periods, led to rapid decentralization of the human community in America.

The Depression—The Urbanization Process Slows

As America's industrial infrastructure emerged in the first quarter of this century, population inexorably clustered in metropolitan centers. Between 1900 and 1930, metropolitan population increased from 42 percent to over 54 percent of the total. This rapid increase created social and environmental problems which led many residents to consider urban living unpleasant. In addition, therefore, to the "push" effect of supersession which converted open and agricultural lands at the urban periphery to residential use, the late 1920s witnessed a brief period of "pull." This flurry of residential construction in previously undeveloped areas reflected the convergence of several forces. First, many people, especially those who had benefited most by America's rapid economic growth, became disenchanted with the city as experienced in the 1920s. The problems described in previous chapters heightened America's latent rural-romanticism (White & White, 1964) and produced a class of people wanting to move to more pastoral settings. Such moves became increasingly possible as the automobile became universally available, road systems improved, and disposable income increased. Many families chose to spend their increased wealth on overcoming friction and realizing their dream: a home in the suburbs.

These trends slowed when the industrial system stagnated during the Great Depression. The rural and small town migration to metropolitan areas relented (see Table 8-1) as economic bases stopped growing. As disposable income slid below the level of the late 1920s, suburbanization stalled, leaving many tracts of land unsold for a decade. From 1930 to 1940 the system of collection, production, and distribution languished, and American communities incurred the social costs described by the ecologists (Mitchell, 1951).

Table 8-1. Growth of Metropolitan and Nonmetropolitan Population

Decade	Conterminous United States, Total	Constant Criteria		Constant Area	
		Metropolitan	Nonmetropolitan	Metropolitan	Nonmetropolitan
		Numerical Increase, in Millions			
1900-10	16.0	10.6	5.4	7.5	8.5
1910-20	13.7	11.5	2.2	8.5	5.2
1920-30	17.1	16.0	1.1	12.4	4.7
1930-40	8.9	5.9	3.0	5.0	3.9
1940-50	19.0	17.6	1.4	14.4	4.6
1950-60	27.8	27.5	.2	21.6	6.2
1960-70[a]	20.8	22.5	−1.7	15.1	5.7
		Percentage of Increase			
1900-10	21	44	10	31	16
1910-20	15	33	4	25	9
1920-30	16	35	2	27	8
1930-40	7	10	5	8	6
1940-50	14	26	2	21	7
1950-60	18	32	0	25	10
1960-70[a]	12	20	−3	13	9
		Percentage Distribution of Increase			
1900-10	100	66	34	47	53
1910-20	100	84	16	62	38
1920-30	100	94	6	72	28
1930-40	100	66	34	56	44
1940-50	100	92	8	76	24
1950-60	100	99	1	78	22
1960-70[a]	100	108	−8	73	27

[a]U.S. Bureau of the Census, *1970 Census of Population*, preliminary figures.
Source: Hawley, Duncan, and Goldberg, op. cit., p. 149.

The War Effort—Increased Urbanization and Income, but Few Diversions

The American economy remained weak from the crash in late 1929 until the nation mobilized to become the "armory of the free world." The huge capital investment in war production infrastructure renewed the movement of population from small town and rural America into metropolitan areas. While the metropolitan population had increased by only 10 percent (five percent non-metropolitan increase) from 1930 to 1940, the succeeding decade saw a 26 percent increase (two percent nonmetropolitan increase). This rush to the industrial centers was not accompanied by increases in urban amenities. Capital could not be diverted from the war effort to build sufficient housing, or expand transportation, sewer, and water systems. Zoning ordinances were suspended. Public transportation was idled by lack of gas and tires. Life was not pleasant for many drawn to the industrial city by the war effort.

During the war years, the economic status of most American families changed drastically. Every able-bodied citizen, male and female, was mobilized into some productive role. Average disposable income increased dramatically. While per capita income decreased from $677 in 1929 to $536 in 1939, the next six years witnessed an incredible doubling to $1,080 in 1945. This jump was not accompanied by an expansion of consumer choices. The goods and services available during the war were extremely limited. There were no new cars, new homes, appliances, or recreational diversions. The result was a huge increase in savings. Between 1940 and 1944, savings increased nearly ten-fold from $29 per capita to $270. The $37.3 billion held in savings in 1944 was not surpassed until 1967 when savings totaled $40.4 billion. The combination of unpleasant urban living conditions and the huge increase in disposable income and savings would probably have sufficed to trigger the mass suburban migration experienced at mid-century. However, two government programs, The Federal Aid Highway Act of 1956 and federal mortgage subsidy plans, accelerated the expansion.

In the late 1940s and 50s, Americans began to construct what may eventually be viewed as the Western world's most significant public works project: the interstate highway system. By 1960 many American cities had major high-speed highways leading from their central areas into the surrounding undeveloped areas. These highways were paid for by a trust fund financed by gasoline and tire taxes. While the monies raised through these taxes paid for highway construction and maintenance, they did not reflect the social costs incurred by American society as a result of highway construction. In effect, the cost of friction was being reduced below its "true" level. Americans also had begun spending their savings and increased income on new automobiles and houses. The home building and buying splurge of the 1950s and 60s was spurred by federal mortgage plans, such as the Veterans Housing Administration and the Federal Housing Administration. These plans guaranteed repayment of bank loans made to those who might not qualify in the conventional mortgage market.

The convergence at mid-century of increased economic power, unpleasant wartime urban experiences, an artificially low cost of friction, and subsidized home mortgages led to a dramatic and continuing expansion of urban systems.

The Suburbanization of America

The human community is a socioeconomic (not political) unit. The urban system which concerns us is divided into political jurisdictions which render services essential to social mobility and the amelioration of human costs. Among these jurisdictions is the political city or municipality. All metropolitan areas have a "central city," usually the oldest and largest municipality in the economic organism. Resorting to the simple concentric zone model and the attendant understanding of the human community as an expanding system, visualize the central city as the political jurisdiction in which the community began and spread to fill. With the rapid expansion of metropolitan areas since the end of World War II, the outer rings of Burgess' model are now outside of the central city. With the acceleration of this suburbanization process since 1950, America has become a predominantly suburban nation. Table 8-2 shows that, from 1900

Table 8-2. Population Growth in Central Cities and Outside Central City Areas of Standard Metropolitan Statistical Areas, by Decades, 1900-70

Decade	SMSA's	Central Cities	Outside Central City Areas	Central City Growth per 100 Increase, Outside Central City Areas
		In Thousands		
1900-10	10,176	7,337	2,839	258.4
1910-20	10,496	7,519	2,977	252.6
1920-30	14,204	8,428	5.776	145.9
1930-40	5,864	2,403	3.461	69.4
1940-50	16,387	6,664	9,723	68.5
1950-60	23,421	5.573	17,848	31.2
1960-70	19,152	850	18,301	4.6

Source: U.S. Bureau of the Census, *U.S. Census of Population. Selected Area Reports: Standard Metropolitan Statistical Areas*, Final Report PC(3)-1D. U.S. Bureau of the Census, *Current Population Reports*, Series P-23, No. 37, "Social and Economic Characteristics of the Population in Metropolitan and Nonmetropolitan areas: 1970 and 1960."

Table 8-3. Percentage of Increase of Population in Metropolitan Areas (By Date of Inception of Metropolitan Area and by Type of Place [Constant Area])

Date of Metropolitan Area Inception and Type of Place Within Areas	1960-70*	1950-60	1940-50	1930-40	1920-30	1910-20	1900-10
All areas							
Total	13.3	24.7	21.2	8.3	26.7	24.2	31.6
Central cities	4.2	7.0	12.9	5.3	22.6	25.6	41.9
Remainders of areas	21.7	48.3	34.4	13.3	34.8	21.5	30.7
1850 and before							
Total	8.6	15.3	12.6	5.8	21.8	17.2	29.0
Central cities	−3.2	−2.9	6.3	4.2	15.4	17.1	27.5
Remainders of areas	19.5	42.3	23.3	8.7	35.2	17.5	31.6
1860							
Total	14.0	22.8	24.2	7.4	28.1	24.8	23.9
Central cities	−6.6	−3.4	10.3	3.9	22.2	22.4	24.6
Remainders of areas	31.2	60.1	51.4	15.3	45.3	33.1	42.8
1870							
Total	7.6	19.4	16.2	5.3	31.2	37.6	37.0
Central cities	−10.1	−4.5	8.2	1.1	26.2	43.1	37.1
Remainders of areas	20.7	48.5	27.8	12.1	40.4	27.6	36.8
1880							
Total	16.7	23.2	16.8	3.7	22.4	24.0	27.6
Central cities	17.5	7.9	12.0	1.4	19.0	31.8	36.4
Remainders of areas	11.8	49.2	26.4	8.7	30.7	8.4	13.1
1890							
Total	17.4	32.7	28.1	15.5	41.0	28.0	34.8
Central cities	8.7	14.3	16.4	9.6	31.8	28.7	40.2
Remainders of areas	24.6	63.3	47.3	26.8	62.8	26.8	23.7
1900							
Total	14.7	19.8	21.3	5.5	15.8	23.9	42.1
Central cities	−1.9	13.0	19.1	2.4	14.8	29.2	60.9
Remainders of areas	29.9	27.2	23.8	9.1	18.9	17.6	24.8
1910							
Total	16.7	28.2	32.4	10.6	29.5	35.0	−
Central cities	12.1	26.7	28.0	7.8	36.6	45.4	−
Remainders of areas	22.3	31.8	39.3	15.0	12.6	23.4	−
1920							
Total	16.2	36.9	27.1	10.4	34.6	−	−
Central cities	11.5	29.7	14.3	10.2	29.6	−	−
Remainders of areas	20.8	44.5	46.8	10.7	27.3	−	−
1930							
Total	20.6	38.5	33.0	18.9	−	−	−
Central cities	17.4	−4.3	28.5	16.6	−	−	−
Remainders of areas	23.6	85.7	38.1	21.5	−	−	−
1940							
Total	21.8	52.3	51.0	−	−	−	−
Central cities	19.1	91.9	48.5	−	−	−	−
Remainders of areas	25.7	10.4	53.6	−	−	−	−
1950							
Total	21.2	26.1	−	−	−	−	−
Central cities	14.0	32.0	−	−	−	−	−
Remainders of areas	28.5	19.1	−	−	−	−	−
1960							
Total	48.7	−	−	−	−	−	−
Central cities	45.2	−	−	−	−	−	−
Remainders of areas	51.6	−	−	−	−	−	−

*1970 figures are preliminary.
Source: U.S. Bureau of the Census, *Censuses of Population.*

224

Table 8-4. Central City as a Percentage of
Standard Metropolitan Statistical Area Population, 1900-70

	1900 %	1930 %	1950 %	1960 %	1970 %	City Rank 1900	City Rank 1970
East							
Baltimore, Md.	73.8	77.6	67.6	54.5	43.7	6	7
Boston, Mass.	42.5	36.0	33.2	26.9	23.3	5	16
Newark, N.J.	47.0	35.4	29.9	24.0	20.2	16	36
Buffalo, N.Y.	69.3	62.9	53.3	40.8	34.3	8	28
New York, N.Y.	90.1	86.9	82.6	72.8	68.2	1	1
Rochester, N.Y.	74.6	77.4	68.2	54.3	33.5	24	49
Philadelphia, Pa.-N.J.	68.4	62.2	56.4	46.1	40.5	3	4
Pittsburgh, Pa.	41.7	33.1	30.6	25.1	21.7	11	24
Midwest							
Chicago, Ill.	81.5	74.9	69.9	57.1	48.2	2	2
Indianapolis, Ind.	85.8	86.2	77.4	70.6	67.1*	21	11
Detroit, Mich.	66.9	72.0	61.3	44.4	36.0	13	5
Minneapolis-	79.6	83.4	72.4	53.7	41.0	19	32
St. Paul, Minn.						23	46
Kansas City, Mo.-Kans.	63.6	60.1	36.1	45.9	40.4	22	26
St. Louis, Mo.-Ill.	69.6	59.3	49.8	36.4	26.3	4	18
Omaha, Neb.-Iowa	50.3	68.3	68.5	65.9	64.3	35	41
Cincinnati, Ohio-Ky.-Ind.	61.3	63.8	55.7	46.9	32.7	10	29
Cleveland, Ohio	82.8	72.4	62.4	48.8	36.4	7	10
Columbus, Ohio	76.3	80.5	74.7	69.0	58.9	28	21
Toledo, Ohio	85.8	83.6	76.8	69.6	55.4	25	34
Milwaukee, Wis.	78.1	74.4	66.6	62.1	51.1	14	12
South							
Birmingham, Ala.	27.4	60.2	58.3	55.7	40.7	94	48
Atlanta, Ga.	45.3	58.5	46.6	47.9	35.8	43	27
Louisville, Ky.-Ind.	68.5	72.1	64.0	53.9	43.7	18	39
New Orleans, La.	93.4	90.8	83.2	72.3	56.8	12	19
Oklahoma City, Okla.	17.2	67.5	62.0	63.4	57.2	19	37
Memphis, Tenn.-Ark.	66.5	82.6	82.1	79.3	81.0	37	17
Dallas, Tex.	20.2	56.8	58.4	62.7	54.2	58	8
Houston, Tex.	70.0	81.4	73.9	75.5	62.1	85	6
Norfolk, Va.	50.8	76.4	65.8	72.7	49.5	80	47
West							
Los Angeles-	55.1	59.3	50.9	41.9	45.1	—	3
Long Beach, Calif.							40
San Diego, Calif.	50.4	70.6	60.1	55.5	51.3	—	14
San Francisco-	75.5	68.1	51.8	41.8	34.6	9	13
Oakland, Calif.							38
Denver, Colo.	72.8	74.8	67.9	53.1	41.9	25	25
Portland, Ore-Wash.	60.0	66.3	53.0	45.3	37.9	42	35
Seattle, Wash.	60.2	67.4	55.4	50.3	37.4	48	22

	1900	1930	1950	1960	1970†
U.S. Total, SMSA	62.1	64.6	58.6	51.4	45.8
Over 3,000,000 in 1960	81.1	75.8	68.5	66.1	44.4 (over 2,000,000)
1,000,000-3,000,000 in 1960	60.0	57.0	50.5	42.6	44.1
500,000-1,000,000 in 1960	57.6	65.5	59.0	52.7	49.2
250,000- 500,000 in 1960	48.6	58.0	52.9	49.0	44.3
100,000- 250,000 in 1960	50.3	59.9	57.5	56.8	—
Less than 100,000 in 1960	63.4	69.1	74.1	77.0	55.5 (less than 250,000)

*Consolidation.
†1970 categories are not identical with those of earlier years due to definitional changes.
Source: U.S. Bureau of the Census, *Selected Area Reports: Standard Metropolitan Statistical Areas*, Final Report PC(3)-10.

Table 8-5. Population Change, Central City (CC) and Outside Central City (OCC) of Cities of Standard Metropolitan Statistical Areas, by Race and by Size, 1960-70

Size of Area	All Classes			White			Negro		
	Total	CC	OCC	Total	CC	OCC	Total	CC	OCC
	Numbers in Thousands								
2,000,000 or more	5,590	-424	6,013	2,773	-2,489	5,262	2,302	1,755	547
1,000,000-2,000,000	5,966	1,034	4,931	4,940	295	4,645	820	637	182
500,000-1,000,000	3,346	763	2,583	2,767	299	2,468	437	407	30
250,000-500,000	2,769	768	2,002	2,238	462	1,875	321	248	72
Less than 250,000	2,122	1,053	1,070	1,877	826	1,051	174	186	-11
U.S. Total	19,793	3,194	16,598	14,695	-607	15,300	4,054	3,234	820
	Percent Change								
2,000,000 or more	12	-2	29	7	-13	24	40	37	59
1,000,000-2,000,000	27	10	42	24	3	41	39	39	38
500,000-1,000,000	18	8	30	17	4	31	22	26	8
250,000-500,000	17	10	22	15	7	22	20	24	13
Less than 250,000	14	13	16	14	11	17	13	21	-2
U.S. Total	17	5	28	14	-1	27	32	33	29

Source: U.S. Bureau of the Census: *1970 Census of Population.*

Table 8-6. Percentage of Families with Incomes Under $3,000 and Over $10,000, by Race of Head of Family and Size of SMSA for Central Cities (CC) and Outside Central Cities (OCC), 1959

Size of Area	All Classes			White			Negro		
	Total	CC	OCC	Total	CC	OCC	Total	CC	OCC
Percentage Under $3,000									
3,000,000 and over	12.6	15.4	8.9	10.6	12.7	8.3	27.9	28.6	24.0
1,000,000-3,000,000	13.0	17.1	10.0	10.8	13.4	9.2	32.6	32.6	32.5
500,000-1,000,000	17.2	19.8	14.2	14.7	16.4	13.1	37.9	37.8	38.3
250,000-500,000	17.6	18.7	16.6	15.3	15.3	15.2	46.1	44.4	51.0
100,000-250,000	19.5	19.6	19.3	16.1	15.6	16.6	52.3	49.5	59.3
Less than 100,000	20.7	18.8	27.2	18.2	16.6	24.1	57.2	54.5	64.5
U.S. Total	15.2	17.6	12.5	12.8	14.4	11.4	36.7	35.8	40.4
Percentage Over $10,000									
3,000,000 and over	23.0	19.5	27.6	24.9	21.9	28.3	7.4	7.2	9.1
1,000,000-3,000,000	20.8	16.6	23.9	22.5	19.2	24.5	6.2	6.0	6.9
500,000-1,000,000	16.4	14.6	18.4	17.6	16.3	19.0	6.0	5.9	6.5
250,000-500,000	14.6	14.7	14.5	15.6	16.2	15.0	2.8	2.8	2.8
100,000-250,000	13.7	14.3	12.9	14.9	15.9	13.6	2.3	2.4	1.9
Less than 100,000	13.8	14.4	12.0	14.7	15.2	12.8	1.6	1.6	1.7
U.S. Total	18.8	16.5	21.2	20.3	18.5	21.9	5.3	5.2	5.3
Ratio: Number Over $10,000 Per 100 Under $3,000									
3,000,000 and over	183.0	126.7	311.5	234.1	172.8	340.4	26.6	25.1	37.7
1,000,000-3,000,000	160.5	97.3	238.9	208.5	143.3	265.9	19.0	18.4	21.3
500,000-1,000,000	95.6	73.8	129.3	120.0	99.6	144.9	15.9	15.7	16.9
250,000-500,000	82.8	78.6	87.4	101.8	105.7	98.3	6.1	6.3	5.6
100,000-250,000	70.3	73.1	66.6	92.5	101.5	82.0	4.3	4.9	3.2
Less than 100,000	67.0	76.3	44.0	80.5	91.4	53.2	2.8	2.9	2.7
U.S. Total	123.9	93.5	169.4	157.9	128.9	191.9	14.3	14.6	13.1

Source: U.S. Bureau of the Census, U.S. Census of Population: 1960. Selected Area Reports. Standard Metropolitan Statistical Areas. Final Report PC(3)-1D.

to 1930, central cities absorbed most of the growth in metropolitan population. Migrants to the city lived in the zone in transition, and those whose improved economic status allowed them to move into the workingmen's and commuter zones also remained inside the central city. During the Depression, however, the population increases in metropolitan areas began to be larger *outside* the central city. This trend has accelerated to the point where, in the last decade, a one person increase in the central city was accompanied by a 25 person increase outside. The rapidly expanding system has pushed the commuter and, in some SMSA's, the workingmen's zones beyond the political boundaries of the central city. Table 8-3 shows that this phenomenon has been most pronounced in the older metropolitan areas where there has been an absolute loss of central city population in the two decades since 1950. As a result of this disproportionate growth, America, as shown in Table 8-4 became a predominantly suburban nation sometime in the 1960s.

The Black Migration and Maldistribution of Rich and Poor

The major changes in the American economy occasioned by World War II and subsequent industrialization profoundly impacted America's blacks. As reflected in Table 8-5, the demand for industrial workers and the mechanization of southern agriculture created a large pool of black laborers willing to move to urban areas to improve their economic status. The southern Europeans and white rural Americans, who had traditionally accounted for most of the migrants to the transitionary zones of metropolitan areas, were, by 1955, being replaced by blacks.

The economic status of the typical migrant black family was similar to that of the preceding migrant—poor. Because economic expansion had, by 1960, delivered most middle class families to the suburbs, and because the transitionary zones remained in the central city, the maldistribution of rich and poor between political jurisdictions became pronounced. As shown in Table 8-6, the central cities, by 1960, were increasingly black and poor; the suburbs, white and middle class.

REDUCED SOCIAL MOBILITY

The implications of the rapid change in America's economy and urban system have become increasingly clear over the last decade. The altered spatial distribution of wealth and of races across communities and jurisdictions has created serious problems. Many poor Americans no longer believe that they have the opportunity to increase the benefits received from the economic system. Educational and work opportunities have not allowed the children of the most recent migrants to increase their relative economic status and their choice of residential environments. The forces which reduced social mobility have not abated, and deserve fuller explication.

The Zones in Transition Become Chronic

Burgess hypothesized that the zone in transition was being invaded by business district land uses as competition for central sites increased. The displaced land uses, usually low-rent residences and heavy industry, were in the zone in transition because they could not outbid banks and retailers for central sites, but still needed to be as close to the point of highest accessibility as possible.

Low-rent residences in the zone of transition were of two types. The first were old structures allowed to decay by owners waiting for central business district land users to purchase the land at increased prices. To invest in a home that would be torn down and was worthless, relative to the land on which it stood, was economically unwise. The tenants, moreover, were unskilled laborers who worked in the nearby factories and could not afford the higher rents that would come with better maintenance.

The second type of residence, the high density tenement, was an economically wise use of zone-in-transition land not faced with immediate prospects of succession. Industrial workers could not afford to buy homes in better districts and commute, so a high density tenement near the factories could be filled, despite its unattractive environment. The owner, to profit on expensive land with low rents, often increased the ratio of units to covered surface area to the technological or legal limit.

As industrial uses superseded tenements, the latter would, as Burgess hypothesized, appear in the zone of workingmen's homes, which, in turn, expanded into the commuter zone, and so on. This supersessional model assumed that the zone in transition would move outward, encompassing newer units, rather than remain in the same absolute position. The lower rent housing stock, it was assumed, would never become totally dilapidated since it was "filtering down" at a pace proportional to growth of the entire housing stock. If upper and middle income housing was built more quickly, the quality of filtered down housing—being newer—was expected to improve. Whether the filter down effect ever worked is debatable, but, by 1960, it clearly was not. The supersession process, theoretically moved from the center, had halted with the age of cheap mobility.

As the interstate highway system was built, location options expanded for manufacturers located at the periphery of central business districts. Before large-load trucks and ubiquitous highways were available, the manufacturer was reluctant to move very far from the central location and rail terminal. The cost of friction was so high that relocation was kept to a minimal distance, reflecting the Burgess supersession model in which the industrial zone encroached predictably into the zone in transition. When trucks became widely available and highways were built, however, the cost of moving materials through space dropped, especially in terms of time. A manufacturer could move, for the sake of the example, five times the distance for the same cost of friction. Rather than move to a new site in the zone in transition and incur site clearance costs and expensive multistory construction, the entrepreneur took advantage of the

Table 8-7. Manufacturing Employment, Central City (CC) and Outside Central City (OCC),* 1958, 1963, and 1967 (in Thousands), 37 Largest Standard Metropolitan Statistical Areas

	1958		1963		1967		% Increase, 1958-67	
	CC	OCC	CC	OCC	CC	OCC	CC	OCC
East								
Washington, D.C.	21.3	13.4	22.1	28.0	23.1	32.4	+8.5	+141.8
Baltimore, Md.	113.4	84.4	103.9	86.6	106.7	103.0	−5.9	+22.0
Boston, Mass.	90.2	210.8	82.5	210.9	79.6	236.6	−11.8	+17.0
Newark, N.J.	78.8	166.8	73.7	176.5	68.5	195.2	−10.3	+12.2
Patterson-Clifton-Passaic, N.J.	62.9	95.6	62.8	113.7	62.1	127.9	−1.3	+33.8
Buffalo, N.Y.	68.0	105.9	57.0	105.9	66.7	109.5	−1.9	+3.4
New York, N.Y.	998.6	185.4	927.4	219.8	895.3	252.1	−10.3	+36.0
Rochester, N.Y.	96.5	20.2	97.3	24.0	114.2	31.5	+18.3	+55.9
Philadelphia, Pa.-N.J.	298.5	238.4	264.9	270.9	263.9	309.9	−11.6	+30.0
Pittsburgh, Pa.	99.3	206.4	81.7	190.5	85.6	214.0	−13.8	+3.7
Providence, R.I.	62.6	64.6	65.0	60.9	65.4	72.6	+4.5	+12.4
Midwest								
Chicago, Ill.	569.4	287.8	508.4	352.2	546.9	436.2	−4.0	+51.6
Indianapolis, Ind.	70.1	35.5	70.2	45.6	86.3	48.4	+23.1	+36.3
Detroit, Mich.	213.5	253.9	200.6	293.3	209.7	374.8	−1.8	+47.6
Minneapolis-St. Paul, Minn.	113.5	32.5	110.3	53.5	123.6	80.0	+8.9	+146.2
Kansas City, Mo.-Kans.	64.9	38.2	62.1	49.0	65.1	64.3	0	+68.3
St. Louis, Mo.-Ill.	146.8	115.7	129.1	130.6	131.9	163.6	−14.9	+41.4
Cincinnati, Ohio-Ky.-Ind.	76.4	80.1	76.6	77.5	84.5	82.3	+10.6	+2.7

Cleveland, Ohio	180.8	92.9	168.9	111.4	171.3	135.5	−5.3	+42.6
Columbus, Ohio	55.4	17.6	65.9	14.3	65.4	17.6	+18.1	0
Dayton, Ohio	78.2	19.0	81.2	23.0	88.3	37.9	+12.9	+99.5
Milwaukee, Wis.	126.6	63.9	119.3	74.5	118.6	97.9	−6.3	+55.6
South								
Miami, Fla.	19.4	17.4	19.2	24.0	20.5	37.8	+5.7	+116.0
Tampa-St. Petersburg, Fla.	23.7	8.5	23.8	12.9	24.6	24.1	+3.8	+280.0
Atlanta, Ga.	49.6	33.9	52.4	43.3	54.0	63.2	+8.9	+86.4
Louisville, Ky.-Ind.	55.7	31.0	58.0	29.6	64.0	46.0	+16.7	+48.4
New Orleans, La.	30.1	16.8	31.1	18.0	33.8	21.7	+12.3	+29.2
Dallas, Tex.	79.7	15.5	86.3	23.2	113.1	35.8	+41.9	+131.0
Houston, Tex.	68.8	35.7	77.3	31.3	97.9	40.2	+41.6	+12.6
San Antonio, Tex.	19.3	1.6	2.4	2.2	24.8	2.6	+28.5	+62.5
West								
Los Angeles-Long Beach, Calif.	327.2	401.8	304.0	538.9	361.0	494.4	+10.3	+23.0
San Diego, Calif.	56.8	14.6	43.7	11.6	42.9	20.6	−24.5	+27.5
San Francisco-Oakland, Calif.	99.5	90.8	91.6	104.6	80.5	117.4	−23.5	+29.3
San Bernardino-Riverside-Ontario, Calif.	11.7	17.5	14.0	23.5	18.4	28.0	+57.3	+60.0
Denver, Colo.	37.9	15.8	36.1	33.4	40.5	33.6	+6.9	+112.7
Portland, Ore.-Wash.	35.2	23.1	35.6	29.7	41.0	38.8	+16.5	+68.0
Seattle-Everett, Wash.	86.5	28.4	84.1	37.5	64.3	97.9	−25.7	+244.7
Weighted Average	—	—	—	—	—	—	−1.8	+36.0

*Not adjusted for annexation.
Source: U.S. Census of Manufacturing.

highway to "leapfrog" over the zone in transition into suburban areas, where lower land prices and taxes permitted cheaper, single-level construction.

As leapfrogging became more common, supersession from inner zones decreased, lowering land values in transitionary areas. Land owners lost money and began to abandon structures. Racial discrimination precluded many blacks and minorities from buying homes in suburban or even working class areas. With no supersession from the center and with discrimination and increasing prices in the suburban and working class areas, the zone in transition became stagnant and chronic. The environment in which the lower socioeconomic class population prepared for upward social mobility worsened at a time when most Americans were moving to their "dream houses."

The Loss of Manufacturing and Retailing Job Opportunities

The leapfrogging of manufacturing firms, from central locations to suburban areas, not only added to the stagnation of the zones of transition, but it also reduced social mobility. Traditionally the semiskilled manufacturing job was regarded as the income source which started the migrant family on its ascent to the middle class. One advantage to being in the transitionary areas was proximity to unskilled employment opportunities. By mid-century, however, automation had reduced the number of unskilled or semiskilled jobs, and the suburbanization of manufacturing made those that were available difficult for minorities in the central city to reach. As Table 8-7 shows, in the 37 largest SMSA's manufacturing jobs *decreased* an average of 1.8 percent in the central city, while increasing 36 percent outside, between 1958 and 1967.

In addition to the loss of employment opportunities in central cities, other traditional means to upward social mobility were disappearing by the mid-1960s. The retailing function traditionally identified with "downtown," or the "central business district," began to follow customers to the suburbs. As shopping centers with acres of parking began to appear over the suburban landscape, fewer middle class shoppers chose to drive to the congested central city. Table 8-8 shows the result of decentralized retailing. Central cities, which accounted for an average of 63 percent of all sales in the 37 largest SMSA's in 1958, represented only 49.3 percent in 1967.

With the loss of manufacturing and retailing jobs in the central cities, the latest migrants to the "staging areas" of America's economic system were severely hampered. Because these migrants were racially different, the opportunities were probably even fewer than statistical count would indicate. As the traditional means to socioeconomic mobility became more elusive, the public sector assumed the task of keeping the relative difference in standard of living, between the majority of Americans and the urban poor, from widening beyond politically acceptable parameters.

Table 8-8. Percentage Increase in Retail Sales, Deflated by General Price
Increase, Central City (CC) and Outside Central City (OCC) Areas, 1958-67,
and Percentage Retail Sales in Central City (CC) 1958 and 1967,
37 Largest Standard Metropolitan Statistical Areas

Area	% Retail Sales in CC (CC/SMSA)			% Increase (Real) Retail Sales, 1958-67	
	1958	1963	1967	CC	OCC
Washington, D.C.	52.1	42.1	32.9	10.5	134.8
Baltimore, Md.	71.4	58.1	53.4	4.9	128.2
Boston, Mass.	38.9	31.2	26.0	--1.4	79.2
Newark, N.J.	30.0	25.8	21.2	−14.1	37.1
Paterson-Clifton-Passaic, N.J.	36.0	23.9	24.6	0.9	74.5
Buffalo, N.Y.	52.2	40.1	38.9	–9.9	54.7
New York, N.Y.	72.9	67.1	64.8	9.7	60.2
Rochester, N.Y.	60.4	52.9	48.5	18.1	91.3
Philadelphia, Pa.-N.J.	51.1	43.4	40.2	6.2	65.4
Pittsburgh, Pa.	37.5	34.1	33.5	7.8	28.7
Providence, R.I.	55.7	50.4	31.2	−36.3	73.1
Northeast	(50.7)	(42.6)	(37.7)	(−0.3)	(75.2)
Chicago, Ill.	65.3	56.9	51.5	5.3	86.6
Indianapolis, Ind.	76.8	65.5	60.4	20.0	160.8
Detroit, Mich.	51.1	42.7	36.1	0.7	86.4
Minneapolis-St. Paul, Minn.	73.4	61.5	54.4	7.9	149.7
Kansas City, Mo.-Kans.	59.9	63.3	50.1	55.2	64.3
St. Louis, Mo.-Ill.	48.1	37.5	32.7	−7.8	76.3
Cincinatti, Ohio-Ky.-Ind.	64.2	57.0	45.0	4.6	129.4
Cleveland, Ohio	74.0	54.8	39.6	−15.2	269.1
Columbus, Ohio	80.2	69.0	67.2	22.8	141.9
Dayton, Ohio	60.5	47.4	41.3	3.6	125.5
Milwaukee, Wis.	73.1	63.1	58.4	7.5	108.3
Midwest	(66.0)	(56.2)	(48.8)	(9.5)	(127.1)
Miami, Fla.	54.9	40.4	37.5	−2.5	98.2
Tampa-St. Petersburg, Fla.	75.4	66.6	65.8	30.9	108.9
Atlanta, Ga.	71.4	62.8	57.6	37.7	153.9
Louisville, Ky.-Ind.	70.5	64.0	57.5	14.0	101.8
New Orleans, La.	79.0	71.3	65.3	21.0	141.9
Dallas, Tex.	77.7	71.2	68.4	36.6	119.2
Houston, Tex.	75.7	82.4	74.8	55.9	63.3
San Antonio, Tex.	91.2	90.0	89.6	36.4	79.9
South	(74.4)	(68.6)	(64.5)	(28.7)	(108.3)
Los Angeles-Long Beach, Calif.	48.8	41.3	39.9	22.2	75.4
San Bernardino-Riverside, Calif.	44.9	42.1	NA	NA	NA
San Diego, Calif.	64.0	56.4	53.9	25.6	91.8
San Francisco-Oakland, Calif.	54.5	48.0	43.4	16.3	81.6
Denver, Colo.	70.5	55.9	53.3	11.1	132.4
Portland, Ore.-Wash.	76.3	58.8	59.6	28.1	180.3
Seattle, Wash.	71.7	63.5	54.3	18.0	152.5
West	(61.5)	(52.3)	(49.0)	(20.2)	(119.0)
Unweighted average, 37 SMSA's	63.0	54.1	49.3	12.6	105.8

Source: U.S. Bureau of the Census. *Census of Business—1958*, Vol. II, *Census of Business—1963*, Vol. II; and *Census of Business—1967*, Vol. II.

Fiscal Disparities

The health and behavioral problems indigenous to a dynamic economy inevitably evoke controversy over who should pay for their amelioration. Such services as police and fire fighting have traditionally been regarded as functions that government should provide at public expense. While private charities provide some health services, public health and sanitation services have also become primarily public functions. The public sector has become increasingly responsible for providing food, clothing, and shelter for the needy. Besides these functions, education and other services intended to improve the lot of the citizenry have been publicly organized and funded. To ensure that all these services are rendered to those who need them, governments have been given the power to tax. Local government, cities, and school districts in particular, usually raise funds through the property tax. While levied against all material goods owned by individuals, the largest sources of property tax income are land and the structures built upon it. Jurisdictions "assess," or estimate the value of, a house, store, apartment building, or factory, and the owner pays a percentage of the value in taxes. The logic underlying the property tax is that those who benefit most from the social contract and who have the most property to protect should pay the most to enforce and maintain that contract.

When the central city was coterminous with the urban system, the entire socioeconomic strata would be taxed for services. The rich and the middle class, and the industrial and service corporations probably paid their share of the cost incurred in providing police, social workers, sanitation, public health services, public housing, welfare payments, and education to those who would eventually become productive, taxpaying citizens. Until early in this century, in fact, the cities were the center of wealth and new investment. Tax receipts increased without rate increases as competition drove up property values faster than inflation. As long as the city was the focus of supersession, and the outer rings remained much within its boundaries, tax revenues would seem to be equal to the costs of helping those who were attracted by its economic success.

When the postwar suburbanization of residential, manufacturing, and service functions began, central cities faced a new and threatening fiscal environment. On the demand side, the central city was being asked to supply all the traditional services needed by migrants and lower socioeconomic classes, as well as increased welfare payments brought on by job losses described above. With the stagnation of the housing stock available to the lower classes, government had to clear abandoned units and provide new housing. Much of the infrastructure—roads, sewers, libraries, police stations, schools—was reaching the end of its useful life by mid-century, meaning a major investment in new construction was necessary. While demand on the public treasury was steadily increasing, revenues were not. Manufacturers and retailers were moving outside the city. The commuter zone, in Burgess' terms, had now moved over the city boundaries, denying its property taxes to the city coffers. City taxes had to be raised, but this was often self-

Table 8-9. Taxable Real Property Values, 1961-66, School District Basis,
Central City (CC) and Outside Central City Areas (OCC)

	% Values in CC		% Growth in Real Values	
	1961	1966	CC	OCC
East				
Baltimore, Md.	47.9	40.6	4.3	40.3
Boston, Mass.	23.1	16.7	2.3	52.8
Newark, N.J.	20.8	17.6	109.0†	157.9†
Buffalo, N.Y.	44.6	42.1	0.3	11.0
New York, N.Y.	79.8	78.3	22.1	48.5
Rochester, N.Y.	49.4	41.6	2.5	40.8
Philadelphia, Pa.-N.J.	58.4	48.4	8.8	62.6†
Pittsburgh, Pa.	30.2	27.9	2.2	14.5
Midwest				
Chicago, Ill.	49.4	44.5	4.5	26.8
Indianapolis, Ind.	50.1	43.4	14.0	49.5
Detroit, Mich.	48.9	37.2	−4.6	54.3
Minneapolis, Minn.	37.9	31.3	2.0	56.0
St. Paul, Minn.	21.7	17.8	1.5	56.0
Kansas City, Mo.−Kans.	55.0	52.8	13.8*	24.1
St. Louis, Mo.-Ill.	32.8	29.8	5.7	21.2
Omaha, Neb.-Iowa	66.2	67.2	53.3*,†	46.6†
Cincinnati, Ohio-Ky. Ind.	42.3	30.6	7.4	67.5†
Cleveland, Ohio	40.4	34.3	−5.1	23.6
Columbus, Ohio	57.9	56.0	21.9*	31.6*
Toledo, Ohio	51.8	67.7	24.2*	−11.6*
Milwaukee, Wis.	51.6	46.5	9.7	34.9
South				
Birmingham, Ala.	55.1	44.3	4.9	64.5
Atlanta, Ga.	43.5	33.7	24.7	88.4
Louisville, Ky.-Ind.	50.9	49.1	227.3†	251.8†
New Orleans, La.	83.0	78.2	10.2	49.6
Oklahoma City, Okla.	NA	61.1	NA	NA
Memphis, Tenn.-Ark.	76.0	76.3	33.2	31.8*
Dallas, Tex.	NA	NA	31.8	NA
Houston, Tex.	NA	NA	41.7	NA
Norfolk, Va.	NA	45.7	20.5	NA
West				
Long Beach, Calif.	4.3	4.8	57.0	39.4
Los Angeles, Calif.	36.4	36.8	43.0*	39.4
San Diego, Calif.	54.5	54.3	26.2	27.3
San Francisco, Calif.	27.9	23.0	17.7	57.4
Oakland, Calif.	11.7	10.2	24.2	57.4
Denver, Colo.	55.7	49.0	11.2*	40.8
Portland, Ore.-Wash.	56.0	40.2	−23.4*,†	28.8†
Seattle, Wash.	55.5	46.7	21.2	72.4
Average	47.0	40.8		

*Annexation.
†Reassessment.

Source: U.S. Bureau of the Census, *Census of Governments: Taxable Property Values.*

defeating. Those individuals and firms whose location decisions were tenuous would now move to the suburbs to avoid higher central city taxes. Each time a middle class homeowner left the central city, rather than invest in his house, the burden on remaining middle class homeowners increased. With each increase, more left, creating a vicious circle. As shown in Table 8-9, growth in assessed valuation of central city property was considerably slower than in the suburbs between 1961 and 1966, and in several instances actually decreased. Considering the fact that there was an eight percent inflation over those five years, several central cities became net losers of property tax base.

The comparison between the steadily increasing demand for services and the stable, if not decreasing, tax base of the many central cities, and the low service demands and increasing tax base of the suburbs has been referred to as "fiscal disparities." Table 8-10 shows the impact of this disparity in terms of revenues

Table 8-10. Summary of Fiscal Disparities Inside and Outside
Central City, 37 Largest Standard Metropolitan Statistical Areas,
1964-1965

| | 37 Largest SMSA's | | | | Remainder of Nation (Weighted Average) |
| | In Central City | | Outside Central City | | |
Item	Weighted Average	Unweighted Average	Weighted Average	Unweighted Average	
Per capita total general expenditures	$ 332	$ 304	$ 278	$ 265	$ 203
Per capita educational expenditures	100	99	146	141	107
Per pupil current expenditures	NA	449	NA	573	NA
Per capita general non-educational expenditures	232	205	132	124	96
Per capita total general revenues	340	301	268	253	212
Per capita taxes	200	173	152	137	103
Per capita Federal and State aid	88	78	80	78	76
Percent of general expenditure	26.5%	25.7%	28.8%	29.4%	37.4%
Percent of taxes	44.0	45.1	52.6	56.9	73.8
Per capita income	2,607	2,482	2,732	2,552	1,789

NA = Data not available.
Source: U.S. Government publication.

and expenditures. Central cities, and jurisdictions overlaying them, must tax their citizens more heavily than suburban citizens are taxed. With more police, fire fighting, physical maintenance, and social services needed in the central cities, a larger amount of revenues must be expended on non-educational functions than on schools. In the suburbs, even after non-educational functions are paid for, there is a higher per capital expenditure for schools than in the central city, even though the tax burden is lower.

Educational expenditures were singled out, above, because schools have traditionally played an important role in preparing migrants and the poor to participate in America's economic system. Not only have manufacturing and service firms moved to the suburbs, but the jobs that remain available often require more education than those previously filled by migrants. If schools are to remain a viable means to economic assimilation, they must teach useful skills, as well as transmit the norms and behavior expectations of the dominant society. The shift in the mix and spatial distribution of metropolitan populations, occasioned by suburbanization of mid-century, seems to have precluded this.

Schools—A Case Study of the Impact of Ecological Change on Human Wellbeing

Education is highly valued by American society. While there is controversy over how much one's school performance influences future earnings (Jencks, 1972), schooling is crucial to success in America. Without credentials, jobs are extremely difficult to find. Beyond the obvious credentialing function, schools provide the basic reading, writing, and calculating skills needed to function in any level of a complex economy. More importantly, schools perform the crucial function of transmitting the behavioral prerequisites to achievement in society. These prerequisites include interpersonal, social, and language skills not always learned from teachers. Schools are among the principal institutions used to shape behavior into societally sanctioned, "normal," patterns.

As the educational function has become increasingly controversial due to its cost and use as an instrument of social policy, researchers from numerous disciplines have become interested in measuring the impact of school on children. Among the best known of these studies has been the Coleman report (1966). In the Civil Rights Act of 1964, Congress directed the Commissioner of Education to survey educational opportunities available to minority groups. The Commissioner, Harold Howe, contracted with a staff of researchers, led by James Coleman of Johns Hopkins University. Their report, issued in 1966, focused on three questions:

1. Do schools attended by minority groups in America differ from those attended by most American children?
2. If yes, what are the differences?
3. Do those differences affect student achievement?

As expected, the researchers found that schools attended by minority group children did differ from those attended by most American children. The two primary differences related to classmates and to the schools themselves. The classmates of minority students tended to also be from minority groups, and their schools were usually older and less well equipped. These differences reflected the suburbanization and segregation of metropolitan areas which greatly accelerated at mid-century. School districts overlaying the central cities served increasingly black populations and found it increasingly difficult to raise revenues to replace, or refurbish, old schools.

Coleman's most controversial finding concerned the determinants of scores on standardized achievement tests. After tests were administered to a sample of first, third, sixth, ninth, and twelfth grade white and minority group students across the United States, Coleman used statistical techniques to determine if test scores could be predicted by differences in family background, or in schools. Analysis determined that the best predictors of student test scores were the educational attainment and income of parents. Children whose parents had more years of schooling and higher incomes did better as a group than those with less well educated parents. While genetic interpretations of this finding have been offered (Scarr & Weinberg, 1978), most explanations assert that the more education a person has the higher the value he places on school achievement, and the more he insists that his children perform successfully in school. For minority students, Coleman found that the income of parents was especially predictive. The higher the income of minority families, the higher the children tended to score. Once again, it is assumed that successful parents insist that their children be successful in competitive endeavors, such as school. The most important variable in explaining the variation in test scores appeared to be the degree to which the student's home environment was achievement oriented.

The second most important variable in predicting test scores was the achievement orientation of classmates. Students whose parents' educational attainment and economic status were comparatively low scored higher than others with similar family backgrounds, when their classmates were from homes with more educated and higher income parents. This effect has been explained as a product of peer group pressure or behavior modeling. If a student with little interest in school achievement is placed in an environment in which his peers are highly motivated to succeed, he will eventually model their achievement drive. If two students from similar home environments were placed in different schools, one with peers whose parents had more education and higher incomes and the other with peers from homes similar to his own, the Coleman findings would predict the former would eventually score higher on achievement tests than the latter.

The third most predictive variable was the characteristics of the schools and teachers. Assuming two groups of students with the identical mix of family backgrounds were assigned to two schools varying significantly in the amount of lab space, library size, and teacher experience, Coleman's analysis indicated the

Table 8-11. Educational Characteristics Based on
Selected Urbanized Areas, 1960

Area	Percent of Persons 14 to 17 Years of Age Not in School		Median School Years Completed, Persons Over 25 Years of Age	
	Central City	Urban Fringe	Central City	Urban Fringe
Los Angeles-Long Beach, California	10.2%	9.2%	12.1	12.1
San Bernardino-Riverside-Ontario, California	5.6	8.0	12.2	11.6
San Diego, California	13.2	8.0	12.2	12.2
San Francisco-Oakland, California	9.8	7.4	11.9	12.3
Denver, Colorado	14.0	8.2	12.1	12.4
Washington, D.C.	15.2	7.5	11.7	12.6
Miami, Florida	14.1	9.0	10.6	12.0
Tampa, Florida	13.9	12.0	10.2	11.3
St. Petersburg, Florida	10.1	15.7	11.0	11.2
Atlanta, Georgia	15.1	9.9	10.5	12.3
Chicago, Illinois	14.2	9.8	10.0	12.1
Indianapolis, Indiana	16.3	8.9	10.8	12.2
Louisville, Kentucky-Indiana	18.7	12.0	9.3	11.1
New Orleans, Louisiana	15.0	12.9	9.0	11.1
Baltimore, Maryland	19.2	11.6	8.9	10.9
Boston, Massachusetts	18.2	9.7	11.2	12.3
Detroit, Michigan	11.6	8.6	10.0	11.7
Minneapolis-St. Paul, Minnesota	8.7	6.1	11.6	12.4
Kansas City, Missouri-Kansas	16.1	10.6	11.5	12.1
St. Louis, Missouri-Illinois	17.7	9.0	8.8	10.9
Newark, New Jersey	10.4	7.9	9.0	11.8
Paterson-Clifton-Passaic, New Jersey	12.1	7.9	9.1	11.8
Buffalo, New York	11.9	8.1	9.6	11.3
New York, New York	14.6	7.9	10.1	18.8
Rochester, New York	10.9	3.8	10.1	12.2
Cincinnati, Ohio-Kentucky-Indiana	15.7	10.1	9.7	10.9
Cleveland, Ohio	13.6	6.5	9.6	12.2
Columbus, Ohio	15.0	5.4	11.2	12.5
Dayton, Ohio	13.0	8.4	10.4	12.1
Portland, Oregon-Washington	6.0	5.0	12.0	12.2
Philadelphia, Pennsylvania-New Jersey	15.6	9.1	9.6	11.7
Pittsburgh, Pennsylvania	13.8	9.5	10.0	11.3
Providence, Rhode Island	18.4	18.3	9.6	10.5
Dallas Texas	16.8	12.2	11.8	12.2
Houston, Texas	14.3	10.8	11.3	12.0
San Antonio, Texas	19.0	49.7	9.6	12.8
Seattle, Washington	4.8	6.0	12.2	12.4
Milwaukee, Wisconsin	8.9	5.1	10.4	12.1
U.S. average	13.5	9.0	10.7	12.0

Source: U.S. Bureau of the Census, *U.S. Census of Population, 1960, Selected Area Reports, Standard Metropolitan Statistical Areas*, Final Report PC(3)-1D.

Table 8-12. Current Educational Expenditures Per Student, Total Educational and Noneducational Expenditures Per Capita, and Total Nonaided Educational Expenditures Per Capita (Tax Proxy) for Central City and Outside Central City Areas, 1962
(School District Basis)

	Current Education Expenditures Per Pupil, $		Total Education Expenditures Per Capita, $		Total Non-aided Education Expenditures Per Capita, $		Total Noneducation Expenditures Per Capita, $	
	CC	OCC	CC	OCC	CC	OCC	CC	OCC
East								
Baltimore, Md.	366	421	81	113	61	81	206	93
Boston, Mass.	385	465	50	101	44	93	227	142
Newark, N.J.	496	522	94	112	78	100	201	151
Buffalo, N.Y.	447	561	59	137	34	78	161	184
New York, N.Y.	537	684	77	194	47	128	276	161
Rochester, N.Y.	580	573	79	159	55	92	185	185
Philadelphia, Pa.-N.J.	393	493	55	106	37	81	154	84
Pittsburgh, Pa.	368	451	51	96	40	62	117	91
Midwest								
Chicago, Ill.	408	474	66	113	51	92	177	137
Indianapolis, Ind.	353	468	70	144	51	116	116	116
Detroit, Mich.	462	434	94	128	70	89	163	131
Minneapolis, Minn.	414	442	61	157	42	110	155	146
St. Paul, Minn.	416	442	58	157	40	110	143	146

Kansas City, Mo.-Kans.	409	351	75	157	54	126	95	108
St. Louis, Mo.-Ill.	387	434	55	101	37	76	145	76
Omaha, Neb.-Iowa	283	395	49	137	44	126	128	101
Cincinnati, Ohio-Ky.-Ind.	373	398	63	118	55	95	171	151
Cleveland, Ohio	371	459	65	114	58	101	156	141
Columbus, Ohio	327	332	61	98	52	70	130	130
Toledo, Ohio	379	512	80	161	72	113	129	120
Milwaukee, Wis.	378	469	65	125	52	113	220	190
South								
Birmingham, Ala.	194	224	50	61	18	24	75	75
Atlanta, Ga.	273	288	57	90	36	51	147	121
Louisville, Ky.-Ind.	301	478	43	134	25	106	97	77
New Orleans, La.	272	233	42	67	13	28	131	98
Oklahoma City, Okla.	269	292	57	84	44	70	76	66
Memphis, Tenn.-Ark.	228	246	49	97	27	64	131	132
Dallas, Tex.	302	325	74	100	47	62	114	99
Houston, Tex.	290	450	64	144	32	92	116	116
Norfolk, Va.	265	289	47	88	30	59	347	72
West								
Long Beach, Calif.	426	555	86	132	50	72	180	199
Los Angeles, Calif.	437	555	101	132	50	72	204	199
San Diego, Calif.	414	539	105	156	68	82	168	168
San Francisco, Calif.	468	546	69	132	45	74	240	182
Denver, Colo.	418	381	81	151	67	116	164	94
Portland, Ore.-Wash.	422	480	79	149	58	96	111	105
Seattle, Wash.	410	416	89	138	47	59	153	121

Source: U.S. Bureau of the Census, *Census of Governments, 1962.*

group in the better equipped school would do better. The amount of resources available to a school district, reflected in per pupil expenditure, would be the best predictor if the student socioeconomic mix held constant across districts. Teacher-related variables, such as education, experience, and family economic status, did influence the scores of black students, but had little impact on white student scores.

The impact of the suburbanization and segregation of metropolitan populations on schools as a means to social mobility can be best understood in light of Coleman's findings. The key to Coleman's first two predictors is how important a student's family and peers regard school achievement. Achievement orientation of parents is best measured by their own educational attainment and income. The best measure for peers is parental educational attainment and income. Coleman's data indicates that the child least likely to succeed is one whose parents are relatively less educated and earn lower incomes, whose classmates come predominantly from similar households, and whose school district has low per pupil expenditures. These conditions are typical of central city school districts and further impede upward mobility. Table 8-6 shows that the central cities are typically poorer than suburbs. Table 8-11 shows that educational attainment of the typical central city parent is considerably less than that of his, or her, suburban counterpart. Table 8-12 indicates the nearly universal pattern of suburban school districts spending more per pupil than central city districts. By all of Coleman's measures, it would seem that the gap between the school achievement of the children of the rich and middle class and that of the urban poor will continue to widen. The system that once appeared able to provide each family with a reward for temporarily filling the most menial of roles in the division of labor, and for enduring the risks of living in transitionary areas had ceased to function by 1964.

The Urban Riots

As has been described in the previous three chapters, rates of disease, abnormal behavior, and crime exhibit ecological gradients as does the age and quality of housing stock. In geopolitical terms, the gradient means the highest rates are in the central cities of metropolitan areas. This situation is not new. The "zones in transition" have traditionally been the homes of those populations most seriously stressed by the dynamism of industrial societies. Economic growth and relative equality of opportunity, however, traditionally allowed the populations attracted to transitional areas by the promise of increased economic wellbeing to improve their position in the socioeconomic strata. The American dream of a good home and comfortable life style seemed within reach of those willing to endure initial adversity and to work hard. The very success which enabled many white American families to move to suburban areas, however, accelerated the processes of segregation and political balkanization which reduced the chances of similar success for minorities. Manufacturing and service firms moved to

Table 8-13. Median Annual Income of White and Nonwhite Males
(1939-1969)

Year	1 White Males	2 Nonwhite Males*	3 White/Nonwhite Difference	4 Percent of Nonwhite to White†
1939	$1112	$ 460	$ 652	41
1945	2176	1158	1018	53
1946	2223	1367	856	61
1947	2357	1279	1078	54
1948	2510	1363	1147	54
1949	2471	1196	1275	48
1950	2982	1828	1154	61
1951	3101	1708	1393	51
1952	3255	1784	1471	55
1953	3396	1870	1526	55
1954	3359	1678	1681	50
1955	3542	1868	1674	53
1956	3827	2000	1827	52
1957	3910	2075	1835	53
1958	3976	1981	1995	50
1959	4208	1977	2231	47
1960	4297	2258	2039	53
1961	4432	2292	2140	52
1962	4460	2291	2369	49
1963	4816	2507	2209	52
1964	4936	2797	2139	57
1965	5290	2848	2443	54
1966	5592	3097	2495	55
1967	5862	3448	2414	59
1968	6267	3827	2440	61
1969	6765	3935	2830	55

*95 percent of this group are black.
†100 percent indicates perfect income equality; 0 percent indicates perfect inequality.

Source: U.S. Bureau of the Census, *Current Population Reports—Consumer Income*, Series P-60, "Income of Families and Persons in the United States," annual issues.

outside city locations, making employment for adults difficult to secure. The public schools, the mechanism which helped children to escape the transitionary areas whether parents were successful or not, have become predominantly poor, underfunded, and increasingly ineffective. Those minorities fortunate enough to overcome the increased impediments to economic success often found that racial discrimination precluded their full participation in American life (Simkus, 1978). The system of collection, production, and distribution which brought migrant populations to the transitionary areas was apparently condemning them to remain there, despite the general prosperity around them (Table 8-13). This realization precipitated the destruction and killing which plagued the stagnant zones in transition in the mid 1960s.

UNINTENDED OUTCOMES

The situation described above is the product of many decisions. Many were made by individuals, some by corporations, and others by government. Each decision was supposedly made on the basis of whether the action in question would return more benefits than costs. The entrepreneur, deciding where to build a new factory, calculates all the costs of alternative sites in the city and suburbs and chooses the one which will be most profitable. The worker who will take a job in that factory likewise considers where he will locate, trading off distance from work with attractiveness of neighborhood. Thousands of these decisions are made each year in any metropolitan area. The decision makers gather as much data as they think necessary for an informed choice and, depending on the economy and restrictions placed upon them by law, act. If each decision maker did the most rational thing for his family or firm, would the sum of all such decisions maximize the well being of the whole of the community? The example of the asbestos factory cited in Chapter 3 demonstrates that the answer is not necessarily. The individual decision maker does not have to bear all costs generated by his action. The accounting and proper assignment of these costs is government's most important and controversial function. The public sector has the right, indeed the duty, through the social contract, to preclude someone from harming the general welfare for individual gain, and to either internalize, or preclude, the social costs of actions which affect the general public. With our communities plagued by adaptation and pollution-linked health problems, and by crime, alcoholism, drug addiction, and other behavioral problems, one is entitled to ask whether the increase in goods and services created by each advance in economic organizations has been worth the human pain and suffering incurred? And is the public sector, indeed anyone, accounting the human cost of change so that the most enlightened decisions can be made and costs corrected assigned? While the answer to the first question is as yet unclear, the second can be answered no.

In fact, the public sector, which has apparently failed in its duty to supervise the impact of private actions on public health and welfare, has committed some of the worst offenses. Were the costs of air pollution, traffic deaths, resource depletion, and segregation calculated and considered in deciding whether to build the interstate highway system? Were the same costs considered in deciding to fund housing subsidy programs? Have the human costs of unemployment vis-a-vis inflation been accounted to insure that national economic policies are as well informed as possible? The answer to many, if not all, of the above is no. The federal government has been remiss in assessing how policy alternatives can influence population distribution, and the implications of that distribution for the incidence and control of problems. State and local governments have been equally lax in assessing the impact of private decisions on wellbeing, and in properly assigning the costs of change. The next chapter will suggest two factors responsible (or involved in) the failure to account the human costs of public and private actions: 1) the ideology and structure of government in America, and 2) the lack of knowledge of human costs, and the need for social ecological research.

Table 8-14. Criteria Followed in Establishing
Standard Metropolitan Statistical Areas

A standard metropolitan statistical area always includes a city (cities) of specified population which constitutes the central city and the county (counties) in which it is located. A standard metropolitan statistical area also includes contiguous counties when the economic and social relationships between the central and contiguous counties meet specified criteria of metropolitan character and integration. A standard metropolitan statistical area may cross State lines. In New England, standard metropolitan statistical areas are composed of cities and towns instead of counties.

A standard metropolitan statistical area is generally designated on the basis of population statistics reported in a census, conducted by the Bureau of the Census.

A standard metropolitan statistical area is sometimes designated on the basis of population estimates published by the Bureau of the Census which have been accepted for use in the distribution of Federal benefits. An area designated on the basis of such estimates shall lose its designation, if it does not qualify for designation on the basis of population statistics reported in the next succeeding census conducted by the Bureau of the Census.

Basic Criteria

1. Each standard metropolitan statistical area must include at least:
(a) One city with 50,000 or more inhabitants, *or*
(b) A city with at least 25,000 inhabitants, which, together with those contiguous places (incorporated or unincorporated) having population densities of at least 1000 persons per square mile, has a combined population of 50,000 and constitutes for general economic and social purposes a single community, provided that the county or counties in which the city and contiguous places are located has a total population of at least 75,000.
2. A contiguous county will be included in a standard metropolitan statistical area if
(a) At least 75.00% of the resident labor force in the county is in the non-agricultural labor force, *and*
(b) At least 30.00% of the employed workers living in the county work in the central county or counties of the area.
3. A contiguous county which does not meet the requirements of criterion 2 will be included in a standard metropolitan statistical area if at least 75.00% of the resident labor force is in the nonagricultural labor force and it meets two of the following additional criteria of metropolitan character and one of the following criteria of integration.
(a) Criteria of metropolitan character.
　　(1) At least 25.00% of the population is urban.
　　(2) The county had an increase of at least 15.00% in total population during the period covered by the two most recent Censuses of Population.
　　(3) The county has a population density of at least 50 persons per square mile.
(b) Criteria of integration.
　　(1) At least 15.00% of the employed workers living in the county work in the central county or counties of the area, *or*
　　(2) The number of people working in the county who live in the central county or counties of the area is equal to at least 15.00% of the employed workers living in the county, *or*
　　(3) The sum of the number of workers commuting to and from the central county or counties is equal to 20.00% of the employed workers living in the county.

9 Avoiding and Minimizing the Human Costs

The social costs of change in the physical and social environment are inexorably tied to the issues which perplex our communities. The health and behavioral implications of change are at the base of a controversy which has separated the world into blocs or nations defined by political ideology. This chapter briefly sketches the market and socialist positions on the controversy over minimizing and distributing the costs of economic change.

Also addressed in this last chapter is the problem of imperfect knowledge. Even if a market or socialist nation decided to minimize social costs and distribute them equitably, there would still be the problem of devising methods for accounting those costs. The study of the health and behavioral costs of adaptation to change has not, unfortunately, come very far since Haig's plea for human cost accounting in 1926.

Assuming that there were a political system which was sensitive to social costs and that progress were made toward understanding and predicting these costs, community service professionals would still have to cope with adaptation-related disorders. This is true first because there would undoubtedly be many times when a society would feel the benefits of change outweigh the costs. The community service professional would be expected in these cases to minimize the costs by enhancing the adaptation skills of the population and dealing effectively with the "casualties." Second, adaptation requiring change is not always, or even usually, the result of explicit societal decisions, but rather the product of millions of individual decisions uninformed of true costs. There will, therefore, be much unintended adaptation-related disorder to be dealt with in the community.

MINIMIZING HUMAN COSTS: THE MARKET AND SOCIALIST FAILURES

All modern economies are "managed" in the sense that the nation state influences the collection of raw materials, and the production and distribution of goods and services. How much management occurs, and which variables are claimed to be maximized, varies among nations depending on ideology. The simplest classification of ideologies is the market/socialist dichotomy. Both ideologies believe that the ultimate goal of organized society is to reduce pain and suffering by producing as many goods and services as possible, given the natural resources and human skill available. Both also agree that the most efficient economy can be had only when as many individuals as possible are motivated to use their productive abilities to the fullest. Socialist and market ideologies differ most basically on how to generate that motivation. The market system assumes that entrepreneurial ability is a limited resource which can be developed to its fullest only when everyone is enticed to bring his product or service to market by the promise of profit. Not everyone, of course, is an entrepreneur, and not all entrepreneurs will be successful, but those who are will supply the others with employment and the income to purchase the goods and services which reduce pain and suffering. This system means that the most clever of the entrepreneurs will have more income to purchase goods and services than the less capable who will still, however, have more income than the nonentrepreneurial worker. The resulting maldistribution of goods and services is seen as inevitable, if society is to raise the survival chances of its members above those of the pre-industrial feudal system.

The government plays a key role in this simplified model of the market system. Through its power to tax, spend, borrow, and lend, it can control the relative distribution of costs and benefits generated by the economy. It can, for example, tax the rich to supply services to the poor. By increasing spending or reducing taxes, the government can increase the number of successful entrepreneurs and, therefore, the number of jobs available to the nonentrepreneurial. At times it can tax more heavily to decrease demand, thereby lowering inflation or prices. The role of government in a modern market economy is, in short, to manipulate several key variables—such as taxes, money supply, and public sector spending—to keep the system of collection, production, and distribution working most efficiently.

The market ideology recognizes that social costs will result as employment fluctuates and populations shift from area to area and from social class to social class. Market economists, as a rule, believe that these costs are unavoidable and inherent in a healthy economy. Unemployment, for example, should never be so low as to allow labor to demand wages which would be so high as to spur inflation. Physical mobility of the labor force, moreover, is seen as essential to an efficient industrial system. If the labor force were stationary, new plants would have to be built in existing population centers, regardless of the geometry of industrial location, thereby leading to unnecessarily high production costs. Social mobility, as reflected in economic status and residential choice, is, moreover, assumed to be among the primary benefits of organized economies. The human costs of such mobility is assumed to be much lower than the benefit of increased wealth. The market ideology also recognizes that some human costs can be lessened through the pricing system. "True pricing" an automobile, for example, would mean adding to its selling price its share of the obvious social costs of cleaning up air pollution, treating emphysema cases, maintaining roads and traffic control systems, relocating persons moved by highways, and the cost of disposing of the auto when no longer useful. Not so obvious costs, such as the long term impact of lead on children, the pain and suffering of accident victims, and the costs of premature suburbanization, might also be added to make an auto's selling price reflect what it really costs society. If that were done, there would, obviously, be fewer autos in America. To do it in the last half of the twentieth century, however, may be irrational for the social costs of readjusting our entire economic system may be greater than continuing to allocate a major portion of our human energy and resources to repairing the damage done by automobiles. Another, and probably more controversial, outcome of true pricing would be the increased differences among classes. If autos were true priced, only the rich could afford them. The same would be true of suburban homes and other goods whose costs are absorbed by those who neither produce nor consume them. Such a situation would be unacceptable to any egalitarian society. The use of true pricing, therefore, even though it is compatible with market ideology, is not likely to become widespread.

Socialist ideology, also, assumes that the object of organized society is to reduce pain and suffering by producing as many goods and services as possible, given the available natural resources and human skills. Unlike the market ideology, which assumes economies evolve most efficiently only when entrepreneurial skills are rewarded through profit, the socialist ideology believes that a population is best motivated to organize and work efficiently when all the costs and benefits generated by such organization are equally distributed. Rather than encouraging everyone to devise products and services to be brought to market, the socialist model posits that the population should decide which goods it needs to improve its existence, and then organize to produce them at the lowest cost, and to distribute them equally at their true price. To paraphrase a common socialist slogan, each adds whatever skill he can to the task of production and receives back whatever he needs to maintain himself at the standard of living established by the group. The "means of production," as the socialists refer to the system of collection, production, and distribution, are owned by everyone (not entrepreneurs), and everyone pays and benefits equally.

The socialist ideology grew out of the concern intellectuals felt when they witnessed the staggering social costs incurred by the working classes during the industrial revolution. Socialism, therefore, is, in its theoretical expression, preoccupied with social costs. Indeed, the object of having everyone decide which goods are to be produced is to allow those who will incur the costs and benefits to decide if that product or service is a net asset or liability. By having everyone share equally in costs and benefits, moreover, no one will urge investment in a product because others are paying more and receiving less than he.

While the market and socialist positions seems worlds apart in theory, the actual economies which claim to be one or the other are similar along several dimensions of importance to this discussion. Both market and socialist economies are, in reality, managed to produce as many goods and services as possible without much regard for social costs, other than those which would cause political disruption. While the distribution of benefits measured in income is more equitable in socialist nations, the distribution of costs measured in health and behavioral problems is, in all economies, skewed toward the poor who bear the brunt of the change generated by all dynamic economies. Neither system is very good at accounting human costs, and neither has explicitly devised national management systems, which pose investment decisions as tradeoffs between easily described material gains and difficult to measure human costs. While the willingness to consider human costs may be greater in one economy than another, knowledge about those costs as well as about decision systems which can weigh them against material gains is equally lacking. This fact means that major changes in the world's systems of collection, production, and distribution are likely to continue, regardless of the human costs involved. The task of ameliorating those costs will fall on community service agencies, regardless of the ideological position of the national government.

PAYING THE COST OF HUMAN SERVICES

If America continues to experience changes in her economic system, her communities will have to deal with the health and behavioral problems precipitated by adaptation processes. The effectiveness of these ameliorative efforts will depend on the fiscal resources and knowledge base available to community service agencies.

Reforming Local Government

How well any publicly supported program performs will depend heavily on how much funding and political cooperation it receives. As we saw in the last chapter, the problems created by economic evolution are concentrated in the central political cities, but the resources available to solve them are usually outside those jurisdictions. In most cases, those resources take the form of taxable property, but in those few instances in which the problem centers around behavior modeling, such as school achievement and, perhaps, juvenile delinquency, the resource may be majoritarian values.

There have been several reforms suggested to make the property wealth of suburban districts available to the entire metropolitan area. The most obvious is to replace smaller jurisdictions with a single government that would circumscribe the entire metropolitan area. This metrogovernment could tax all areas and deliver services where they are most needed. Metrogovernment would internalize the costs and benefits of change. If schools, police, and other services would be funded by the entire area, middle class suburban areas would become concerned with the effectiveness of these services in the former central city. The major drawbacks of such a scheme are the loss of accountability and the standardization of service districts. A large centralized government would certainly be more distant and less responsive to its citizens than are smaller jurisdictions. The police and school functions have been especially guarded by the typical American community. Any suggestion of metropolitanizing these services meets with great resistance. Besides being less accountable than more decentralized schemes, metrogovernment requires that all services be rendered at the SMSA level, even those that might be rendered most cost-effective locally. Water and sewer systems, air pollution control, and roads may be most efficiently provided at the SMSA level; but schools, sanitation, and fire services may be more rationally rendered by smaller service areas. The shift to metrogrovernment might not only mean less accountability but also unnecessarily expensive service costs.

To gain the advantages of metrogovernment, and to minimize the costs, some have suggested "two-tier government." This system would create a SMSA-wide tax assessment and collection jurisdiction which would render those services which are most efficiently offered on a metro-wide basis. Several smaller jurisdictions would be created to provide those services over which people desire more control, such as police and schools. These districts could not tax, but would be funded by the SMSA-wide taxing jurisdictions. Two-tiered government would, therefore, maintain accountability while making the SMSA's property wealth available to the entire population.

Such reforms must be viewed in the context of geopolitical reality. The United States Constitution explicitly gives all powers not expressly delegated to the federal government to the states. This separation of power means that local government is totally controlled by the state. Any merger or redrawing of local governmental boundaries, such as the cities in an SMSA merging into a metrogovernment, must approved by the state legislature. Before the mid 1960s, states tended to create legislative districts which favored small town and rural interests. A rural district with X number of people, for example, would have one representative, as would a district which overlays a city with 100X persons. As a result, many legislatures were controlled by rural interests unsympathetic to urban problems. A coalition of cities and citizens which went to court to fight this unequal representation claimed that residents of rural districts had more power to influence democratic processes than city dwellers. In 1962, the Supreme Court ruled, in Baker v. Carr,[1] that unequal districts were unconstitutional, and that states would have to be redistricted to create districts relatively equal in population size. This was a Pyrrhic victory. By the time Baker v. Carr went into effect, most Americans lived not in the central cities, or the rural areas, but in the suburbs of metropolitan areas. Suburbanites were even less willing to allow central cities to tap suburban property taxes than were rural voters. Any reform of local government which broadens central city tax bases is not very likely to be realized.

Schools—A Bleak Dilemma

Perhaps the best example of the unwillingness of American society to reform local government is the desperate plight of central city schools. The Coleman data show that schools which are poorly funded and attended principally by students from lower socioeconomic families are least likely to successfully prepare children for American society. The schools most likely to be in this situation are those in central cities. In a recent case,[2] the Supreme Court ruled that children in America do not have a right to equally-funded education. That is, the fact that some school districts are extremely poor and others wealthy does not violate the right to education. This ruling means that with the exception of California, where unequal educational funding has been found in violation of the state constitution,[3] there is no legal reason for states to attempt to close the per pupil expenditure gap between central city and suburb. This situation has moved the federal government to help central city schools, but this aid has only kept the gap from growing wider, rather than closing it.

Even more perplexing than the Supreme Court's allowing states to perpetuate grossly unequal school expenditures has been its recent ruling on the limits of integration. In the early 1950s the Court, in a series of cases, ruled that segregated schools were not equal schools. This ruling, which began the controversial process of school integration, applied only to school districts. That is, no district could be segregated if it had different races represented in its population. For the reasons described in detail in previous chapters, most minority students were in central city neighborhoods near the CBD. Where a city was so large that students could not walk from their neighborhood schools to one which was to be integrated, they were bused. Fear of busing and integrated schools, plus the realization that suburban school districts did not have to be integrated because they were all white, led many parents to move from the central city areas. Racial integration schemes, therefore, accelerated the exodus of middle class families from the central cities, leaving behind a predominantly poor population which was racially mixed. By the early 1970s many central city school districts had become predominantly lower socioeconomic class, regardless of race. Integration schemes which mixed poor whites with poor blacks created much resentment, but, as Coleman indicated, may have had little effect on achievement. This realization led to court suits which asked that integration schemes reach across school district boundaries. The Supreme Court ruled in 1974 that its previous directives did not apply to more than one district.[4] This ruling, coupled with the resistance of suburban America to either racial or socioeconomic integration, has sealed the fate of central city schools.

The low probabilities of governmental reform cloud the prospects of political and fiscal support of community service agencies throughout the metropolitan area, and in the central cities in particular. This inescapably leads to the judgment that whatever interventions are made in the near future to ameliorate human costs will most likely be made through existing institutions at their current relative level of support. If these institutions are to be more effective in the future, the difference will have to be the skill and knowledge base of the community service professionals who staff them. These persons must anticipate the human impact of changes in the physical and institutional environment, and improve their remedial and preventive efforts. This can only be done by improving the knowledge base upon which community service professionals act.

TOWARD MORE ECOLOGICAL RESEARCH

As stated in the introduction, there were two principal reasons for preparing this volume. The first was to increase the likelihood that those preparing to pursue the community service professions would be sensitized to the interrelationships among community problems and to the impact of ecological factors on these problems. The second was to motivate researchers to test the hypotheses fully stated, or implicit, in the previous chapters. These goals are complementary. If the latter is achieved, effectiveness of the community service professions will increase.

The research suggested by an ecological perspective on the health and behavioral problems plaguing the modern community falls into three general categories. The first, and perhaps most difficult, is the monitoring of metropolitan areas to test the basic hypothesis that a measurable relationship exists between economic change and the incidence of health and behavioral problems among the population as a whole and its sub sets. While previous chapters cite research suggesting such a relationship, the lack of sound historical data to describe metropolitan areas has precluded the type of longitudinal retrospective analyses needed for predictive models. Researchers must identify indicators of economic change and of health and behavioral well-being, and monitor those indicators for test and comparison of communities over time. Predictive models from such monitoring would be of great value to community service agencies. Agencies could allocate resources more rationally by preparing for increased or decreased demand for different types of services. The chances of successful prevention strategies would also be increased.

The concept of preventive strategies suggests a second class of research questions. Can an individual be prepared to cope with changes requiring adaptation? It is not clear that forewarning alone makes adaptation physiologically, or psychologically, less stressful. There is evidence, however, that several training routines reduce stress reactions. If these routines prove effective, and if the ecological monitoring described above can predict high stress periods and populations at risk, an exciting opportunity to reduce human costs would seem to exist. Coping skills could be taught to high risk populations to reduce stress reactions. This training could be brought to the work, school, church, or other setting as have been other public health measures, such as polio immunization.

The possibility of preparing populations to cope with stress suggests an even more basic strategy to reduce the human costs of adaptation. The object of education has traditionally been to transmit the skills and behavior expectations needed to assume a role in the economic system. Certainly a crucial element of preparing an individual to function in a dynamic economy is to alert him to the fact that adaptation demands will result from his own decisions, as well as from changes over which he has little control. Individuals should be taught how to, at least crudely, calculate the likely human as well as material costs and benefits of decisions they will face. Coping skills should also be taught to help reduce the cost of adapting to changes one has elected or over which one has no control.

The third type of research suggested by an ecological perspective on human problems involves devising cost accounting techniques and decision systems so findings of ecological monitoring can affect public decision making. Recent federal and state actions now make it possible for human cost accounting to influence decision making (Catalano and Monahan, 1975; Catalano & Reich, 1975; Catalano, Simmons & Stokols, 1975; Wolfe, 1975), but two factors limit these opportunities. First, the ideological reluctance of market economies to consider human costs, and second, the lack of accounting techniques which express such costs in a form compatible with existing decision systems. Economists, social ecologists, and political scientists must study these systems to determine how human costs can be reflected in public decision making.

It is clearly irrational that society should run the risk of incurring avoidable pain and suffering due to uninformed decisions, and to intellectuals who blindly observe discipline boundaries while admitting those boundaries confound, rather than facilitate, the accumulation of knowledge. Hopefully, this volume demonstrates that the task of measuring the human costs of economic evaluation is one intellectual effort which can immediately involve several disciplines and generate knowledge useful in improving the human condition.

Notes

1. *Baker* v. *Carr*, 369 U.S. 186 (1962). See also *Reynolds v. Sims*, 84. S. Ct. 1362 (1964).
2. *San Antonio Independent School District* v. *Rodrigues*, 411 U.S. 1 (1973).
3. *Serrano* v. *Priest*, 5 Cal. 3d 584, 487. Pac. 2d 1241.
4. *Milliken* v. *Bradley*, 94 S. Ct. 3112 (1974).

References

Ackertnecht, E. Medical practices. In J. Steward (Ed.) *Handbook of South American Indians*. Washington, D.C.: Government Printing Office, 1949.

Alexander, F. & Healy, W. *The roots of crime*. New York: A.A. Knopf, 1935.

Alexander, F. & Staub, H. *The criminal, the judge, and the public*. New York: Macmillan, 1931.

Arieti, S. Manic-depressive psychosis. In S. Arieti (Ed.), *American Handbook of Psychiatry*. New York: Basic Books, 1959.

Astrup, C. & Odegaard, O. Internal migration and disease in Norway. *Psychiatric Quarterly*, (suppl.), 1960, *34*, 116.

Baillou, G. *On epidemic and ephemeral diseases*. Paris: Quesnel, 1640.

Bandura, A. *Principles of behavior modification*. New York: Holt, Rinehart, and Winston, 1969.

Banfield, E. *The unheavenly city*. Boston: Little, Brown, 1968.

Barker, G. Family factors in the ecology of juvenile delinquency. *Journal of Criminal Law and Criminology*, 1940, *30*, 681-91.

Barker, R.G. & Barker, L.S. The psychological ecology of old people in the Midwest. *Journal of Gerontology*, 1961, *16* 144-49.

Barker, R.G. & Gump, P.V. *Big school, small school*. Stanford, California: Stanford University Press, 1964.

Barker, R.G. & Shoggen, P. *Qualities of community life*. San Francisco: Jossey-Bass, 1973.

Beilen, H. The pattern of postponability and its relation to social class mobility. *Journal of Social Psychology*, 1956, *44*, 33-48.

Berry, B. *Geography of market centers and retail distribution.* Englewood Cliffs, N.J.: Prentice-Hall, 1967.

Binder, A. An experimental approach to driver evaluation using alcohol drinkers and marijuana smokers. *Accident Analysis and Prevention*, 1971, *3*, 237-56.

Blomberg, R.D. & Preusser, D.F. Narcotic use and driving behavior. *Accident Analysis and Prevention*, 1976, *6* 23-33.

Bollens, J. & Schmandt, H. *The metropolis.* New York: Harper, 1970.

Borgatta, E. On the existence of Thurstone's oblique reference solution. *American Sociological Review*, 1968, *33*, 598-600.

Boughey, A. *Fundamental ecology.* London: Intext, 1971.

Bowlby, J. *Maternal care and mental health.* Geneva: World Health Organization, 1952.

Brenner, M.H. Economic changes and heart disease mortality. *American Journal of Public Health*, 1971, *61*, 606-11.

Brenner, M.H. *Mental Illness and the Economy.* Cambridge: Harvard Press, 1973.

Brenner, M.H. Fetal, infant and maternal mortality during periods of economic stress. *International Journal of Health Sciences*, 1973, *3*, 145-59.

Brenner, M.H. Trends in alcohol consumption and associated illnesses: Some effects of economic changes. *American Journal of Public Health*, 1975, *65*, 1279-92.

Brenner, M.H. Estimating the costs of national economic policy: Implications for mental and physical health, and criminal aggression. (Report to the Congressional Research Service of the Library of Congress and the Joint Economic Committee of Congress). Washington: Government Printing Office, 1976.

Bromberg, W. & Thompson, C. The relation of psychoses, mental defect and personality types of crime. *Journal of Criminal Law and Criminology*, 1937, *28*, 70-89.

Budd, W. *Malignant cholera: Its mode of propagation.* London: John Churchill, 1849.

Burchinal, B. Characteristics of adolescents from unbroken, broken, and reconstituted families. *Journal of Marriage and Family Living*, 1964, *26*, 44-51.

Burgess, E. The growth of the city: An introduction to a research project. In R. Park & E. Burgess (Eds.), *The city.* Chicago: University of Chicago Press, 1926.

Burt, C. *The young delinquent.* New York: D. Appleton, 1925.

Cadogan, W. *An essay upon nursing and the management of children.* J. Roberts, London, 1748.

Caldwell, C. *Elements of phrenology.* Lexington, Kentucky: T.T. Skillman, 1824.

Cameron, C. Accident proneness. *Accident Analysis and Prevention*, 1975, *6*, 125-41.

Carlson, W.L. & Klein, D. Familial vs. institutional socialization of the young traffic offender. *Journal of Safety Research*, 1970, *2*, 13-25.

Carus, N. *Grundzuge einer neuen und wissenschaftlicken kranioscopie.* Stuttgart, 1840.

Cassell, J. & Tyroler, H. Epidemiological studies of culture change, I: Health status and recency of industrialization. *Archives of Environmental Health*, 1961, *3*, 31-38.

Catalano, R. Community stress: A preliminary conceptualization. *Man Environment Systems*, 1975, *5*, 307-10.

Catalano, R. Health costs of economic expansion: The case of accident injuries. Paper presented to the American Sociological Association, San Francisco, 1978.

Catalano, R. & Dooley, C.D. Economic predictors of depressed mood and stressful life events. *Journal of Health and Social Behavior*, 1977 (a), *18*, 292-307.

Catalano, R. & Dooley, C.D. The economy as stressor, a sectoral analysis. Paper presented at the meeting of the Pacific Division of the American Association for the Advancement of Science, April, 1977 (b).

Catalano, R. & Monahan, J. The community psychologist as social planner. *American Journal of Community Psychology*, 1975, *3*, 327-34.

Catalano, R. & Reich, R. Local government and the environmental impact report: The California experience. *American Bar Association Urban Lawyer*, in press.

Catalano, R., Simmons, S. & Stokols, D. Adding social science knowledge to environmental decision making. *Natural Resources Lawyer*, 1975, *8*, 29-41.

Chilton, R. Continuity in delinquency area research: A comparison of studies for Baltimore, Detroit, and Indianapolis. *American Sociological Review*, 1964, *29*, 71-83.

Chilton, R. & Markle, G. Family disruption, delinquent conduct, and the effect of sub-classification. *American Sociological Review*, 1972, *37*, 93-99.

Christaller, W. *The central places of Southern Germany*. Englewood Cliffs, N.J.: Prentice-Hall, 1966.

Christensen, W. & Hinkle, L. Differences in illness and prognostic signs in two groups of young men. *Journal of the American Medical Association*, 1961, *177*, 247-53.

Clausen, J.A. & Kohn, M.L. Relation of schizophrenia to the social structure of a small city. In B. Pasamanick (Ed.), *Epidemiology of mental disorder*. Washington, D.C.: American Association for the Advancement of Science, 1959.

Cloward, R. & Ohlin, L. *Delinquency and opportunity: A theory of delinquent gangs*. New York: The Free Press, 1960.

Coddington, R. The significance of life events as etiologic factors in the diseases of children. *Journal of Psychosomatic Research*, 1972, *16*, 205-13.

Coleman, J. *Equality of educational opportunity*. Washington, D.C.: U.S. Dept. of Health, Education and Welfare, 1966.

Coughlin, R. Attainment along goal dimensions in 101 metropolitan areas. *Journal of the American Institute of Planners*, 1973, *39*, 413-25.

Crawford, W.A. Accident proneness: An unaffordable philosophy. *Medical Journal of Australia*, 1971, *2*, 905-09.

Crockett, H. The achievement motive and differential occupational mobility in the United States. *American Sociological Review*, 1962, *27*, 191-204.

Darwin, C. *On the origin of species*. London: John Murray, 1859.

Darwin, C. *The Descent of Man*. New York: D. Appleton, 1882.

Dohrenwend, B.S. Social status and stressful life events. *Journal of Personality and Social Psychology*, 1973, *28*, 225-33.

Dohrenwend, B.S. & Dohrenwend, B.P. *Stressful life events: Their nature and effects*. New York: Wiley, 1974.

Dohrenwend, B.S., Krasnoff, L., Askenazy, A. & Dohrenwend, B.P. Exemplification of method for scaling life events. *Journal of Health and Social Behavior*, 1978, *19*, 205-30.

Dooley, C.D. & Catalano, R. Economic, life and disorder changes: time-series analysis. *American Journal of Community Psychology*, in press.

Dooley, C.D. & Catalano, R. Money and mental disorder: Toward behavioral cost accounting for primary prevention. *American Journal of Community Psychology*, 1977, *5*, 217-27.

Douvan, E. Social status and success strivings. *Journal of Abnormal and Social Psychology*, 1956, *52*, 219-23.

Douvan, E. & Edelson, J. The psychodynamics of social mobility in adolescent boys. *Journal of Abnormal and Social Psychology*, 1958, *56*, 31-44.

Drahms, A. *The criminal: His personnel (sic) and environment*. New York, 1900.

Dubos, R. Second thoughts on the germ theory. *Scientific American*, 1955, *192*, 31-35.

Dunham, H.W. The ecology of the functional psychoses in Chicago. *The American Sociological Review*, 1937, *2*, 467-79.

Durkheim, E. *Suicide: A study in sociology*. Paris: Alcan, 1897.

Eaton, W. Life events, social supports, and psychiatric symptoms: A re-analysis of the New Haven data, *Journal of Health and Social Behavior*, 1978, *19*, 230-234.

Eiseley, L. *Darwin's century: Evolution and the men who discovered it*. Garden City, N.Y.: Doubleday, 1958.

Eysenck, H.J. The effects of psychotherapy: An evaluation. *Journal of Consulting Psychology*, 1952, *16*, 319-24.

Eysenck, H.J. *Crime and personality*. Boston: Houghton Mifflin, 1964.

Eysenck, H.J. & Rachman, S. *The causes and cares of neurosis*. San Diego: Knapp, 1965.

Faris, R.E.L. & Dunham, H.W. *Mental disorders in urban areas*. New York: Hafner, 1960.

Feldman, D. Psychoanalysis and crime. In Rosenberg, et al. (Eds.), *Mass society in crisis*. New York: Macmillan, 1964.

Ferreira, J. & Silverman, A. The impact of Massachusetts' reduced drinking age on auto accidents. *Accident Analysis and Prevention*, 1976, *8*, 141-63.

Ferrero, G.L. *Criminal man according to the classification of Cesare Lombroso*, New York: Putnam, 1911.

Firey, W. Sentiment and symbolism as ecological variables. *American Sociological Review*, 1936, *1*, 180-89.

Forbes, T.W. *Human factors in highway traffic safety research*. New York: Wiley, 1972.

Fracastoro, G. *On contagion, contagious diseases and their treatment*. Venice, 1546.

Frank, J. *System of a complete medical policy*. Vienna, 1779.

Freidlander, K. *The psychoanalytical approach to juvenile delinquency*. New York: International Universities Press, 1947.

Freud, A. & Dann, S. An experiment in group upbringing. In R.S. Eissler, et al. (Eds.), *The psychoanalytic study of the child* (Vol. 6). New York: International Universities Press, 1951.

Freud, S. *The ego and the id* (standard ed., Vol. 4). London: Hogarth, 1960.

Freud, S. *The psychopathology of everyday life* (standard ed., Vol. 6). London: Hogarth, 1960.

Galen. *On the Natural Faculties*. Translated by A.J. Brock. London: Putnam, 1916.

Gall, F. *On the functions of the brain*. Paris: F. Shuell, 1825.

Gleuck, S. & Gleuck, E. *Unraveling juvenile delinquency*. Cambridge: Harvard University Press, 1950.

Goffman, E. *Asylums*. Garden City, N.Y.: Anchor Books, 1961.

Goldfarb, W. Effects of early institutional care on adolescent personality. *Child Development*, 1943, *14*, 213-23.

Goldfarb, W. Infant rearing as a factor in foster home replacement. *American Journal of Orthopsychiatry*, 1944, *14*, 162-73.

Goldfarb, W. Psychological privation in infancy and subsequent adjustment. *American Journal of Orthopsychiatry*, 1945, *15*, 247-55.

Goode, W. Family disorganization. In R.K. Merton & R.A. Nisbet (Eds.), *Contemporary social problems* (2nd ed.). New York: Harcourt, Brace, and World, 1966.

Gordon, R. On the interpretation of oblique factors. *American Sociological Review*, 1967, *33*, 601-20.

Gore, S. The effect of social support in moderating the health consequences of unemployment. *Journal of Health and Social Behavior*, 1978, *19*, 157-65.

Goring, C. *The English convict: A statistical study*. London: His Majesty's Stationery Office, 1913.

Gossen, H. The physician in ancient Rome. *Ciba Symposia*, 1939, *1*, 2-39.

Gras, N. *An introduction to economic history*. New York: Harper & Bros., 1922.

Green, H.W. *Persons admitted to the Cleveland State Hospital, 1928-1937*. Cleveland: Cleveland Health Council, 1939.

Guerry, A. *Essay on the moral statistics of France*. Paris: l'Academie des Sciences, 1833.

Haan, N. The relationship of ego functioning and intelligence to social status and social mobility. *Journal of Abnormal and Social Psychology*, 1964, *69*, 544-605.

Hackler, J. Boys, blisters, and behavior: The impact of a work program in an urban area. *Journal of Research in Crime and Delinquency*, 1966, *3*, 155-64.

Hackler, J. & Hagan, J. *Work, programs, and teaching machines.* Mimeographed manuscript available from Edmonton: The University of Alberta, Department of Sociology, 1972.

Haig, R. *Major economic factors in metropolitan growth and arrangement: A study of trends and tendencies in the economic activities within the region of New York and its environs.* Robert C. McCrea (consultant.) Reprinted by Arno Press, 1974.

Haig, R. Understanding the metropolis. *Quarterly Journal of Economics*, 1926.

Harmon, D., Masuda, M. & Holmes, T. The social readjustment rating scale: A cross cultural study of Western Europeans and Americans. *Journal of Psychosomatic Research*, 1970, *14*, 391-400.

Hathaway, S. & Monachesi, E. The personalities of predelinquent boys. *Journal of Criminal Law, Criminology, and Police Science*, 1957, *68*, 149-63.

Hawley, A. (Ed.) *Roderick McKenzie on human ecology.* Chicago: University of Chicago Press, 1968.

Hawley, A. *Urban society.* New York: Ronald Press, 1971.

Hawley, A. Ecology and population. *Science*, 1973, *179*, 1196-99.

Healy, W. & Bronner, A. *New light on delinquency and its treatment.* New Haven: Yale University Press, 1936.

Heller, K. & Monahan, J. *Psychology and community change.* Homewood: Dorsey, 1977.

Henle, J. *Pathologische untersuchungen.* Berlin: Hirschwald, 1840.

Hinkle, L.E. The effects of exposure to culture change, social change, and changes in interpersonal relationships on health. In B.S. Dohrenwend and D.P. Dohrenwend (Eds.), *Stressful life events: Their nature and effects.* New York: Wiley, 1974.

Hinkle, L.E., Pinsky, R., Bross, I., & Plummer, N. The distribution of sickness disability in a homogeneous group of healthy adult men. *American Journal of Hygiene*, 1956, *64*, 220-42.

Hodgkiss, M. The influence of broken homes and working mothers. *Smith College Studies in Social Work*, 1933, *3*, 254-74.

Hollingshead, A.B. & Redlich, F.C. *Social class and mental illness: A community study.* New York: Wiley, 1958.

Holmes, T. & Rahe, R. The social readjustment rating scale. *Journal of Psychosomatic Research*, 1967, *11*, 213-18.

Hook, S. *Science and mythology in psychoanalysis.* In S. Hook (Ed.), *Psychoanalysis, scientific method, and philosophy.* New York: New York University Press, 1959.

Jencks, C. *Inequality.* New York: Harper, 1972.

Jonassen, C. A re-evaluation and critique of the logic and some methods of Shaw and McKay. *American Sociological Review*, 1949, *14*, 608-17.

Jones, H.C. A laboratory study of fear: The case of Peter. *Journal of Genetic Psychology*, 1924, *31*, 308-15.

Jones, W. *Hippocrates.* Cambridge: The Loeb Classical Library, Harvard University Press: William Heinemann, 1923.

Joroff, S. & Navarro, V. Medical manpower: A multivariate analysis of the distribution of physicians in urban United States. *Medical Care*, 1971, *9*, 428-38.

Kantor, M. *Mobility and mental health.* Springfield: Charles C. Thomas, 1965.

Kapp, K. *The social cost of private enterprise.* New York: Schocken, 1950.

Kass, N. *The impact of functional specialization on population characteristics.* Ann Arbor: University Microfilms, 1972.

Kelly, J. Ecological constraints on mental health services. *American Psychologist*, 1966, *21*, 535-39.

Kobrin, S. The conflict of values in delinquency areas. *American Sociological Review*, 1951, *16*, 653-61.

Koch, G. & Reinfurt, D.W. An analysis of the relationship between driver injury and vehicle age. *Accident Analysis and Prevention*, 1974, *6*, 1-19.

Kohn, M.L. Social class and schizophrenia: A critical review. In D. Rosenthal & S.S. Kety (Eds.), *The Transmission of Schizophrenia*. Oxford: Pergamon Press, 1968.

Komaroff, A., Masuda, M., & Holmes, T. The social readjustment rating scale: A comparative study of Negro, Mexican and White Americans. *Journal of Psychosomatic Research*, 1967, *12*, 121-28.

Kraepelin, E. *Lectures on clinical psychiatry, 1904*. New York: Hafner, 1968.

Kraepelin, E. *Textbook in psychology*. Leipzig: Barth, 1896.

Kuhn, T. *The structure of scientific revolutions*. Chicago: University of Chicago Press, 1968.

Kurella, H. *Cesare Lombroso, a modern man of science*. New York: Rebman, 1910.

Lamarck, J. *Zoological philosophy*. Paris, 1809.

Lander, B. *Towards an understanding of juvenile delinquency*. New York: Columbia University Press, 1954.

Lavater, J. *Physiognomical fragments*. Munich: Heimeran, 1775.

Lauvergne, H. *The convicts: Considerations of the moral, physical and intellectual relationships observed at the prison of Toulon*. Paris: J. B. Baillière, 1841.

Leff, M.J., Roatch, J.F. & Bunney, W.E., Jr. Environmental factors preceding the onset of severe depressions. *Psychiatry*, 1970, 33, *3*, 298-311.

Lewin, K. *Field theory in social science*. New York: Harper and Row, 1951.

Lewis, N.D. *A short history of psychiatric achievement*. New York: Norton, 1941.

Liem, R. & Liem, J. Social class and mental illness reconsidered. *Journal of Health and Social Behavior*, 1978, *19*, 139-56.

Lombroso, C. *The criminal man*. Milan: Hoepli, 1876.

Losch, A. *Die raumliche ordung der wirtschaft*. Jena: Fischer, 1941.

Maller, J. Are broken homes a causative factor in juvenile delinquency? *Social Forces*, 1932, *10*, 531-33.

Malthus, T.R. *Essay on the principles of population*. London: J. Johnson, 1798.

Marden, P. A demographic and ecological analysis of the distribution of physicians in metropolitan America, 1960. *American Journal of Sociology*, 1967, *72*, 290-300.

Masuda, M. & Holmes, T. The social readjustment rating scale: A cross cultural study of Japanese and Americans. *Journal of Psychosomatic Research*, 1967, *11*, 227-37.

May, J. *The ecology of human diseases*. New York: M.D. Publications, 1958.

Mayer, H. & Kohn, C. *Readings in urban geography*. Chicago: University of Chicago Press, 1954.

Mayhew, H. *The criminal prisons of London and scenes of prison life*. London: C. Griffin Bohn, 1862.

Mayhew, H. *London labour and the London poor*. London: C. Griffin Bohn, 1864.

McDonald, A. *Le criminal-type dans quelques formes graves de la criminalito*. Paris: C. Masson, 1893.

McGuire, F. A typology of accident proneness. *Behavioral Research in Highway Safety*, 1970, *1*, 32-41.

McKenzie, R. The ecological approach to the study of the human community. In R. Park & E. Burgess (Eds.), *The city*. Chicago: University of Chicago Press, 1926.

McMullen, T., et al. Air quality and community characteristics. Paper presented at the Annual Meeting of the Air Pollution Control Association, Cleveland, 1967.

McMurray, L. Emotional stress and driving performance: The effect of divorce. *Behavioral Research in Highway Safety*, 1970, *1*, 100-14.

Merton, R. Social structure and anomie. *American Sociological Review*, 1938, *8*, 672-83.

Merton, R. *Social theory and social structure*. Glencoe, Ill.: Free Press, 1957.

Meyer, A. *Collected papers of Adolf Meyer* (4 vols.). Baltimore: Johns Hopkins Press, 1948.

Meyer, A. The life chart and the obligation of specifying positive data in psychopathological diagnosis. In E.E. Wynters (Ed.), *The collected papers of Adolf Meyer*. (Vol. III). Baltimore: Johns Hopkins Press, 1951.

Mills, R. & Kelly, J. Cultural and social adaptations to change: A case example and critique. In S. Golann & C. Eisendorfer (Eds.), *Handbook of Community Mental Health*. New York: Appleton-Century-Crofts, 1972, 157-205.

Mitchell, W. *What happens during business cycles: A progress report*. Washington: National Bureau of Economic Research, 1951.

Monahan, T. Family status and the delinquent child: A reappraisal and some new findings. *Social Forces*, 1957, *35*, 250-58.

Morel, B.A. *Traite des degenerescences physiques, intellectuelles et morales de l'espece humaine*. Paris: J.B. Bailliere, 1857.

Morselli, E. Cesare Lombroso e "anthropologia generale". *L'opera di Cesare Lombroso nella scienze e nella sup applicazioni*. Torino: Bocca, 1908.

Moynihan, D. *Maximum feasible misunderstanding: Community action in the war on poverty*. New York: The Free Press, 1969.

Myers, J.K. & Bean, L.L. *A decade later: A follow-up of social class and mental illness*. New York: Wiley, 1968.

Nagle, E. Methodological issues in psychoanalytic theory. In S. Hook (Ed.), *Psychoanalysis, scientific method, and philosophy*. New York: New York University Press, 1959.

National Criminal Justice Information and Statistics Service. *Criminal victimization surveys in the nation's five largest cities*. Washington: Government Printing Office, 1975.

National Safety Council. *Accident facts*. Chicago: National Safety Council, 1976.

Nettler, G. *Explaining crime*. New York: McGraw-Hill, 1974.

Noyes, W. The criminal type. *Journal of Social Science*, 1888, *24*, 31-42.

Nye, F. Child adjustment in broken and unhappy unbroken homes. *Journal of Marriage and Family Living*, 1957, *19*, 366-71.

Ottolenghi, S. *Trattato di polizia scientifica*. Rome: Societa Editrice Libraria, 1932.

Ozolins, G. *A rapid survey technique for estimating community air pollution emissions*. Cincinnati: U.S. Department of Health, Education and Welfare, 1966.

Panum, P. *Veber krankheiten und krankheitsverhaltnesse auf Island und den Faroer-Inseln*. (A. Hatcher, Ed. and Trans.) New York: Delta Omega Society, 1940.

Park, R. Suggestions for investigation of human behavior in the urban environment. In R. Park & E. Burgess (Eds.), *The city*. Chicago: University of Chicago Press, 1926.

Park, R. & Burgess, E. (Eds.) *The City*. Chicago: University of Chicago Press, 1926.

Paykel, E.S., Meyers, J., Dienelt, M., Klerman, G., Linderthal, J. & Pepper, M. Life events and depression. *Archives General Psychiatry*. 1969, *21*, 753-60.

Pende, N. *Trattato sintetico di patalogia e clinica medica*. Messina: Principato, 1928.

Piggott, S. *Prehistoric India to 1000 B.C.* Harmondsworth: Penguin Books, 1950.

Polk, K. Urban social areas and delinquency. *Social Problems*, 1969, *14*, 320-25.

Porte, J. *The human physiognomy*, 1586.

Price, R.H. *Abnormal behavior: Perspective in conflict*. New York: Holt, Rinehart, and Winston, 1972.

Pyle, G.F. *Some examples of urban-medical geography*. M.A. Thesis, Chicago: University of Chicago, 1968.

Rahe, R. & Paasikivi, J. Psychosocial factors and myocardial infarction: An outpatient study in Sweden. *Journal of Psychosomatic Research*, 1971, *15*, 33-39.

Queen, S.A. The ecological studies of mental disorder. *American Sociological Review*. 1940, *5*, 201-09.

Recklass, W. The distribution of commercialized vice in the city: Sociological analysis. *Publications of the American Sociological Society*, 1926, *20*, 164-76.

Reenie, T.A.C. & Fowler, J.B. Prognosis in manic-depressive psychosis. *American Journal of Psychiatry*. 1942, *98*, 801-14.

Reid, J.S. *The municipalities of the Roman Empire*. Cambridge: University Press, 1913.

Robertson, L.S. & Baker, S. Motor vehicle size in 1,440 fatal crashes. *Accident Analysis and Prevention*, 1976, *3*, 167-77.

Robins, R. *The story of water supply*. London: Oxford University Press, 1946.

Robinson, W.S. Ecological correlations and the behavior of individuals. *American Sociological Review*, 1950, *15*, 351-57.

Rodenwaldt, E. & Jusatz, H. *World atlas of epidemic diseases* (3 vols.). Hamburg: Falk, 1961.

Rogers, A. *The economics of crime*. Hinsdale, Ill.: Dryden Press, 1973.

Rosen, G. *The history of miners' disease*. New York: Schumans, 1943.

Rosen, G. *A history of public health*. New York: M.D. Publications, 1958.

Rosen, L. & Turner, S. An evaluation of the Lander approach to ecology of delinquency. *Social Problems*, 1967, *15*, 184-200.

Rosenhan, D.L. On being sane in insane places. *Science*. 1973, *179*, 250-58.

Royce, J. *The encapsulated man*. Princeton: Van Nostrand, 1964.

Ruch, L. & Holmes, T. Scaling of life change: Comparison of direct and indirect methods. *Journal of Psychosomatic Research*, 1971, *15*, 221-27.

Ruffer, M.S. *Studies in the paleopathology of Egypt*. Chicago: University of Chicago Press, 1921.

Sacks, S. *City Schools/Suburban Schools: A history of fiscal conflict*. Syracuse: Syracuse University Press, 1970.

Sarbin, T.R. Schizophrenic thinking: A role theoretical analysis. *Journal of Personality*. 1969, *37*, 190-206.

Satterthwaite, S.P. An assessment of seasonal and weather effects on the frequency of road accidents in California. *Accident Analysis and Prevention*, 1976, *8*, 87-97.

Scarr, S. & Weinberg, R. Influence of Family background on intellectual attainment. *American Sociological Review*, 1978, *43*, 674-93.

Schafer, S. *Theories in criminology*. New York: Random House, 1969.

Scheff, T.J. *Being mentally ill: A sociological theory*. Chicago: Aldine, 1966.

Schroeder, C.W. Mental disorders in cities. *American Journal of Sociology*. 1942, 47, 40-47.

Schuessler, KK. & Cressey, D. Personality characteristics of criminals. *American Journal of Sociology*, 1950, *55*, 476-84.

Selling, L.S. *Men against madness*. New York: Garden City Books, 1943.

Selye, H. *The story of the adaptation process*. Montreal: Acta Inc., 1952.

Selye, H. The general adaptation syndrome and the diseases of adaptation. *Journal of Clinical Endocrinology*, 1946, *6*, 117-230.

Selzer, M.L. Alcoholism, mental illness, and stress in 96 drivers causing fatal accidents. *Behavioral Science*, 1969, *14*, 1-10.

Selzer, M.L., Rogers, J.E. & Kerns, S. Fatal accidents: The role of psychopathology, social stress and acute disturbance. *American Journal of Psychiatry*, 1968, *124*, 1028-36.

Selzer, M. & Vinokur, A. Life events, subjective stress, and traffic accidents. *American Journal of Psychiatry*, 1974, *131*, 903-06.

Shaw, C., & McKay, H. *Juvenile delinquency and urban areas*. Chicago: University of Chicago Press, 1942.

Shaw, C., Zorbaugh, F. McKay, H. & Cottrell, L. *Delinquency areas*. Chicago: University of Chicago Press, 1929.

Shuster, D. & Guilford, J. The psychometric prediction of problem drivers. *Human Factors*, 1966, *6* 393-421.

Simkus, A. Residential segregation by occupation and race in ten urbanized areas. *American Sociological Review*, 1978, *43*, 81-92.

Simmel, G. The metropolis and mental life. In K. Wolfe (Ed.), *The Sociology of Georg Simmel*. Glencoe: The Free Press, 1950.

Simon, E. *The golden hand*. New York: Putnam, 1959.

Skinner, B.F. *Science and human behavior*. New York: Macmillan, 1953.

Skinner, B.F. *Beyond freedom and dignity*. New York: Knopf, 1971.

Smith, S. *Epidemics*. Edinburgh: Edmonston & Douglas, 1856.

Snow, J. *On the mode of communication of cholera*. 2nd ed. London: J Churchill, 1855.

Spitz, R. Hospitalism: A follow-up report. In R.S. Eissler et al. (Eds.), *The psychoanalytic study of the child* (Vol. 2). New York: International Universities Press, 1946.

Srole, L., Langer, T.S., Michael, S.T., Opler, M.K. & Rennie, T.A.C. *Mental health in the metropolis: The midtown Manhattan study*. New York: McGraw-Hill, 1962.

Stacey, B. Some psychological aspects of inter-generational occupational mobility. *British Journal of Social and Clinical Psychology*, 1965, *4*, 275-86.

Steuart, J. *An inquiry into the principles of political economy*. Chicago: University of Chicago Press, 1966.

Steward, G. & Voos, H. Determinants of sickness in marine recruits. *American Journal of Epidemiology*, 1968, *89*, 254-63.

Stone, S. Psychiatry through the ages. *Journal of Abnormal Social Psychology*, 1937, *32*, 131-60.

Sutherland, E. *Principles of criminology*. Philadelphia: Lippincott, 1939.

Sydenham, T. *Opera universe*. London: Kettilby, 1685.

Szasz, T.S. The myth of mental illness. *American Psychologist*. 1960, *15* (2), 113-18.

Theis, S. *How foster children turn out*. New York: State Charities Aid Association, 1924.

Theorell, T. Life events before and after the onset of a premature myocardial infarction. In S.S. Dohrenwend and B.P. Dohrenwend (Eds.), *Stressful life events: Their nature and effects*. New York: Wiley, 1974.

Theorell, T. & Rahe, R. Psychosocial factors and myocardial infarction. *Journal of Psychosomatic Research*, 1971, *15*, 25-31.

Thomas, W. & Znaniecki, F. *The Polish peasant in Europe and America*. New York: Alfred A. Knopf, 1920.

Thompson, P. Some factors in upward social mobility in England. *Sociology and Social Research*, 1971, *55*, 384-400.

Thorndike, E.L. *The psychology of wants, interests and attitudes*. New York: Appleton-Century-Crofts, 1935.

Thrasher, F. *The gang: A study of 1,313 gangs in Chicago*. Chicago: University of Chicago Press, 1927.

Tittle, C., Villemez, W. & Smith, D. The myth of social class and criminality. *American Sociological Review*, 1978, *43*, 643-56.

Trasler, G. *The explanation of criminality*. London: Routledge and Kegan Paul, 1962.

Trickett, E., Kelly, J. & Todd, D. The social environment of the high school. In S. Golann & C. Eisendorfer (Eds.), *Handbook of Community Mental Health*. New York: Appleton-Century-Crofts, 1972, 331-406.

Ullman, L.P. & Krasner, L. *A psychological approach to abnormal behavior*. Englewood Cliffs, N.J.: Prentice-Hall, 1969.

Varron, S. Housing in antiquity. *Ciba Symposia*, 1945, *7*, 137-47.

Vidoni, G. *Valone e limiti dell endocrinologia nello studio del delinquente*. Torino: Bocca, 1923.

Villemin, J. *Etudes sur la tuberculose*. Paris, 1868.

Viner, J. & Tamanini, F.J. Effective highway barriers. *Accident Analysis and Prevention*, 1973, *5*, 203-14.

von Thunen, J. *Der isolierte staat in beziehung auf landwirtschaft und nationalekonomie*. Hamburg, 1826.

Voss, H. & Petersen, D. *Ecology, crime and delinquency*. New York: Appleton-Century-Crofts, 1971.

Waller, J.A., Lamborn, K.R. & Steffanhagen, R.A. Marihuana and driving among teenagers: Reported use patterns, effects, and experiences related to driving. *Accident Analysis and Prevention*, 1974, *6*, 141-62.

Watson, J.B. *Behavior: An introduction to comparative psychology*. New York: Holt, 1914.

Watson, J.B. & Raynor, R. Conditioned emotional reactions. *Journal of Experimental Psychology*. 1920, *3*, 1-14.

Weber, A. *The growth of the city in the nineteenth century: A study in statistics*. (1899) Ithaca, N.Y.: Cornell Press, 1963.

Weber, A. *Theory of industrial location*. Chicago: University of Chicago Press, 1968.

Weir, J. Criminal Anthropology. *Medical Record*, 1894, *45*, 42-45.

Weissman, H. (Ed.). *Justice and the law in the mobilization for youth experience*. New York: Associated Press, 1969.

Welson, J. & Stevens, B. *Air quality and its relationship to economic, meteorological, and other structural characteristics of urban areas in the United States*. Philadelphia: Regional Science Research Institute, 1970.

White, M. & White, L. *The intellectual v. the city*. New York: Mentor Books, 1964.

Wicker, A.W. Undermanning, performances, and students' subjective experiences in behavior settings of large and small high schools. *Journal of Personality and Social Psychology*. 1968, *10* (3), 255-61.

Willems, E.P. Sense of obligation to high school activities as related to school size and marginality of student. *Child Development*, 1967, *38* (4), 1247-60.

Willems, E.P. The interface of the hospital environment and patient behavior. *Archives of Physical Medicine and Rehabilitation*. 1972, *53*, 115-22.

Wilner, D. & Walkley, R. Effects of housing on health and performance. In L. Duhl (Ed.), *The urban condition*. New York: Simon and Schuster, 1963.

Wolfe, C.P. *Social impact assessment*. The 1975 Proceedings of Environmental Design Research Association (Vol. 5). Washington, D.C.: Environmental Design Research Association, 1975.

Wolpe, J. *Psychotherapy by reciprocal inhibition*. Stanford, California: Stanford University Press, 1958.

Ziboorg, G. & Henry, G.W. *A history of medical psychology*. New York: Norton, 1941.

Zylman, R. A critical evaluation of the literature on alcohol involvement in highway deaths. *Accident Analysis and Prevention*, 1974, *6*, 163-204.

Name Index

Subject Index

About the Author

Ralph Catalano (Ph.D. Maxwell School, Syracuse University) is an Associate Professor of Social Ecology at the University of California at Irvine. This book is an outgrowth of his teaching the introductory course for the interdisciplinary program in Social Ecology. The program Faculty and coursework represent such diverse disciplines as Public Health, Psychology, Sociology, Regional Planning and Law. In addition to his teaching and research activities, Catalano is Associate Director of the University's Public Policy Research Organization.

PERGAMON GENERAL PSYCHOLOGY SERIES

Editors:　Arnold P. Goldstein, *Syracuse University*
Leonard Krasner, *SUNY, Stony Brook*

TITLES IN THE PERGAMON GENERAL PSYCHOLOGY SERIES
(Added Titles in Back of Volume)

The terms of our inspection copy service apply to all the above books. A complete catalogue of all books in the Pergamon International Library is available on request.

The Publisher will be pleased to receive suggestions for revised editions and new titles.

TITLES IN THE PERGAMON GENERAL PSYCHOLOGY SERIES (Continued)